Madeleine Bunting is a columnist on the *Guardian*. She joined the paper in 1989 as a general reporter and has been a leader writer as well as reporting on religious affairs, Europe and development issues. She has won several awards for her journalism and is a regular broadcaster. Her previous book, *The Model Occupation*, on the Second World War history of the Channel Islands, was published in 1995. Born in Oswaldkirk, North Yorkshire, she studied at Cambridge before winning a postgraduate scholarship to Harvard. She lives in East London with her husband and three children.

For automatic updates on Madeleine Bunting visit harperperennial.co.uk and register for AuthorTracker.

'Madeleine Bunting examines the important place of work in our lives today: what it means to us, where things go right and where things go wrong. Passionately written with up-to-the-minute research, she queries our attraction (economic and psychological) to the long hours culture and makes us think again about what we are up to. Read it'   SUSIE ORBACH

'Brilliantly thorough and thoroughly brilliant'   *Guardian*

'This is a book that can stimulate a dramatic response from its readers. It raises questions about how we live our lives, and sparked off two long and intense debates among friends of mine on the topic. At least one resolved to change her work–life balance'   *Wall Street Journal*

'Excellent'   SUZANNE MOORE, *Mail on Sunday*

By the same author

The Model Occupation: The Channel Islands
Under German Rule, 1940–1945

MADELEINE BUNTING

WILLING SLAVES

How the Overwork Culture Is
Ruling our Lives

HARPER PERENNIAL
London, New York, Toronto and Sydney

Harper Perennial
An imprint of HarperCollins*Publishers*
77–85 Fulham Palace Road
Hammersmith London W6 8JB

www.harperperennial.co.uk

This edition published by Harper Perennial 2005
1

First published by HarperCollins*Publishers* 2004

A catalogue record for this book
is available from the British Library

ISBN 0 00 716372 X

Set in Minion with Trade Gothic Display by
Rowland Phototypesetting Limited, Bury St Edmunds, Suffolk

Printed and bound in Great Britain by Clays Ltd, St Ives plc

To Simon

Contents

Contents

Acknowledgements

My first thank-you goes to dear Simon, without whose inspiration, care and encouragement this book simply wouldn't have been written. Another thank-you is owed to nine-year-old Eleanor and seven-year-old Luke for their patience – 'Isn't the book finished yet?' – and to one-year-old Matthias for his tolerance.

I owe a great debt to the Joseph Rowntree Foundation for their generous fellowship and to the *Guardian*'s Alan Rusbridger and Georgina Henry for their agreement to a generous leave of absence and their encouraging support.

I've been very lucky to have had the help of two wonderfully cheerful researchers. Louise Norton was unfailingly patient and James Walter did invaluable work on Chapters 5 and 10.

Thank you also to the Work Foundation, in particular Will Hutton, John Knell, Andy Westwood and Alex Jones for help at different stages and to the research department's vigorous debate on the book in its early stages. I'm grateful to Professor Shirley Dex, who bore with my journalistic approach with great patience and perseverance in the midst of a hectic timetable – I hope I didn't add too much to her burden of overwork. A huge range of people gave generously of their time, contacts and thoughts to answer my questions. Many of them are quoted in the text, but in particular

Acknowledgements

I'd like to thank: Gurnek Bains, Chris Ball of Amicus, Mike Bold of Unison, Frances Cairncross, Shirley Conran, Jock Encombe, Richard Finn, Lisa Harker of the Daycare Trust, Sarah Jackson of Working Parents, Oliver James, Neil Jamieson of the East London Communities Organisation, Richard Jolly of the London Business School, Paul Kent of the West Midlands Low Pay Unit, David Ladipo, Penelope Leach, Charles Leadbeater, Andrew Macdonald, Peter Maxwell, Julie Mellor of the Equal Opportunities Commission, Susie Orbach, Jack O'Sullivan and Tom Beardshaw of Fathers Direct, Katharine Rake of the Fawcett Society, Richard Reeves, Adrian Rickard, David Robey, Andrew Samuels, and Paul Sellers. Special thanks to Kath Viner for fitting in time to read a draft, also thanks to Robin Piper and colleagues with whom I've discussed these issues in recent years, including Camilla Nichols and Liz Mcgregor. There are many others to whom I'm very grateful, but who prefer to remain anonymous.

I am greatly indebted to the work of many academics who have worked assiduously to clarify our understanding in the areas over which I have trampled in my research. For those interested, the endnotes point to the papers and books they have written; in the meantime, I hope I haven't done too much damage to the subtlety of their thinking. In particular I'd like to thank Julia Brannen, Cary Cooper, Yiannis Gabriel, Jonathan Gershuny, Francis Green, Paul Heelas, Suzan Lewis and Rhona Rapoport. Many thanks to all those who attended the Cumberland Lodge seminar for their stimulating intellectual companionship. My gratitude to Zygmunt Bauman for his inspiration, encouragement and delicious strawberries and cream.

Hundreds of people have emailed me through the *Guardian*'s 'Working Lives' website with comments on the columns I'd written there. I'm grateful for all of the emails, many of which I followed up with interviews. The sheer volume of the response exceeded my ability to reply to all of them individually – here is a very heartfelt

Acknowledgements

thank-you. I hope the book is what you hoped for. Your emails were a rich source of ideas, and many of you will recognise excerpts from them which I've included. Some names and identifying details have been changed.

Thanks are also due to the companies who allowed me to interview their staff. It's a tribute to their organisational cultures that these staff were only occasionally accompanied by press officers, and that so many of them spoke so freely about their working lives.

Finally, many thanks to my agent Natasha Fairweather, whose judicious judgement I've come to trust better than my own. Book writing is lonely, hard work from the initial spark of an idea to the final proofs, but Natasha's gentle coaxing of the proposal into shape and her encouragement along the rest of the way have been invaluable. Similarly, Richard Johnson at HarperCollins has been an unfailing source of calm encouragement, while Robert Lacey's editing has smoothed out infelicities in the text and, as on a previous book, has saved me from many a scandalous mistake.

Madeleine Bunting
February 2004

Introduction

The starting point for this book has been readers of my column in the *Guardian*. Whenever I touched on the subject of overwork, I would be overwhelmed by the volume and emotion of the emails I received in response. It was like a burst water main – a torrent of anger, bewilderment and sometimes despair. Here was a source of deep frustration beneath the surface which fitted awkwardly into the public space allocated to it in the national conversation. 'Work–life balance' was an inadequate label for the set of issues which stirred these passionate emails and letters. When I started researching the book, one of the first things I did was to set up a column on the *Guardian*'s website called 'Working Lives'. I appealed to readers for their experiences, opinions and ideas on how things could change. The response was astonishing, as the emails poured in on every aspect of their work. Few of them, if any, could be put down merely to the sender's grumbles about his or her job; I made a point of steering clear of individual injustices to focus on the mainstream. The underlying theme was the sheer invasive dominance of work in people's lives, and the price it exacted on their health and happiness.

'It's not that I completely hate my job, it does have its good points. It's just the amount of my valuable time that it takes up.

Introduction

Employers these days want blood, and if you're not prepared to give it, you're not part of the "team". Our society should learn to relax more and stop working as slaves to the "economy". It's time to call a halt to this never-ending pursuit for more and more money. It's time to reclaim our lives back from the so-called "employers" and it's time to start living our lives as they should be lived, more life, less work,' wrote a storeman in Hertfordshire.

His sentiments were echoed by an engineer who compared German and British working practices and concluded that the latter had 'taught me that left to their own devices, companies will happily take your lifeblood'.

A civil servant from Yorkshire wrote that 'I enjoy what I do and I work hard. But, and it is a growing but, I feel owned and more so every day. Due to all the mission statements, "values", imposed ways of behaving and having to be always get-at-able (you must be accessible by mobile phone, must give an address when you are on leave, must leave a number when you are at meetings . . .) I feel that I have no privacy left.'

A woman in the oil industry in Scotland wrote, 'Over the past ten years I have seen large companies continuously cut back on staff, whilst still expecting the same quality of work. Being thirty-something, our circle of friends are in a similar age group, starting families and suffering the same strain of long hours and not enough time with their families. Don't get me wrong, I love my work. However, it takes such a toll on my family life that I have no choice but to seek a different career.'

A redundant banker decided not to try to find another job, because 'Every week I hear similar stories of friends or friends of friends who, like me, worked sixty- or seventy-hour weeks, arrived home after dark each night, ate dinner and crawled into bed before getting up again the next morning whilst still dark to repeat the whole thing again, but who have now lost their jobs.'

A woman in advertising voiced what became a recurring theme

when she wrote: 'I feel that there is an expectation that work should be treated as a vocation, and that working hard is just not quite enough. But I don't feel that my job is really that important (to society or to me) to really want to take on the extra and damage my home life. Not all of us have a vocation – what about those of us who want to do a good job, but want time to see partners, friends etc. after work?'

For a woman who had suffered a nervous breakdown because of the pressures of her job in television, 'It is high time we re-evaluated our work ethic in this country – we are damaging ourselves and our children by not having the time or energy for caring, and trying to enrich our lives by buying more consumer goods only perpetuates the cycle . . . Where is it written that life should be endured, not enjoyed?'

The point is not that people don't like their work; they often do. They appreciate the sense of fulfilment and usefulness it brings. They often find it stimulating, exciting and rewarding. This book is not a diatribe against work; it would be foolish not to acknowledge all the evidence that work is a crucial source of self-respect – and that the lack of work saps the confidence of individuals and communities. But as work gains an ever tighter grip on certain sections of the population, we have to face a new set of questions about the place it occupies in our lives.

Time and again, email contributors circled round the same point – it shouldn't have to be like this; why hasn't wealth and technological development brought us the leisure it was predicted to? Why, instead, has it brought even harder work? From John Maynard Keynes to Alvin Toffler, thinkers predicted that the twenty-first century would be an Age of Leisure, while in the seventies increasing automation even led policy-makers and politicians to worry how people would usefully fill their time. For some, this dawning era promised abundant opportunities for human beings in industrialised countries to reach their full potential. It would be the fulfilment of a long-cherished dream that we would finally be freed from the oppressive toil of long hours at work. The realisation of Aristotle's belief that it is only in leisure that we are most human would be within reach of us all. Marx dreamt of society reaching a point where people could spend the morning thinking and the afternoon fishing.

It never happened. Quite the contrary: the historic decline in working hours has gone into reverse in the last two decades. Such are the demands of many jobs that leisure has been reduced to simply a time to recuperate before the gruelling demands of the next week's work. British workers have a roughly one in three chance of finding at some time in the course of their working lives that those demands exceed their capacity to cope; the odds are even higher if you're a woman. Ours has become a more work-centred society than ever; it demands more of us than ever, and it also purports to fulfil more of our needs than ever. One sociologist has identified five categories of experience as vital for well-being: time structure, social contact; collective effort or purpose, social identity or status and regular activity.[1] With the decline in community, political parties and faith institutions, and the fragmentation of family, employment has become the main, often the sole, provider of all five. We look to work for a sense of integration and connection to society, while our grandparents would have been able also to look to their neighbourhood, their church, their political party, perhaps also an extended family nearby. This gives employers unprecedented purchase over our lives: how they are organised, how we perceive ourselves, and how we shape our relationships with others – both colleagues at work and personal relationships outside it.

The nature of work is changing, and its demands are increasing. These two trends have coincided over the last two decades with the move of women into paid employment. Family life no longer revolves around one breadwinner and one carer, but typically around one full-time and one part-time earner; in a generation we have seen a dramatic shift of time and energy from the unpaid caring economy into the paid labour market. The disinvestment of women in the caring economy has not been accompanied by sufficient compensating investment by men. The result is a care deficit – a shortage of time and energy to invest in relationships. It begins with a deficit of care towards ourselves, in which our work culture makes us ill, and at its worst can kill. There is also a deficit in the care of children, and across the myriad of interdependent relationships which sustain us in families, friendships and neighbourhoods. The result is an emotional impoverishment of all our lives: the office is now where the heart is, not the home, as the complexities of the workplace demand an ever larger share of our emotional resources. Women's participation in the labour market did not need to exact such a steep price.

The emails I received echoed some of my experience as one of the generation of Thatcher's teenagers, whose understanding of public affairs developed in the shadow of the severe recession of the early eighties, soaring unemployment and the miners' strike. The harsh rhetoric of public debate in those years dismantled the post-war consensus – the role of the welfare state was challenged, old institutions such as trade unions emasculated. Dependency became a term of abuse, independence the ultimate aspiration; individualism was to be forged by work and upward mobility; these ideas seduced many, particularly women, determined not to be caught as their mothers had been in the confines of the home and child-rearing. 'The only way is up,' as the hit single went. The fact that many were left behind only underscored the 'survive or die' mentality. So we worked hard, very hard.

And then . . . we had children, and the whole game-plan had to be redrawn. None of the operating principles on which we had built our careers was of any use; we learnt for the first time the satisfactions and fulfilment of dependence and interdependence. But we also ran smack into the traditional separation between work and family, and found ourselves uncomfortably trying to straddle the two. 'We were betrayed by feminism,' said one contemporary of mine recently. In fact, it was more a case of our generation betraying feminism: we turned our backs on the feminists of the seventies, ignoring their warnings that the entire way we worked had to be revolutionised.

We cobbled unhappy compromises together – went part-time, gave up the career, put the children into nurseries. We were bemused by the lack of respect for raising children, we grumbled about the exhaustion, and about the re-emergence of old gender stereotypes as our male counterparts' careers surged ahead while we were left, just as our mothers had been, amongst the nappies. So one very personal explanation for writing this book is that my generation are the offspring of an unfinished revolution. 'Work–life balance' is the weaselly term for where feminism – the historic development of women's equality – has now got to.

In the course of my research another set of questions took shape which forms the central thrust of the argument. This book investigates the consequences of two phenomena: two decades of neoliberal economic policy, and the impact of information technology on working lives. In the context of periods of high unemployment, a lightly regulated labour market, increasing inequality and high levels of perceived insecurity, I seek to disentangle how the dictates of the market, with its cult of rationalism and efficiency, extend into people's individual lives. How and why do people collude with a system which, they are well aware, often does not have their interests at heart? What kind of trade-offs do they make, and why? What degree of choice do they have? How *willing* are these wage slaves? And finally, why is it that the choices become individualised, and that many of us have lost virtually all interest in collective reform of our working lives?

It is in the workplace that the pressures of market disciplines such as competitiveness and cost-effective efficiency impinge most directly on people's daily experience. Those disciplines are often at odds with our intuitive understanding of effectiveness, not to mention our ethics and sense of purpose. They distort and erode the quality of relationships with colleagues, students, pupils and patients. This was a rich source of anger for many working in the public sector, where employees struggle to meet requirements for efficiency while maintaining their own vision of the nature – spontaneous, unpredictable, intuitive – of human relationships.

Paid employment is, for many, their only experience of collaboration with other people – in what other way do they work with others to achieve a common goal? – and it is one increasingly poisoned by competition, insecurity and stress. As the economist E.F. Schumacher argued, 'What people actually *do* is normally more important, for understanding them, than what they say, or what they spend their money on, or what they own, or how they vote.'[2] Intense competition is everywhere in our culture, and is used for our entertainment in hugely popular television programmes such as *Big Brother* and *The Weakest Link*. This reflects our fears about how our workplaces are organised, the laws they operate under and our total failure to imagine a process of reform, let alone transformation. 'It's the way of the world, and there's no alternative,' is the refrain. The eighties in Britain saw mass redundancies, high unemployment and savage industrial restructuring which hit manufacturing and the lowest-skilled hardest. The 1990s and the first years of the twenty-first century were no less destructive, although the process was quieter and more insidious, hitting white-collar managerial and professional jobs and leading to a steady intensification of work as people were required to do more with fewer staff. The pressures hit particularly hard in the public sector, undermined by a crisis in the legitimacy of the principle of public provision. Between 40 and 60 per cent of the entire labour force found their workloads increasing, the hours got longer and the stress levels soared.

Introduction

It is this experience which is the main focus of this book: the burnout of white-collar Britain. I wanted to see not the worst examples of British employment (of which there are many, as Polly Toynbee brilliantly describes in her book *Hard Work*), but to find out why 46 per cent – *nearly half* – of those working in even the best companies in the UK say they are exhausted at the end of a day's work. I chose to interview companies that were not the worst employers but the best, and were recognised as such in the *Sunday Times* Best Companies list.

Just what is making work so hard? Technology has played a crucial role: firstly by increasing the mechanisms for accountability for one's work and thus depriving many of autonomy; and secondly by eroding the boundaries around work – the routines of set working hours, the spatial separation between work and home – which for the entire industrial era had given people privacy and rest. The arrival in the nineties of the mass use of mobile phones, email, the internet and home PCs has made workers more available than ever to the pressures that their employers can bring to bear on them. We haven't even started to think how to put in place new boundaries, either legislative or cultural, and instead have been seduced by the rhetoric of the liberation and autonomy brought by technology, when in fact it can bring the reverse of both.

The policies of the eighties and nineties (Tony Blair's Labour government has done little more than modify the Thatcherite model) were based, John Gray argued in his book *False Dawn: The Delusions of Global Capitalism* (1998), on 'the theory that market freedoms are natural and political restraints on markets are artificial. The truth is that free markets are creatures of state power, and persist only so long as the state is able to prevent human needs for security and the control of economic risk from finding political expression.' The speeding-up of communication, trade and capital flows generates unpredictable and constant change: all that filters down to daily lives, where individuals struggle to adjust – to speed up their pace of work, to stretch their working hours to get the job done, to adapt family routines to the 24/7 service economy, to find new jobs and acquire new skills – and to make sense of those constant necessary adjustments. As Gray puts it, 'The imperatives of flexibility and mobility imposed by deregulated labour markets put particular strain on traditional modes of family life. How can families meet for meals when both parents work on shifts? What becomes of families when the job market pulls parents apart?' Both Tony Blair and Gordon Brown proudly point to the present low unemployment rate as the product of the UK's lightly regulated labour market, but they overlook the price we pay in long working hours, exhaustion and rising stress.

The great failure of market economies is that they take no measure of externalities: if something doesn't have a market value, it doesn't exist; this is what economists call 'the tragedy of the commons'. The emergence and development of the environmental movement pioneered the understanding of how markets, in a bid to drive down costs, 'externalise' them – or, to put it more crudely, get someone else (usually the taxpayer) to pay for them; for example, polluting a river is cheaper than processing the waste product and recycling it. In just the same way, markets externalise the social costs of their ways of working; it is left to individuals – and their overworked NHS doctors – to deal with the exhaustion, work-related depression, stress and the care deficit.

Just as the late twentieth century grasped the fact that there was a crisis of environmental sustainability, the twenty-first century is beginning to grasp the dimensions of a comparable crisis, this time of *human* sustainability – a scarcity of the conditions which nurture resilient, secure individuals, families, friendships and communities. Who has time to care for whom in the overwork culture? The price is paid not just by children, but by their exhausted parents, the lost friends and the lonely elderly. The consequences of this crisis can be traced in the rising incidence of depression – by 2020, it is predicted, it will be the world's most prevalent disease – as well as in family breakdown and the rise in loneliness. This crisis of human sustainability is not just an affliction of Western developed nations, but a consequence of neo-liberal economic development, and is evident in the fast-growing cities of developing countries, where rapid urbanisation is coinciding with the rise of female employment.[3] At its most dangerous, the crisis triggers the defensive coping mechanisms of finding substitute security in rigid, clear-cut ways of thinking which spill over into fundamentalism. This crisis cannot entirely be placed at the door of work, but employment is one of the prime causes; it is driving a stress epidemic as more and more is expected of employees, and it is depriving people of both the time and the energy to lead lives with a rich diversity of experience. Lives in which they have time to fulfil their responsibilities to others, be they children, the elderly, friends, neighbours or fellow citizens, and to develop interests and hobbies.

Job satisfaction fell sharply in the nineties. Yet there has been little protest: both trade union membership and the number of days lost to strike action are sharply down since the eighties. There has been no great effort to question why work is getting tougher – we accepted that it was the competitive pressures of the market, or the drive for public sector reform. The result is this undercurrent of frustration, and at its worst quiet despair. Instead of joining a trade union, people sought private solutions, treating themselves to aromatherapy or a nice holiday in the sun instead. The response of the trade union movement, beleaguered by the loss of members and of jobs in its manufacturing heartland, still battling to re-establish its legitimacy in national life, has often been piecemeal and ineffective. The unions were slow to push working time, rather than their traditional priority of pay, to the top of their campaigning agenda. They have been slow to revitalise the old struggle over working time which they so successfully championed in the nineteenth century. They are only now reconnecting to that radical agenda first laid out by the International Association of Working Men (later the First International) which commemorated its first meeting over 140 years ago with a specially made watch, the face of which was inscribed: 'We require eight hours work, eight hours for our own instruction and eight hours for repose.'

It's a rallying cry as relevant to the twenty-first century as it was to the nineteenth: the dream of a forty-hour week is for many British workers further from being realised than ever. The trade unions have been held back by prejudices in favour of 'proper' full-time jobs from pushing for the reorganisation of work which is possible in a flexible economy. The undermining of the unions has left a vacuum in Britain. Who speaks for the working man and woman? Where is the campaign to wrest back control of our time, to demand the right to a day's work which leaves one with the energy to do more than stagger home and slump onto the sofa?

The answer, I was repeatedly told by those defending the status quo, is that people make their own choices. If they want to work hard, that is up to them. If they want to opt out, to downshift and live the good life, they can do so. It is all up to them. This is a powerful rubric for those defending neo-liberalism, and has success-fully debilitated any collective consensus about what is wrong and what needs to be put right. Some people *don't* have any choice; they have poorly-paid jobs which require long hours, and even then they don't make what would be commonly described as a 'decent living'. But the bulk of this book is focused on the predicament of the broad swathe of what might now constitute the British middle classes, ranging from skilled factory workers to white-collar man-agers. For the vast majority there is a degree of choice in how hard they work. But the choices we make are not made in isolation: they are the product of the particular organisational culture of our workplaces, which promote concepts of success, of team spirit so that we don't let colleagues down, and a powerful work ethic. We are also influenced by a culture which reinforces that work ethic and its cycle of continual achievement and consumption as measures of self-worth, and that has developed a tight grip on exactly those workers in white-collar professional and managerial jobs whose conditions deteriorated most significantly in the nineties, yet who have potentially the most bargaining power in the labour market. These are the classes whose grandparents saw leisure as a sign of status. Now, it is overwork that has become a sign of status – the laptop on holiday, the permanently ringing mobile and the bulging inbox.

In the seventies, commentators and policy-makers worried that the work ethic was in terminal decline. They needn't have: it was reformulated, and is now stronger than ever, particularly amongst the most educated. It is through work that we seek to satisfy our craving for a sense of control, of mastery, of security and autonomy in a chaotic, insecure world: this is the gold at the end of the rainbow. The craving is never satiated, we are always promised more if we work that bit harder.

A work ethic has evolved that promotes a particular sense of self and identity which meshes neatly with the needs of market capitalism, through consumption and through work. Put at its simplest, narcissism and capitalism are mutually reinforcing. What is pushed to the margin are the time-consuming, labour-intensive human relationships, and doing nothing – simply being. Clever organisations exploit this cultural context, this craving for control, self-assertion and self-affirmation, and design corporate cultures which meet the emotional needs of their employees. This is where corporate power aims to reach into the interstices of our characters and even our souls, and manipulate them to its own interests. A chart on the wall of Microsoft's Reading office shows a large 'S' curve which begins by identifying individual character strengths, and through a number of stages translates them into a share price increase. Human beings are instrumentalised as the means to an end – the share price.

Introduction

We have become familiar with the debate about corporate power extending into political life and subverting the power of the state, and we are aware of the way in which corporate power has infiltrated every aspect of civic life; but we also need to recognise how corporations attempt to mould and manipulate our inner lives through new styles of invasive management which sponsor our 'personal growth'. The 'absorptive corporation' is a well-known phenomenon in American business life. The British are sceptical, but who knows whether corporate formulations of community, mentoring and teamwork will prove a powerful seduction for an increasingly lonely nation?

Throughout my research for this book I encountered a powerful sense of restlessness. We have reached a tipping point, a pervasive, inarticulate feeling that there must be another way, that enough is enough. Wealth should bring leisure, not hard work. Our rising GDP should have some payoff in increasing well-being – or what's the point? Surveys show that a growing number of people want to trade pay for time. Interestingly, the anger and frustration seems to be increasing even though the deterioration in the quality of our working lives has eased slightly since 1997–98; for example, the implementation of the European Union's Working Time Regulations, which limit the working week to forty-eight hours, has halted the increase in the average number of hours worked, although the incidence of stress has continued to soar. But on this plateau, the exhaustion has accumulated; the extra effort and time was not for a short sprint, but for an endless marathon – it has become institutionalised.

What gives me hope is that the point of revolution is not when things are at their worst, but when they're beginning to get better. But we are crippled by one of the strongest illusions of our age, namely that we seek 'biographic solutions to structural contradictions', as the German sociologist Ulrich Beck puts it. We look for personal, private solutions to our problems, rather than identifying with others and achieving reform. Many of those 'biographic solutions' are only available to a small minority (how many people can downshift to a cheaper housing market?) or act as an opiate, a fantasy which is endlessly postponed.

There are many points of hope: the eighteen to twenty-four age group view the working culture of their parents with horror. Sociologists have charted a shift to post-modern values, with people in Western industrialised nations growing disenchanted with materialism and looking for self-expression and fulfilment. The growing preoccupation with well-being and health may also spur a challenge to the overwork culture. On the other hand, the re-envisaging of success and achievement needed is no mean task in a culture intoxicated by public recognition and celebrity. We have little place in our pantheon of admirable attributes for what Words-worth described as 'those little unremembered acts of kindness which are the best part of humankind'. Nor is sufficient value placed upon those times of reflection and idleness which are so often the wellspring of human creativity, wisdom and well-being. Bertrand Russell, in his essay 'In Praise of Idleness' (1932), lamented how the 'cult of efficiency' had inhibited the capacity for 'light-heartedness and play'; how horrified he would be at the extent to which that cult of efficiency has now been rolled out across much of our national life.

It is this cultural debate about success, achievement, the limits of efficiency and what it is to be human which needs to be linked to a political debate. The work–life balance agenda is where philosophical questions about what is the good life and what is the common good intersect with the political. We need to challenge the centrality of work in our lives, and reconsider the price we pay for our wages. We need to question the way work is organised: why shouldn't we have a three-day weekend, or Wednesdays off? Time is both a personal and a political issue. This book argues that we need to find again the space to imagine social transformation – and what better place to start than in work, where we spend so many of our waking hours? We need to see more clearly the 'structural contradictions' – of long hours, work intensification – which determine our lives, and to find again ways to express our desire for freedom in our working lives. The employment agenda should not be ruled by the dictates of business needs, but by human needs – such as rest, leisure, caring for dependants, the welfare of children and giving individuals the opportunity to reach their full human worth; the economy should be the servant of our needs, not our master. The sociologist Zygmunt Bauman writes that we have shifted our aspirations for freedom from work to consumption. It's time to shift them back. It's time to break through the conundrum which Bauman expresses as 'Never have we been so free, and so unable to change things.'

Part One

The Meaning of Overwork

1

Working All Hours

*You spelt out how drab our lives are. Now, what about tomorrow?
Do we don our seventies lapels, stir the masses, and stage a walk-out?
I work in a part of the private sector that is cut-throat, our number
has been pared down to a point that hardly sustains its own weight.
Stirring these masses would result in a very feeble affair – and provide
a sure route to joblessness to boot. This job is the only security I have.
My parental responsibility doesn't allow for jacking it all in to go off
and massage whales or whatever's hip these days. I've got to get two
kids through puberty and university yet. And where will they live?
What percentage of new graduates can raise the money to buy a garden
shed, let alone a house of any description?*

*And better this depth of shit than the one that comes with skiving
off. You only take a sicky here knowing that tomorrow's deadlines are
the day after's heart attacks. In addition to the stockpiled workload,
there are the accusatory silences of jaded colleagues. Best avoided,
believe me. And anyone still waiting for some meaningful and positive
intervention from management hasn't yet shed the delusion that gives
way to abject despair.*

*So working oneself into an early grave seems the sensible thing to
do. In reality, I needed to be reminded of how bad things really are,
and you did just that. I'm buggered if I'm going to spend this year in*

this particular drab room doing this particularly thankless task. I've resolved to get the hell out and find something else.

When I met Pete, I found none of the bitter flamboyance of the email he'd sent me. It would be hard to imagine a man less likely to stage a walk-out. He was in the RAF for fourteen years, and it still shows in his reserve and slight formality of manner. He's a technical consultant for a French multinational, working out of an office in the Midlands, but is often on the road. He makes an unlikely revolutionary.

He is contracted to work 37.5 hours a week, and he reckons that he has to put in, on average, another twelve hours or so. Add in the hour-long commute to and from the office, and most of his conscious life is taken up by work – it even wakes him in the small hours. Sometimes, in the run-up to a launch or when he's travelling a lot, it will be more. For all that, he's on £31,000 a year, and of course there's no overtime pay; if there was, the company would owe him another £646 a month – that's an extra 23 per cent of his salary, he says, working it out on his calculator as we talk.

The pressure and the hours have been getting worse. His department has been downsized by a third, but it's still expected to meet the same revenue targets. He has colleagues who work much harder than him, taking large amounts of work home, and his boss (eleven years younger than forty-five-year-old Pete, and with no children) has 'enormous amounts of energy which he pours into his job and does the work of more than one person'.

There's a steadiness to Pete which is probably much valued by his clients, and it probably also stands him in good stead in holding off the pressure of these colleagues' commitment – 'They live to work,' he comments. He takes pride in his work and regards himself as diligent and conscientious, but he vehemently rejects any idea of ambition. It simply costs too much.

He's tried talking to his boss about the long hours and the

workload. His boss is sympathetic, and promises to make representations to senior management, but nothing has happened. Pete
believes that he didn't make the representations clearly enough, for
fear that it would harm his own reputation. Pete doesn't know any
of the senior management – they work at another office – so this
is effectively a headless organisation, where responsibility always
belongs to someone else. There is one senior executive Pete knows,
but he is afraid that if he bypassed his boss to talk to him his job
would be at risk. He heard about the European Union Working Time
Regulations which limit the working week to forty-eight hours, but
it had no impact on him – the paperwork was shoved behind a cupboard, he says. In any case, they have had little impact in the UK
because of an opt-out which allows companies to ask employees to
sign a waiver – a fifth of the British workforce have signed.[1]

Inevitably, the pressure of the job spills over into his home
life. Pete's partner is a further education lecturer and works three
evenings a week, so the household timetable is a precarious juggling
act, with Pete spending time with his children from his former
marriage. He emailed:

> *Anyone who strives to meet the demands of work overload will take
> this stress home with them: poor sleep quality, an inability to engage in
> evening conversation, a 'Fuck it' attitude to bills, shopping, housework,
> parent phoning, friend phoning, eating and sex. I rescue each of these
> when they reach crisis point but it usually coincides with when I'm least
> able to act. Collectively, and to me at least, these indicate psychological
> depression, though not serious enough to be recognised as such by my
> unsympathetic GP.*

The point about Pete is that he is unexceptional. He's not in a
high-pressured metropolitan labour market where telephone-
number salaries are the recompense for demanding hard work. He
does a good job for a good company, yet none of that is enough.

He has a profound sense that the demands his job makes on him are unjust, and that his company is making profits from his free labour.

Things should be better for Sarah. She works in the public sector, and her office allows flexitime. But it isn't working out that way, and the demands of the job are affecting her health. A twenty-seven-year-old with two degrees working for the Department of Health in Yorkshire, she's at a middle management level, but after only eighteen months in the job she's already had enough. She works an average of forty-five hours a week – eight more than she is contracted for:

My immediate boss is a very old-fashioned civil servant, and although the department has flexitime, he doesn't grasp it. Sometimes I put my foot down; I've tried sticking to the contracted hours, but if the work's there, I'm expected to do it. I've laid down some ground-rules – I have to leave early on Wednesdays to attend a class, but I make up for it by getting in before 7.30 a.m. I'm often at work between 7.30 and 8 a.m., and stay until 6 p.m.

Unlike Pete, she's made the decision to leave. It will mean a cut of 50 per cent in her and her husband's joint income, so they're moving to a cheaper housing market to reduce their mortgage: 'I was diagnosed with an underactive thyroid, and I feel it was because I couldn't manage my diet and exercise properly; I was eating two meals a day at my desk. I didn't have a lunch hour, perhaps just a quick surf on the net for twenty minutes with a sandwich.'

Her husband, also in the civil service, has a long commute on top of his long hours; he has to be up at 5.30 a.m. to beat the traffic, and he's often not home until after 7 p.m.:

By the time we've had supper and washed up, we're shattered. There's a huge amount of recovering at the weekends as well as the domestic chores we just can't face in the evening such as cleaning, washing and shopping. We're having difficulty conceiving; we've been trying for nearly a year, but we're so shattered and we're not eating properly and not relaxing and all that affects fertility. I've spoken to my GP, and he says rest more and relax. The decision to leave is not one I've taken lightly. I did a degree in politics and social policy and then a masters, but it's just not worth it. I feel I'm just existing – not living.

There are hundreds of thousands of men and women like Pete and Sarah whose donations of time enable organisations in both the public and the private sectors to function. Nearly 46 per cent of men and 32 per cent of women work more hours than they are contracted for.[2] The problem is worst at the upper levels of the labour market, where in 2002 nearly 40 per cent of managers and senior officials were working more than fifty hours a week; over 30 per cent of professionals were doing likewise.[3] But long hours also badly affect blue-collar workers in fields such as construction, manufacturing and transport: between a quarter and a third of plumbers, electricians, lorry drivers and security guards are working over forty-eight hours a week. It's worse in the private sector than the public sector (17 per cent compared with 12 per cent work over forty-eight hours). Long hours are not an occasional blip in working life – they are structural, and they affect four million British workers. For about 2.4 million there's no overtime pay; their organisations depend on motivating the free labour they need because it is one of their cheapest resources. Don't employ more people, just devise an organisational culture which will ensure that people will give you their free time for free. And thousands like Pete do.

At least Tony is paid for his overtime. As a team leader on a car-plant assembly line in the Midlands, Tony often ends up doing a sixty-hour week. He's well paid for it, he admits, but he's increasingly resentful of how the company expects him to be totally available. Overtime can be called as late as 2.44 p.m. in the day, so it's impossible to make any plans to pick up his daughter from school. Nor is there any choice about doing the overtime. Although the contractual hours are only thirty-nine per week, the overtime is compulsory, and the company can ask for as many as four and a half hours' overtime a day. The company accommodates the usual peaks and troughs of manufacturing by demanding overtime from the slimmed-down workforce. If demand is particularly high, 'production Saturdays' can be imposed, when the entire workforce has to work a Saturday shift. Tony had had three production Saturdays in a row in the weeks before our interview.

'In the last ten days I've done twenty-seven hours overtime, with weekend shifts every weekend. I had to sign the waiver on the Working Time Regulations. I had no choice – if I didn't they would have given me a rubbish job, one of those nobody wants, and I would still have had to do some overtime anyway. Two men did refuse to sign the waiver on the Working Time Regulations and they got moved. I want a better balance. I don't mind some overtime, but not as much as this. I don't want the money. I suppose I'm being bullied.'

There was a period when there was no overtime, and Tony says morale was higher, everyone was more chatty and less tired, the quality of the work improved and productivity rose. The men were happier because their families weren't getting at them. They've tried talking to the manager about it – Tony says he's a nice guy – but he says there is nothing he can do; he's working long hours too. 'They just don't take into account that people have lives. I can't get to my daughter's parents' evenings or school plays because I can't book the time off. I changed my job from being a lorry driver to have better hours, and now I'm back doing the same hours again.'

At this point Tony's wife Linda breaks in. She's very angry. 'I'd like to take my daughter into the company so they could explain to us why they're more important than we are. They say they're a family firm, but they aren't. It seems like we come second. If you work at the company, it has to come first. He's out before seven in the morning and back at about 7.15 in the evening. He has a bath, has his tea and then sits down on the sofa and falls asleep. I can live with that in the week, but not when he gets up at 6 a.m. on Saturday and then spends Sunday sleeping because he's so tired. It gets to the point that when he's there, he's not there because he's that tired.'

They know of plenty of men at the company whose relationships and marriages have broken up. Tony and Linda can't arrange to see friends, they can't arrange to go out as a family. The only thing they all make a point of doing together is the family hobby of kick-boxing on a Sunday evening. 'I had a day off and I took my daughter to the swimming pool,' says Tony. 'I bumped into a mate and we were talking and she interrupts and says, "It's a rare day off for my dad, so don't talk to him."'

Britain's full-time workers put in the longest hours in Europe at 43.6 a week, well ahead of the EU average of 40.3.[4] These figures conceal the increasing polarisation of work between those who have none (16.4 per cent of households have no one in work[5]) and those who have too much. The figure is rising: between 1998 and 2003 British workers put in an extra 0.7 hours a week on average; but this masks the full scale of the accelerating trend of the overwork culture. The number working more than forty-eight hours has more than doubled since 1998, from 10 per cent to 26 per cent.[6] Another survey tracked how the number working more than sixty hours a week is shooting up. Between 2000 and 2002 it leapt by a third, to one in six of all workers,[7] so that a fifth of thirty- to thirty-nine-year-olds are working over sixty hours – a critical proportion of those likely to be at a pivotal point in beginning their own families, and well ahead of any other European country.[8]

Even that dramatic acceleration is outdone by what is happening to women. Here, it's catch-up time. Since 1992 the number of women working more than forty-eight hours a week has increased by a staggering 52 per cent,[9] and the proportion working over sixty hours has more than doubled, from 6 per cent to 13 per cent[10] – one in eight of the female workforce. Long hours is no longer solely a male disease. The average number of working hours for women increased by three and a half hours a week in the period 1998 to 2003.[11]

Add in what is happening to holiday take-up, and the picture looks even worse. According to two surveys, only 44 per cent of workers take all the holiday to which they are entitled – 39 per cent of men and 49 per cent of women.[12] The most frequently cited reason for not taking holidays was that there was too much work to do, followed by fear that taking a break might jeopardise the employee's job. These findings are backed up by another (albeit small-scale) survey which calculated that the average employee loses out on more than three months of holiday over their working life, which was valued at £4 billion-worth of work donated to employers every year. Again, those surveyed said they were simply too busy to get away.[13] Meanwhile the average lunch 'hour' is now estimated to be twenty-seven minutes long according to one study, and 65 per cent of workers report 'rarely taking a full hour's lunch break'.[14] Some argue that simply totting up the number of hours spent at work to calculate working time in a knowledge economy is meaningless, because of the additional time spent on the commute with the mobile or laptop, or puzzling out work problems in the bath. That adds up to another eleven hours on average a week, according to research by the Mental Health Foundation.

These long hours are the biggest cause of the dramatic decline in job satisfaction over the nineties, with the number of men reporting that they are 'very happy' with their hours dropping from 35 per cent to 20 per cent, and for women from 51 per cent to 29 per cent.[15] A quarter of those who work long hours do so reluctantly 'all or most of the time'.[16] The higher the educational qualification, the deeper the unhappiness: commentator Robert Taylor concluded that 'there is a particular malaise among highly educated males'. So here's the puzzle: how is it that men and women like Pete, of a generation brought up to prize their entitlement to autonomy, have lost control of that crucial element of the employment contract, their own time? There were never any negotiations over it, let alone barricades or picket lines; it happened by stealth, piecemeal across thousands of offices, in millions of relationships, where that bit extra was demanded of the workforce . . . and apart from private grumbles, they complied.

There is another side to long hours which is much more straightforward. It is a familiar tale of cheap, low-skill labour which has always relied on long hours of overtime to compensate for low pay. The power relations of the labour contract are more clear-cut and harsh here, but at least the overtime is paid and every extra half-hour is accounted for.

Maev and Joshua work as cleaners in a London hospital. Her average working week is fifty-two hours, twenty-five minutes, because she has chosen to do a double shift. She's at work by 7.30 a.m., and she finally finishes her second shift at 8 p.m. – with a break of an hour and three-quarters between shifts around tea time. Over at the other end of the hospital, Joshua works about fifty-four hours a week, with a similarly broken day. Both of them have had to sign a waiver on the Working Time Regulations, as requested by ISS, the Danish multinational company which employs them.

Maev has been working at this hospital for less than a year. She had a clerical job with better pay, but she wanted to cut down her travelling costs, so she took what the hospital offered her. As she's employed by a contractor, she isn't eligible for the overtime rates, sick pay or pension which NHS staff receive. When I first saw her in the ward she wore the blank, inscrutable expression adopted

11

by those whose presence – let alone their labour – is rarely acknowledged. It was as if she had willed her own absence from her place and her task. But the moment we were introduced, she was transformed. She became human again, with a smile which animated her entire face.

Later, in a small office used by the union she belongs to, Unison, she explained why she works such long hours. She came to Britain in the early nineties; now aged forty-two, she is supporting most of her family back in Africa. She saves more than half her take-home pay to send home.

I send about £100 a week out of about £200 a week take-home pay. My rent is £54.12 and there's phone bills on top of that. I had three sisters and one died last year from AIDS. Another is now very sick and both their husbands have died. I have one niece at university and I pay her fees. If I don't she might have to go out with men and get married quickly – and then I might be left alone. My niece appreciates what I'm doing and has sent me two phone messages saying thank you. I have four other nieces and a nephew who lives with my mother. I'm helping all of them. I want to set up a business back home and I want to build a house there and then I want to devote myself to helping women organise and train themselves.

Several times as she talked, Maev's voice would trail away, and as she fiddled with a piece of paper she stared blankly at the keyboard and desk in front of her. The long silences spoke of her frustrations, of how she has sacrificed her life for her relatives back in Africa, and her anxieties for their welfare. Maev knows she's overqualified for the job, but she takes pride in doing it properly, pointing out that she doesn't have to wait to be told to clean things such as the dirty mop-heads: 'I don't like ISS because of the pay. It's not my joy to be cleaning when I have skills in my head,' she says, and adds that she was the one in her family who went the furthest in her studies, and that she had hoped to get to university. 'But I know it's my responsibility. I know the supervisors don't consider it a big job. I don't see them normally anyway, but you get feedback from other people on the ward.'

Maev refers to the humiliations of the job, and talks of the intense emotions on the ward at times, but she insists that she's 'been brought up not to make a fuss'. She's hoping to get home sometime later in the year to visit her family, but she grimaces at the thought of the expectations of presents which will inevitably greet her on her arrival. Her hopes of change are pinned on the dream of going home with enough money to set up a business – a shop, and flats to rent perhaps – to support her family. That would require better pay, and for that she puts her energies into the union's fight alongside the East London Community Organisation (TELCO) for a 'living wage'. It took nine months to persuade the management of the hospital trust even to meet them, only for them to be told that the wages were set by the contractor. ISS have said they're sympathetic to the campaign, but that market conditions (i.e. their contract with the hospital) don't support a higher wage. Everyone dodges responsibility.

Joshua is in a similar plight to Maev. He's been a cleaner at the hospital for sixteen years. He takes home about £212 a week, out of which he has to pay £50 child support, £60 rent, perhaps another £50 in bills, and he tries to send about £30 a month home to Jamaica for his mother and two children there. He's not eligible for any benefit or tax credits, and some weeks his money runs out, so he has to go hungry until his wages are paid.

'I catch up on one bill and then another, and end up a madman,' he says unhappily. 'I'm in arrears to the council, but there's only £30 left for a week's food and clothing.' He doesn't mind the work – he insists on showing me how clean the carpeted ward is – it's the pay which makes him angry: just £4.79 an hour. He's thought of signing up with an agency and taking a second job, but he'd have to travel, and 'Sometimes I get tired, I'm just a human being.'

Walk into any organisation and there will be plenty of people like Maev and Joshua. They work long hours doing the tedious, repetitive work of cleaning in a burgeoning service economy. Only people with severely limited choices and little negotiating power in the labour market would ever take such jobs, and in London and the south-east that effectively requires a ready supply of immigrant labour. Without immigrants, much of the public sector services in the south-east would be on the point of implosion. They clean, they cook, they do the washing up, and because their work is classed as low-productivity, they earn wages barely sufficient to support one person – let alone the multiple dependants whom both Joshua and Maev support.

The conditions of work have seriously deteriorated as these types of services in the public sector have been contracted out to the private sector. The relationship between employee and employer has been blurred – many of the cleaners I spoke to rarely saw their ISS site manager, who visited the hospital maybe only once or twice a week. They worked alongside NHS staff, but now wore the logo of a company about which they knew nothing. One long-serving employee had once been, several years ago, to a presentation in the centre of London on ISS's corporate vision for the future, and how it aimed at being the world's biggest personal services company. 'ISS is an absentee landlord,' he commented, as incomprehensible and meaningless to him as a French-speaking St Petersburg land-owner might once have been to a Russian peasant.

Even more importantly, contracting out has meant the loss of good overtime pay. Working overtime used to warrant as much as double pay, as did working on Sundays; it was how the low-paid managed to earn a 'living wage'. But employees taken on under the new contracts have had their rights to overtime pay removed, and extra shifts are paid at the standard rate. Weekend work earns only a small premium; the time of these employees costs almost the same regardless of what point in the week or the day they are working. Long-time employees transferred from the NHS to the new contractors who have their pay and working conditions protected say that they are now less likely to get overtime: those shifts go to the more recent employees who aren't entitled to the overtime pay.

It is this kind of development which has helped to loosen the link between low pay and long hours. The lowest levels of overtime working are in the lowest pay brackets, and the higher the hourly wage, the greater the proportion of people working overtime: only 39 per cent of employees earning under £5 an hour ever work overtime, compared to 61 per cent of those earning £10 or more.[17] The introduction of the minimum wage has led to a slight decline in hours as employers cut down their use of labour to save money.[18] Childcare is another constraint on low-paid long hours; its cost simply cancels out the advantage. Also likely is that poorer families opt for both parents to work different shifts and do the childcare between them in a relay, rather than one parent working long hours and the other caring; amongst Maev and Joshua's colleagues, at least, that was the pattern. So the link between low pay and long hours is probably not as strong as it was when a whole family was often dependent on the one breadwinner. Where it is still strong is where overtime pay leverages a worker up into a higher income level, as happens in manufacturing and in skilled trades such as plumbing. It is also strong in some parts of the service sector – hotels and restaurants, for example – in London particularly in the 'black economy', where there are immigrants of uncertain status willing to take the work.

Pete and Sarah, Maev and Joshua may appear to have little in common at first glance, but they all have a powerful sense of being trapped. Pete would be the first to acknowledge that he has considerable advantages and negotiating power in the labour market, but Joshua and Maev have a clearer vision of what needs to change and how. Central to the dilemma of all of them is how their time is not their own. Sarah has gone ahead and made her choice, at the high price of abandoning her career. But for Pete, it isn't clear how he can use his skills and talents to claim back his time. They are all caught up in the politics of time. What their lives reflect is how, over the last decade or so, time has become the battleground for a power conflict between employer and employee, arguably *the* battleground – and we didn't notice.

The Big Squeeze

The traditional patterns of working time and individuals' private lives which provided boundaries between work and rest have been erased. This 'timelessness' is one of the characteristics required of a flexible labour force. It takes on different characteristics in different jobs: shift systems which start early or finish late; on-call requirements; weekend working; an increase in night shifts. Work intrudes into a million bedrooms with pagers, bleepers, alarms to interrupt your rest – to check on financial markets, to make calls to another time zone. As in the television advertisement, you can phone up your bank at 2 a.m. and find someone on the line who is 'perky' and ready to answer your call; they could themselves be in another time zone, such as India. This timelessness is about the employee's availability; instead of extra staffing, employers cut labour costs to the bone, and when there's a surge in work, rely on motivating the extra labour needed from their core workforce – for free.

Where the crunching of the gears comes is in the lives of individuals trying to live simultaneously in two different time frames: the timelessness required by their employer and the 'timeliness' required by intimate human relationships – most markedly, the routine of children's daily lives – and how that connects to a wider network of family and friends and social activities. The knock-on effect of the 24/7 society is to deliver the final blow to those regular rituals which framed most people's lives, such as a family tea or Sunday lunch. These regular rituals originated in the early Industrial Revolution, as a way of giving the family a role in the daily routine after it lost its pre-eminence in the organisation of economic life, with the shift from family workshop to factory. No longer the source of livelihood, the family took on tasks of structuring time, of ritual and emotional support. That is what is now being eroded by the timelessness of a 'flexible' labour market which brings our working lives into direct conflict with our private family lives.

A recent study found that 21 per cent of mothers and 41 per cent of fathers started work between 6.30 and 8.30 a.m. several times a week.[19] A quarter of mothers and nearly half of fathers regularly worked between 5.30 and 8.30 p.m., and one in seven mothers and one in six fathers worked night shifts. Four out of ten mothers worked at weekends and more than half of fathers worked at least one Saturday a month, while a quarter of mothers and just under a third of fathers worked on Sundays at least once a month. Of those, 18 per cent of mothers and 22 per cent of fathers worked both Saturdays and Sundays. What suffered most, the study found, was time spent together as a family and as a couple, particularly in lower-income families where the parents arranged their shifts to operate a relay childcare system and avoid childcare costs.

It is not just the lengthening hours and the atypical hours which put the rhythms of family life under stress, it is also the fact that the family's exposure to this requirement for 'timelessness' has been significantly increased by the flow of women into the labour market over the last two decades. Time frames used to be split along gender roles: the women kept family time, the men adhered to employment time, and the conflict between the two was submerged in the marital relationship. Now, in dual-earner households, both partners are dealing with the conflict in a complex mosaic of employment and caring, and both are spending more time in paid employment. What that has meant for the average household (where at least one adult is employed) is that 7.6 weeks more a year was spent in paid work in 1998 than in 1981;[20] this is made up partly by increasing numbers of women going out to work, and partly by men working longer hours. For most households that transfer of time is probably even higher, because people are travelling further to get to their work (the average distance between home and work increased by a third between 1985 and 1998[21]), spending up to an hour a day commuting on average, and there has also been a decrease in the take-up of holiday. That lost eight weeks could be closer to twelve.

How did this happen? Where did the time go? How were the predictions throughout the first three-quarters of the twentieth century that technological advance would bring greater leisure so comprehensively proved wrong in the last quarter of the century? Now many people are working harder than their grandparents did, and a significant minority of the highest-status jobs require the kind of hours which would have been familiar to Victorian millhands.

What makes this development all the more baffling is that it is not true of other countries in Europe. The British work 8.7 hours a day, compared to the Germans' eight and the French 7.9,[22] but that's only half the story. Even more marked is the difference in holidays between Britain and continental Europe: the UK scrapes in with a mere twenty-eight days on average a year, a long way behind France on forty-seven, Italy on forty-four and Germany on forty-one.[23] A significant part of the difference is the continued observation in Europe of religious holidays and feast days, still widely celebrated even in increasingly secular countries such as France and Italy. When you add up the difference in hours per week and holidays between the UK and Europe, it amounts to the British working almost *eight weeks* more a year than their European counterparts.[24]

*   *   *

In the debate over Britain's overwork culture, we often forget the issue's long historical roots. The negotiation over working time was central to the emergence and development of the trade union movement in industrial capitalism. Karl Marx saw clearly in the mid-nineteenth century how the politics of time was essential to freedom: 'The shortening of the working day [is the] basic prerequisite [for] that development of human energy which is an end in itself, the true realm of freedom.'[25] Time and pay were the two variables over which unions struggled with bosses, and arguably they were more successful on the former than the latter. In 1923 the TUC concluded that reduced working hours was 'the principal advantage secured by over sixty years of trade union effort and sacrifice – the most important achievement of industrial organisation'. Historian James Arrowsmith calculates that from 1856 to 1981 the average total of hours spent at work over the course of a forty-year working life in Britain dropped from 124,000 to 69,000. That historic decline was halted in the early nineties at an average of 68,440. But this figure masks the increasing polarisation of work into the work-rich, time-poor and the work-poor, time-rich. While one-fifth of all households have no one in paid employment, as many as two-fifths are working harder than ever, and suffer from the big squeeze.

The trade union battle to reduce working hours lasted intermittently for nearly two centuries. Children's labour was the first battleground which established the principle of the state intervening to regulate working hours. (It was the moral and child welfare agenda which in the end overrode arguments of economic freedom in the first half of the nineteenth century and ensured legislation on working hours. The question must be whether those agendas are capable of exerting similar power two hundred years later.) There were successive parliamentary Acts throughout the nineteenth and twentieth centuries to reduce working hours. The final gasp was the engineering workers' campaign for a thirty-five-hour basic week in

1989–90, in the last big conflict in the UK over working hours. Employers were finally persuaded to come to settlements of a thirty-eight- or thirty-nine-hour week, just short of the unions' goal; the unions' £15 million strike fund still remains, to be used for any future 'Drive for Thirty-Five'. But the battle had lost impetus long before the eighties, argues Arrowsmith, who points to the fifties, when the trade union commitment to shorter hours was reduced to no more than a paper promise. The real push of union power in the next two decades was to trade time for more pay, which led to the institutionalisation of overtime. That became the 'Trojan horse' which enabled managers to renegotiate working practices through the eighties and nineties, forcing unions to accept flexibility and productivity deals in return for reductions in overtime and pay increases.

The chapter of history in which the struggle over working hours shaped the trade union movement, and vice versa, is largely over. Apart from some notable exceptions such as the teaching unions in their battle over workloads, and the civil service union bid for better work–life balance policies, it is not trade unions which will fight for those worst affected by the long-hours culture, such as managers and professionals, most of whom do not belong to any union. The European Union's Working Time Regulations, implemented in 1998, have been the only attempt to curb long hours in the last decade and a half, and according to the Chartered Institute of Personnel and Development (CIPD) 60 per cent of those working over forty-eight hours before the Regulations were implemented are still doing so, while 21 per cent are working more hours than before, and only 2 per cent have seen their working week reduced below forty-eight hours.[26]

One of the Regulations' biggest weaknesses is that it exempted workers with 'genuine autonomy', which covered anyone who could claim a degree of control over their hours, such as those in managerial or professional work – so the unpaid overtime put in by the likes of Pete does not come within their scope. The Regulations have been more successful in their impact on extending access to paid holidays at the lower end of the labour market than in reducing hours. But for all their inadequacies, they have contributed to employees' sense of entitlement. The CIPD survey showed broad support for them amongst long-hours workers, even if they didn't actually benefit from them personally. The really striking figure in the survey was the pathetic 2 per cent who had actually seen their hours fall since the implementation of the Regulations, which reveals the toothlessness of the government's bid to cut the long-hours culture.

Managing Time

Time at the end of the twentieth and the beginning of the twenty-first century is being restructured. How we collectively organise our use of time is changing, as is how we personally see time. We are in the process of abandoning the time disciplines which structured our working and private lives for much of the last two centuries. This kind of restructuring has happened before, in the late eighteenth century at the beginning of the Industrial Revolution, as the historian E.P. Thompson described in his famous essay 'Time and Work Discipline': 'The transition to a mature industrial society entailed a severe restructuring of working habits – new discipline, new incentives and a new human nature upon which these incentives could bite effectively.'

The dissenting traditions of Puritanism and Methodism provided the concepts of time essential for the development of a disciplined industrial workforce. The restructuring required getting rid of 'St Monday' – the habit of taking Monday and sometimes Tuesday off to recover from the excesses of Sunday – and the regularisation of craftsmen's patterns of short, intense periods of activity interspersed with idleness. Factories required everyone to turn up on time: punctuality was born. They also required a move from paying according to the task, to paying according to the time: instead of paying per pot or piecework, the employer paid per hour. Time became something to be bought and sold, and was intimately bound up with the work ethic in the writings of men such as Benjamin Franklin, who epitomised the spirit of eighteenth-century American self-improvement with his strictures on wasting neither money nor time. The proper use of time was divinely sanctioned, and would form part of that final arbiter of our behaviour, the Last Judgement: we would be held to account for our use of time. Thompson concludes: 'In mature, capitalist society all time must be consumed, marketed, put to *use*.' In 1967, when Thompson wrote his wonderful essay, he presumed that this capitalist exploitation of time had reached its apogee, and speculated on the possibilities of a future leisure age:

> *Puritanism, in its marriage of convenience with industrial capitalism, was the agent that converted people to new valuations of time ... which saturated people's minds with the equation that time is money. One recurrent form of revolt within Western industrial capitalism, whether the bohemian or the beatnik, has often taken the form of flouting the urgency of respectable time values ... if Puritanism was a necessary part of the work ethos which enabled the industrialised world to break out of poverty-stricken economies of the past, will the Puritan valuation of time begin to decompose as the pressures of poverty relax? ... Will people begin to lose that restless urgency, that desire to consume time purposively which most people carry just as they carry a watch on their wrists? ... If we are to have an enlarged leisure in an automated future ... what will be the capacity of experience of people who have this undirected time to live? ... If we become less compulsive about time, people might have to relearn some of the arts of living lost in the Industrial Revolution ... how to fill the interstices of their day with enriched, more leisurely, personal and social relations ... ?*[27]

22

What Thompson didn't bargain for was the insistent call of the mobile phone, filling the 'interstices of the day' which his generation never dreamt would be colonised by the demands of the job: the mobile follows us home, on the school run, even into the toilet. What we have to ask ourselves is, why did we flunk Thompson's challenge? Did we ever have the choice? Instead of learning leisure, our compulsion to see time as a commodity to be spent purposively has intensified, despite the decline of any sense of religious accounting, and despite the easing for the majority of the 'pressures of poverty'.

Thompson did not imagine that in the last decades of the twentieth century time would again be restructured as sharply and as violently as it was in the late eighteenth century. Would he have believed it possible that this would arouse so little resistance – indeed that such a large part of it would rest on voluntarism? No need of a nineteenth-century-style factory supervisor here to enforce timekeeping with disciplinary measures; the disciplines of this restructuring take place inside our heads.

What the Puritan dissenting traditions taught was how to *spend* time, instead of pass time. Now, in the twenty-first century, we are expected to learn how to *manage* time. It takes a tenth of a second for Google to find 9,170,000 items on time management. There are a lot of people out there offering to teach you or to sell you software which will help you manage time. Companies sign up their workforces to what amounts to a massive educational campaign to restructure their use of time. Since when did time become so unruly that it needed this much managing?

As soon as the word 'management' creeps into a sentence, there is reason for suspicion. We talk of *managing* what is often irreconcilable – it's a rhetorical reflex which replaces the conflictual rhetoric of, say, the seventies – and the word usually indicates complex compromises and trade-offs. The responsibility for negotiating those is squarely placed on the individual, because time management is regarded as a personal skill. At the level of micro-management of time, employers cannot always order compliance, particularly from highly skilled workers; they can only hope for efficient time-use by training and by adding pressure to the employee. This is the first characteristic of our restructured time: it's all down to us, individually. The contemporary disciplines of time are not externally imposed by managerial/professional work, but internalised, and we are made into our own timekeepers. We bear that sense of responsibility very keenly, blaming ourselves for our poor time management skills rather than entertaining the possibility that we've got too much to do. Poor time management is regarded as a sign of personal incompetence and inadequacy; we apply to ourselves and our use of time a rationale of efficiency.

The second characteristic of this restructured sense of time is that whereas industrial development required a huge degree of synchronisation – for example, in the factory – our experience of working time is becoming more and more individualised: there is a variety of shift patterns, part-time working and long hours. The debate over Sunday trading was the last gasp of the battle between 'collective' and 'individualised' time: by abandoning many of the restrictions on retailers opening on Sundays we gave up the idea of a communal day of rest, and took on the responsibility of finding and making our own point of rest. We have been decoupled, says sociologist Julia Brannen, from 'shared or collective experiences of time, for example rituals and celebrations; for each of us is compelled to create our own time schedules, live in our own time worlds, deciding when to stop work and when to begin again'.[28] If everyone just does their own thing, that's dandy – only it isn't always, because everyone is doing their own thing in an intensely competitive environment. The individualisation of time cripples any collective struggle over its organisation and how that reflects the distribution of power. There was a degree of protection in regularity and in negotiated hours – you know when the day is over and your job is done – and many of those most afflicted by long hours have lost that formal protection.

The third characteristic of our restructured time is the erosion of the boundaries between personal, private time and work time. E.P. Thompson pointed out that industrialisation drew a sharp division between work and life; we are now in the process of re-integrating them. You can attend a child's school play in work time and then pick up your work emails in the evening at home, just as in earlier centuries the mother might spin some wool for the loom while waiting for the kettle to boil. This is billed as an improvement in working conditions, which provides more auton-omy and enables employees to juggle family responsibilities with work. Will Hutton, head of the thinktank the Work Foundation, argues that this 'time sovereignty' is the panacea to solve the conflict between work and caring, to ease intolerable workloads; if we have control over our working hours, then the demands of the job are tolerable: 'I suspect that what got to [Alan] Milburn [the former Health Secretary who resigned to spend more time with his family] – and the raft of executives who are also resigning from top pos-itions – is not the long hours, but the inability to control them.'[29] Many in the most educated, skilled section of the labour market are prepared to trade time for autonomy, or what appears to be autonomy.

While the lack of boundaries creates some kinds of autonomy for those in senior managerial positions, for many it can become what Barbara Adam described in her book *Timewatch* (1995) as an 'unbearable, unfathomable burden' as workers shift between different forms of time, all of which 'need to be synchronised with lives of significant others and the society'.[30] So that, to prolong the above example, when you get home from the child's play there's an even larger email inbox, with urgent information for the meeting you have to attend the following day; that evening the child runs a temperature, and your mother calls to discuss a hospital test, and there's no time to catch up. Inevitably, shifting back and forth between family time and work time is constantly throwing up conflicts between competing demands which sometimes cannot be *managed*: do you turn up for the meeting with the schoolteacher, or finish off the report for the boss? Robert Reich in *The Future of Success* (2001) describes his dilemma when a critical business meeting was scheduled to clash with his son's sports game. In the end he opted for the latter and forwent the chance of a major work assignment – a decision which requires considerable material and emotional security.

A fourth characteristic of our restructured sense of time is the internalisation of efficiency. There's a reflex by which we calculate a cost/benefit analysis of whether an activity is worth the time we are investing in it. This can apply to doing the shopping, changing a nappy, compiling a report or attending a meeting. Are we doing something in as short a time as possible? It's as if we have absorbed the 'time-motion' studies of the late-nineteenth-century American management theorist Frederick Taylor, and are applying them not just to manufacturing processes but to our entire lives. The American housewife who produced a cookery book on Taylorist principles of time-efficiency in the 1920s was ahead of her time. Closely allied to efficiency is productivity: instead of being asked if we've had a good day, we're now asked if we've had a productive one. Nothing contributes more to frustration and impatience than attempting to live life efficiently. It allows no margin of error, no room for the ebb and flow. Listen to anyone talking about a day that has gone wrong and it's a tale of how their aspirations to efficiency were frustrated by traffic jams, cancelled trains, crashed computers or flight delays. But the aspirations continue, encouraged by the fantasies held out by advertising, which continually promises us more time.

Finally, the fifth characteristic of our restructured time is that we are in the process of shifting back to task-based time rather than the employed time instituted early in the Industrial Revolution. The boss now says, 'I don't care when or how you work, I'm just interested in the results.' All too often, this simply means exacting more work than can feasibly be done in the contracted hours; once again, the burden of resolving the irreconcilable is left to the individual.

Clashing priorities, too much work, and it's all down to us to *manage* it. Of course we fail. No wonder we come to hate time so much – it makes us feel inadequate because we can never control its passage: it's either too fast or too slow. So we blame time and complain that we have too little of it, when in fact time is one of the most democratic of resources. The richer and the more well-educated we are, the more likely we are to be dissatisfied with time. In his book *An Intimate History of Humanity* (1994) Theodore Zeldin quotes a magazine columnist who concludes: 'What we lack more than anything else is time.'[31]

How did we lose control of our time? How did we lose sight of the power relationship which underpins working time – effectively making the bosses' jobs a lot easier for them, because they don't need to supervise the hours of unpaid labour offered by Pete and thousands of others. How did we lose sight of Marx's insight into the essential precondition of human freedom – time and energy? Perhaps by being too busy managing time and trying to cobble together some vestige of shared time with partners, friends or family to understand the freedoms we've lost, let alone to find the time to start imagining which of the old-fashioned protections need to be restored and which new freedoms we need to realise. In the 'extended present', always brimful of preoccupations, comments sociologist Julia Brannen, there is such a constant state of busyness that the future never arrives, and the past is forgotten: 'It not only stops us from imagining the future, it stops us from doing anything about it or making it better.'[32]

2

All in a Day's Work

Time is only one part of the story. For many people it's not so much the time they spend at work, as the effort that is required while they are there. They complain of being rushed off their feet, of always having more work to do than time to do it in, and of there never being enough people to get the job done. By the end of the day they're exhausted: 36 per cent of us are too tired to do anything but slump on the sofa.[1] The nineties marked a significant increase in *work intensification*: workers are required to put in more effort and to work faster. This has been true throughout the economy, affecting most sectors of the labour market. If long hours have particularly hit white-collar Britain, work intensification has been across the board in both the public and the private sector, from school classroom to factory floor. Many of the cost savings attributed to contracting out public sector services have been achieved through work intensification: cleaners have more wards to clean, and catering assistants have more meals to prepare. The killer combination is when both the hours of the job and its intensity have increased, and that is usually the case: surveys show that the single biggest cause of long hours is having too big a workload.[2] 'More for less' is an old tool used by employers to reduce labour costs and improve competitive advantage, and the fight against it has historically been a large part of the trade union struggle, while the challenge to leverage up work effort has been a central preoccupation for management theorists. But the balance of power has tipped decisively against trade unions in Britain. They have lost members and lost battles, and with a few notable exceptions have failed to combat intensification.

One crude, anecdotal measure of job intensification is that the British used to be famous for what the French called 'tea-breakism'. Ask managers about teabreaks now, and they laugh with incredulity at how quickly they have become a distant memory. Office workers sip lattes and espressos at their keyboards: perhaps it's only possible to maintain their workrate with large and regular doses of caffeine. Such is the pace of work that over half the British workforce say they are too busy even to go to the loo.[3]

Economist Francis Green acknowledges that work intensity is notoriously difficult to measure – how can anyone assess how much someone is putting into their work? – but the best available measure is how people regard their own levels of effort.[4] Drawing data from nationally representative samples,[5] he compared responses to the statement 'My job requires that I work very hard.' In 1992, 32 per cent of workers 'strongly agreed' with the statement; by 1997 it had jumped to 40 per cent. Women were slightly more likely to agree than men, and the figures were higher in the public than in the private sector. Top of the intensification league was the education sector, where the proportion strongly agreeing rose by 14 per cent, to well over half of all teachers. These increases are dramatic.

Green also looked at workers' sense of their 'discretionary effort' – how much they choose to put into the job, as opposed to what they feel is asked of them. Again, this showed an increase in the number replying 'a lot', from 68.4 per cent in 1992 to 71.8 per cent in 1997; women indicated a more dramatic increase, from 69.9 per cent to 75.9 per cent. Green then looked at European surveys which asked workers whether they had to work at high speeds, and how often they had to work to deadlines. Those reporting working at very high speed 'all' or 'almost all' of the time rose from 17 per cent to 25 per cent between 1991 and 1996. When Green used these figures to create an index of work intensity for western Europe he found that Britain outstripped all other European countries for the fastest rise in work intensity. Some countries, such as Germany, Denmark and Greece, showed almost no increase at all.

Green's analysis is borne out by the European Working Conditions Surveys (EWCS), which asked respondents in all EU countries whether they had to work to speed or to tight deadlines.[6] The general trend in most countries has been up, but the UK is well ahead. More recent findings from the same survey indicate that the rate of intensification may have eased in the late nineties – a sharp push in the first five years of the decade may have subsequently stabilised.[7]

Green's analysis of the situation in Britain is echoed in the findings of the Job Insecurity and Work Intensification Report of the Joseph Rowntree Foundation, which asked whether employees had experienced an increase in the speed of work and the effort they put into their jobs over the previous five years (1992–97), and found that 64 per cent reported the former and 61 per cent the latter. This was a dramatic increase on a study a decade earlier, in 1986, which reported 55.6 per cent and 38.1 per cent respectively.[8] Intensification began in manufacturing in the eighties, and accelerated in the nineties when it hit professionals and white-collar workers in particular, found the European Working Conditions Surveys for 1995–96 and 2000. The evidence of white-collar blues is underpinned by a 1999 survey for the Institute of Management which found that 69 per cent of its members reported an increased workload in the previous year.

Marx argued that there were three main characteristics of labour under capitalism: it was progressively deskilled as part of the mechanisation process; the surplus value accrued in production was appropriated by the owner of capital; and the latter sought always to reduce the 'porosity' of the working day. By porosity, Marx meant those moments of downtime which were interspersed in the routine of the day – the minutes spent waiting for supplies to arrive on the assembly line, for a machine to be mended or prepared, or for someone to arrive for a meeting. On the first characteristic Marx was plain wrong, but on the third he foresaw one of the central characteristics of the late-twentieth-century labour market – reducing porosity, or intensification, has become a crucial component of efficiency and performance. What managers have sought to do over the last two decades is to whittle away all 'unproductive time'. Shifts have been rescheduled to eliminate breaks, and the organisation of work has been refined to ensure a steady flow of work.

One of the ways in which this last is achieved is through 'functional flexibility'; employees have been trained to do more than one job, so that if a machine breaks down or there is a delay in stocks arriving, they can do something else and then turn back to the original job. Francis Green found a strong link between this kind of flexibility and agreement with the statement 'My job requires that I work very hard.' Companies instituted multi-tasking – giving someone several jobs to do, and leaving them to co-ordinate the different tasks in the most time-efficient way. The aim is to ensure a continuous workflow, so there will be no time wasted waiting at the employer's expense. The conclusion of one study of six organisations was that the whole 'wage–effort' relationship is being restructured in several different ways, by reducing non-working time and by increasing the effort required.[9] The study quotes a machine operative from one of the organisations it looked at: 'We're running the presses with four men, five if you're lucky . . . stress and fatigue are beginning to creep in. Young men in their twenties are tired. I hear of people coming in at six and I say, what are you going to do with the afternoon? "I'm going to bed." . . . There used to be a lot of activity, there used to be football and God knows what else after, they haven't got the time.'

The study described the same process in the public sector, and quoted a local authority employee: 'It's run more like a business . . . whereas before you'd go in and it was like a more friendly basis. You'd go in and you'd do what was required of you and then [the patients] want the company, cup of tea, sit down and have a chat, whereas you can't do that now because time's money.'

Green cites two influential management techniques as important in speeding up workflow: total quality management and just-in-time working: 'The imperative of total quality management is that many more individuals have to take continued responsibility for quality checks and improvements and so on. Rather than wait for someone to tell them what to do, they have to get on and do it.' Just-in-time aims to perfect the logistical flow of materials so that whatever is needed for a task arrives – just in time.

In an attempt to understand the process of work intensification and how it came about, I went to an industrial estate on the outskirts of an old coalmining town in the Midlands. This is the home of Saltfillas – the name has been changed – a small family company. From the windows of its offices could be seen the old coalmining slagheaps and the even older canals which run on either side of the estate. It's an area which has experienced the vicissitudes of industrial change for nearly three hundred years, and the legacy of some of those changes – the bankruptcies and the works closures – is evident in the vacant lots and boarded-up buildings in nearby towns.

The predominantly female workforce of Saltfillas have lived through some of this change, with husbands, fathers, brothers and neighbours who once worked down the pits or at the steelworks. The global economy has ripped out the economic entrails of these towns in the last two decades, and unemployment is above the national average. Survival is a precarious business. That's certainly true of Saltfillas; it's had few spare resources to buffer itself from the pace of globalisation – deregulation, increasing competition and the rapid expansion of European trade – so it's some achievement for Dick and his father, who founded the business in the early sixties, that it's still thriving on a modest but secure footing.

The reason I went to visit Saltfillas is not because they work long hours – on the contrary, the company instituted a 7 a.m.–3.30 p.m. shift pattern because the workforce wanted to get off early, and by 5 p.m. it's empty bar a few evening-shift workers. They can't afford to pay overtime, and they've even managed to stop a long tradition of management coming in on a Saturday morning by reorganising rotas. I went to Saltfillas because the company offered to explain to me how competition drives the intensification of work, how and why they have exacted more work from fewer people, and to give me some insight into why the workforce has gone along with it.

This is not bleeding-edge new economy, and this is not a cut-throat company trying to work its labour force into the ground; on the contrary, it's an old-fashioned firm in many respects, which still holds to a sense of loyalty, and a relationship in which the management will treat employees fairly if they do a fair day's work. Staff turnover is low, and Dick joked that he was buying gold watches for twenty-five years' service in bulk this year.

Saltfillas started out packing salt, and now packs other dry products such as washing powder. It's high-volume, low-margin packing. On the factory floor the noise is deafening, with the clatter of machinery which fills, labels and packs in a mesmerising Heath Robinson-style series of movements. The factory workers' job is to keep the lines moving, sorting out any glitches, ensuring supplies are ready and removing the finished product. It's ceaseless, repetitive hard work. A radio blares out over the noise of the machines, everyone is in hats and overalls and no jewellery is allowed, in order to meet exacting hygiene regulations.

The Meaning of Overwork

Next door in the office, Tracey has been with the company since she started work at fifteen; in twenty-five years she's risen from the factory floor to being production and quality control manager. She is responsible for making sure the company is always using the available labour to its full potential. It's a constant, complex juggling act as she moves from factory floor to her computer terminal and back. There's no doubt in her mind that the workforce have to work harder now than they did when she first started: 'When I first started, we'd go on a line and after a couple of hours, we'd stop the line and all go off for a toilet break. Then we'd be back to work for a while before it was another break, and then the same thing happened in the afternoons. Between 8 and 4.35, we'd stop the lines two or three times on top of the two breaks we were allowed. Sometime in the early eighties, they offered us a bribe – a pay rise in return for stopping that.'

She reckons the toilet breaks were probably not much more than ten minutes or so – perhaps occasionally someone would have a quick cigarette at the same time. That added up to twenty to thirty minutes a day off for each employee. 'No wonder they stopped us. We've had to get more efficient, and there's some long-term employees who've been stuck in a routine who don't like the change. But we talk to them individually and we try to be as honest as we can with them; sometimes you have to say, "If we don't do it like this, we'll lose the contract." We do work harder. In recent years – about the last six – we've never had people with nothing to do, because we now have such a range of products. It's always busy.'

Ed, a senior manager, explains how the 'machines have to work all the time now, there is no quiet time', and any cleaning or maintenance is done after hours. If someone needs to go to the toilet, other packers have to cover for them – the line is never turned off. Computers assist the speed-up of the flow of work to ensure the lines and packers are constantly being juggled to meet orders by the deadlines. The company has diversified into dozens

34

of different products, so the process of aligning into a continuous stream of work the machines, packers, supplies, orders and deadlines is immensely complex. The essential prerequisite for such a system is that employees are 'multi-skilled', so they can work on different lines doing different jobs at different times.

'The labour has to be more intensively managed so that people work more continuously. We've always had every packer trained on every line since 1980 – it's much more flexible. We avoided job descriptions; perhaps if we'd had unions involved, we wouldn't have had that kind of flexibility,' says Ed. 'Two years ago we explained to them that they would have jobs they hadn't done in the past; we told them that "We can give you the pay rise, but that may mean cleaning sometimes." We kept them informed all the time. When people leave the company, they're not being replaced: their jobs are shared out between people, and that might mean new tasks for people, but they understand that. We've not recruited in three years. We tell them that the survival of this company depends on you, and that wins their co-operation. They saw a big company locally which went down – that wakes them up. They see it's a very competitive environment.'

Dick chimes in enthusiastically: 'There's a big change in attitude from the seventies when they'd say, "I'm not doing that, it's not my job." They don't say that now – probably because of the Thatcher years. The attitude now is that we're all in it together. They see workers on the television saying they've done everything they could and yet their companies are going bust. We share much more information with the supervisors, and the pressure from customer complaints and machine breakdowns drips down the hierarchy. The supervisor knows that if we don't get this order out, we'll lose the business.'

The turn-round times have become much tighter as well. Just-in-time delivery ensures that no stocks are sitting around in warehouses (it's a waste of money storing and buying products before they're needed), so the whole system is always working on tight deadlines of a few days – as the petrol blockade of 2000 brought home so powerfully. An entire supermarket network can be a week away from running out of salt. 'We used to say we'll deliver an order in fourteen days, but now it can be expected in three. If they said it must be done in two days, we'll do it. We try to negotiate, but they keep a record of our performance,' said Dick.

Even with the most sophisticated planning, demand can still be unpredictable, leading to sudden intense periods of work: 'There was a marinade powder and they put over £1 million into advertising it, and we went from an order of 5,000 cases to 30,000. We'd bought machines to cope with their predicted capacity, but the demand caught the manufacturers off guard and we were running around like headless chickens. If you can react quickly to unexpected demand, you can do very well.'

For small suppliers like Saltfillas, the relationship with their customers has been revolutionised. For a start, there are far fewer of them, and consolidation and concentration mean that the balance of power has shifted away from the supplier; supermarkets hold such a grip over them that they can pretty much dictate their terms, making or breaking a company on the strength of a few contracts. This is the sharpest contrast for Dick from the days when his father was negotiating with dozens of different co-operative societies. Now he has no relationship of any kind with the supermarket buyers. He's lucky if he gets through to them on the phone. When a European company undercut him on a bid with a long-standing customer, he was told to match their price or lose the contract. He couldn't afford not to, and the company packed the line at a loss until it could invest in more sophisticated machinery which enabled it to cut labour costs.

What I found at Saltfillas is a story familiar throughout UK manufacturing, of how increased competition coupled with de-industrialisation has enabled employers to push through, bit by bit, a process of work intensification. Management's increased communication with workers reinforces the sense of the precariousness of a company's survival in the global market. This awareness reconfigures older perceptions of the distinct and often conflicting interests of management and employees: the 'We're all in this together' line has been amply used by management to exact higher levels of effort or flexibility. This is what labour economist Andrew Scott found in his study of three British factories in the early nineties: threats of closure, unemployment, of being uncompetitive mean that it 'may be that the modern wage–effort bargain has become still more elastic, capable of being stretched well beyond the limits to which it was subject in the past'.[10] Workers find it harder and harder to construct a credible case against this piecemeal encroachment on the pace and nature of their work. 'You can't buck the market,' intoned Margaret Thatcher in the eighties, and her words still resonate on the factory floor.

How Information Technology Makes for Hard Work

The biggest single factor driving work intensification is information technology, argues Francis Green. It enables greater use to be made of time and 'fills up gaps that would otherwise be natural breaks in the pattern of work'. He backs up his argument by pointing to research showing that 42 per cent of workplaces which had introduced new technology in the previous five years experienced a substantial increase in the pace of work, compared with 31 per cent of workplaces where no new technology had been introduced.[11] Often the introduction of information communication technologies (ICT) leads to changes in both the job process and the whole way the work and the organisation is structured. Green found that where there had been reorganisation the rates of intensification were dramatic, with 45 per cent reporting a substantial increase, compared to 29 per cent where there had been no change. If that reorganisation introduced a greater involvement of workers – i.e. they were required to take on more responsibility for tasks – the proportion of workplaces experiencing work intensification increased again, to 48 per cent compared with 30 per cent where there was no increased worker involvement.[12] Nor is such reorganisation a one-off adjustment; it becomes a continuous process as a response to constantly evolving ICT and changing market conditions.

Information technology also increases the pressure on employees to perform, as companies themselves are subject to more exacting regulations and quality control. There is less room for shoddy work, for an absent-minded moment on the assembly line, because the technology enables tracking of products; for example, if a hair was found in one of Saltfillas' packets, the company would be able to track, out of the thousands packed every day, who the packer was at the time the packet went through.

The technology to measure every moment of the employee's performance has enabled the extension of Frederick Taylor's dream into white-collar work, bringing unprecedented control and time efficiency. It transforms the traditional hierarchical structures of bureaucracy, by facilitating supervision and removing the need for layers of managerial control. Here's how Liz, working in the mortgage department of a major bank in Yorkshire, describes how the computer has replaced the clerical supervisor:

We had a laminated sheet of barcodes representing a series of tasks on our desk, and every time we did anything we had to swipe the appropriate barcode with a laser reader pen. We had seventeen minutes to get out a mortgage offer. If the phone went, we had to answer it within two rings and all the calls were recorded and monitored to check whether we were giving out accurate information and the manner with which we dealt with the call. Every time we made a call we had to swipe the pen, and every time we answered the phone we had to swipe. You had to swipe if you were going to the toilet or to get a coffee. If you wanted to talk to a colleague you had to swipe, so that all interactions with colleagues were being monitored. When we had finished for the day, we had to log in and out. The whole thing was then downloaded to the supervisor, who could look at the log to check productivity.

It was like working for Big Brother. Some of my colleagues would say it's for the greater good – trying to get profits up. The people I worked with came from very varied backgrounds. Some women who had worked in factories didn't mind it because they were used to being closely monitored. It was the younger ones who resented it, or those who came from managerial backgrounds or were college-educated; they wanted more freedom and initiative.

The log Liz describes can be programmed to highlight any departure from the required routine – such as too many toilet breaks or too many 'consultations with colleagues'. The level of supervision is superior to anything that even the most beady-eyed boss could achieve.

At the lower levels of the labour market, information technology has frequently been used to increase pressure and reduce autonomy. In professional and managerial jobs the story is rather different: it has increased both pressure *and* autonomy. The higher the level of the employee's computer skills, the greater the degree of anxiety. Research on the impact of information technology on the upper end of the labour market is still in its early stages, but the indications are that it has significantly increased workloads. How do we use email, mobile phones, the internet and laptops, and why haven't they lived up to the promise of the advertising of making our lives easier? Why do so many people say that they have in fact made their jobs more difficult?

There are two separate issues about how technology can increase the burdens of work: the volume of information it makes available to us, and the way in which it increases our own accessibility.

Firstly, the volume of information to which the internet provides access is obvious within a few minutes: a Google search under almost any heading will bring up thousands of relevant items. Eighty-two per cent of managers mentioned the proliferation of the information they had to deal with as a cause of long hours.[13] Material which would once have been kept within the company or department is now widely available on the internet or intranet. The knowledge economy has transformed the circulation of data so that anywhere on the net there could be exactly the information you're looking for. So when do you settle for anything less ?

What accelerates the flow of information is that the whole balance of effort involved in its distribution has reversed: once, a request for a particular bit of information might have required typing it out or photocopying it and putting it in the post; now, it simply requires an email with an attachment. The marginal costs incurred by the sender have shrunk to a few minutes, while the costs to the receiver to read, digest and consider the information are as time-consuming as ever. Far more information is being distributed than ever before, but what has not changed is our capacity to absorb and process it. In fact there is some evidence that the increased flow of information actually hinders our mental processes, making us less productive, not more. Psychologist David Lewis described in *Information Overload* (1999) how the brain becomes tired trying to keep up, and loses its powers of concentration and the ability to think clearly or rationally. He cited Stephen Grossberg's studies of mind and brain, which warned that one of the strategies the brain uses to reduce fatigue is 'to pay attention to anything new, while taking no notice of what is unchanged'.[14]

Secondly, many of the new information technologies transform accessibility. The mobile phone dismantles many of the spatial boundaries of work introduced by industrialisation. It was the development of factories which bounded work spatially, separating it from the home. For the middle classes the spatial differentiation became even more clear-cut with the growth of suburbs and commuting. In the last twenty years mobile phones, laptops, company intranets and home PCs have dissolved the separation between our work and our private lives. It's true that the spillover is both ways – children phoning their parents in the middle of meetings, for example – but we have been better at policing that intrusion of home life into work than work into home. As one civil servant emailed me: 'I frequently get emails from colleagues sent at 2 or 3 a.m. And what's more, copies of replies sent back around the same time. One man at a meeting recently admitted that he "snuck out of bed" in the middle of the night to do his emails, trying not to wake his partner, who "got annoyed about it". He'll be dead before he's fifty.'

A manager for a software company emailed: 'I enjoyed the rush in a way, but . . . I didn't want to see friends or family in the evenings or weekends, it was just more hassle . . . I had a secretary organise my emails into four categories: urgent-important, not urgent but important, not important but urgent, etc., and I would only read and action the most pressing until I could face another long night at home sorting out all the others – only to find fifty new ones the next morning . . . The most apt metaphor to sum the experience up is to imagine yourself standing at the back end of a dumper truck full of gravel. It slowly tips out, covering you. You dig frantically to stop being buried but the gravel keeps on coming and never ceases. If you stop digging, you'll die.'

But the frustration and resentment has not triggered any campaign or collective action to protect privacy. There have been no battles to institute 'no calls outside office hours' contracts, or protests against the home PC being linked up to the company intranet. On the contrary, this Trojan horse has frequently been welcomed; as one female executive explained, 24/7 accessibility is a price worth paying for greater freedom over when she works. The trade-off is privacy and boundaries in exchange for a degree of autonomy –

you may work long, unpredictable hours, your leisure may never be free of the possibility of work intruding, but you have a measure of control and can take off a couple of quiet hours in the middle of the afternoon.

Technology has also transformed accessibility within organisations. That's the appeal of email – private, quick and direct. The barriers of the bureaucratic, hierarchical organisation appear to crumble as we click on the 'send' box; there are no secretaries to brazen our way past, no underlings or deputies to deal with, we can reach anyone anywhere. Email has bred its own character and tone of democratic directness and informality. Of course, senior executives quickly discovered this led to overload, and put their secretaries in charge of their email, but its accessibility and privacy continues to be seductive, and reconfigures office relationships, subverting hierarchies and strengthening more egalitarian networks.

But email has some significant drawbacks. It has evolved as a means of communication very rapidly, with little etiquette or codes of conduct, and has major flaws: email correspondence is very hard to conclude satisfactorily, and because of its brevity and speed it is often very imprecise, thus leading to a much longer correspondence in order to clarify issues. One research study shows that 'more than 65 per cent of all email messages fail to give the recipients enough information to act upon, and ambiguous and poorly-written emails can lead to misunderstandings that can cause tension within the workplace, and may lead to incorrect instructions being carried out'.[15] Judy Bendis, an occupational psychologist, was called in to a major public sector organisation to help tackle the rising tide of emails. The biggest problem was that emails were distracting, she found: people were checking their email inbox two or three times an hour, which broke up their concentration; each check took at least two or three minutes, and then another minute to refocus attention. The whole process, repeated through the day, can take up 25 per cent of the employee's time. One of the chief complaints of managers is constant interruptions, and email is one of the culprits.

But the biggest complaint of all is the sheer volume of emails. The higher you rise in an organisation, the bigger your electronic in-tray: an average of twenty-two emails a day at junior management level increases to forty-seven at the most senior, and the figure is growing all the time.[16] Emails have a disproportionate impact on long and anti-social hours because they are typically dealt with either at the beginning or the end of the day. Asynchronous communication may have seemed initially like a form of liberation – you could find a moment in your own time to reply – but it is indeed often *in your own time*. Bendis found that: 'For managers not at their desks for much of the day because they are in meetings, the only time to catch up is out of normal working hours. A lot of people were printing them out to read on the train or tube or picking them up at weekends.' Those working part-time often have proportionally an even bigger email in-tray to deal with – catching up on the day or days they've been off. Taking a long holiday exacts a heavy price when emails pile up at the rate of fifty to a hundred a day, and many admit to checking up on them while they're away, to prevent the build-up. Mary is a senior executive in an NHS trust:

I have an absolutely enormous electronic in-tray – usually about 250 to attend to. Of those about two hundred will include an attachment which requires my reading and commenting on it. I get about fifty emails a day, and 50 per cent of them I deal with immediately. Another 25 per cent I try and deal with at the end of the day and another 25 per cent get dealt with later. Usually I'll be in at the weekend and have a clear-out. I had some time away recently and got back to find five hundred emails waiting. A lot of them have useful information, especially if you want to keep a breadth of knowledge of what's going on in the organisation. In the past, managers of a particular expertise were left to deal with that but it's all more interconnecting now.

The 'carbon-copy' function of email gets a big share of the blame for its volume. Senior managers are often being copied into emails just to cover the employee's back, or in the hope of drawing attention to their work. Bendis found in her study that email was being used to seek 'positive strokes', particularly from a manager to an underling, the reply being the modern-day equivalent of a pat on the back,

But the carbon-copy email can also be vital. Mary explained how she has to keep abreast of a huge range of information, because she never knows at what point a particular development could impact on her responsibilities. A predecessor in her type of job twenty years ago would have kept his (it probably would have been a man) focus on his own department, she commented, but that thinking is now scorned as creating 'silo' organisations which can't keep up with the speed of information flow and the pace of change. The sociologist Manuel Castells coined the phrase 'the network society' to describe the relationships which open up in the constantly changing and unpredictable digital society. The interconnectedness draws more and more activities into relationship with each other: the company whose stock price rises on rumours of a government initiative, the supplier whose contracts could then be hit, and so on. It's the syndrome of the butterfly flapping its wings in the Bay of Bengal which causes storms elsewhere: small actions can have disproportionate consequences. The quality of the network is what determines the success or failure of the organisation or individual: you never know from what point will come information which may determine opportunity or disadvantage.

The network society has a very clear impact on hard work. The individual who has built up a network of useful relationships is at the nodal point of intersection where information is accurately analysed, decisions are made and power lies, but this is also where information overload is at its most acute. The more points of intersection the node bears, and thus the more flows of information, the more effective the decision-making and the potential for brilliant strategic breakthroughs – and, of course, the more work . . . much more work.

This makes the task of management much more complex – there are many more balls to keep juggling. And it makes the concept of professionalism, where definitions of commitment have always incorporated long hours and availability to the client, positively punishing. The interface with clients becomes more demanding; in the most skilled, lucrative parts of the labour market they want instant access throughout waking hours, while intensified competition accelerates the required turnaround times. The result is the kind of hours common in banking, corporate law, accountancy and consultancy, where seventy-hour weeks can be common and the timelessness of 24/7 global capitalism is unmediated by any reference to human well-being.

The Fast Eat the Slow

The speed with which information is processed and acted upon becomes a critical source of competitive advantage. At the heart of fast-moving competitive sectors of the knowledge economy the pace of work is in unpredictable spurts of intense activity; a far cry from the steady routine which was regarded as a great achievement of industrialised bureaucracies. This is where information technology is transforming our concept of time, hugely speeding up many processes and putting the capacity for human beings to adapt their organisation of work, and to keep up, under constant severe pressure; the computing power of silicon chips doubles every eighteen months, so engineering calculations which would have taken many years in the 1940s took two days by 1969, four hours by 1976, and a mere fifteen minutes today. That kind of speed provides extraordinary opportunities, but the competition is intense. As Klaus Schwab, President of the World Economic Forum, put it,

The Meaning of Overwork

'We are moving from a world in which the big eat the small to a world in which the fast eat the slow.'

For the internet bank egg, that kind of comment has been a driving principle in its short, successful history. egg is about as far from Saltfillas as one could imagine: squeezed into a basement of the great Victorian red-brick palace of Prudential Insurance in central London, it claims to be the biggest finance services provider on the internet, and one of the four most successful creations of the dot.com boom after Amazon, eBay and Yahoo. Mike Harris, who set up the company as its first Chief Executive under the wing of the Prudential, knows a lot about speed and how crucial it is for success; he also knows how it makes for a lot of hard work. He says there is simply nothing he can do about the demanding deadlines, and he recounts the dizzying pace of egg's development:

We launched in October 1998 on an artificially set date to control the amount spent on the launch – to prevent 'creeping sophistication'. We didn't want an overspecified model in the marketplace, because the world will have changed by the time you get round to bringing it out. As soon as you spot a gap in the market, it has to be exploited – a lot of our success has been that we've seen an opportunity and we've got to the market quickest. That urgency is part of the culture, and it causes stress inevitably; there is nothing you can do about that, you can only manage the stress through support and resources. I'm sure we impose unnecessarily tight deadlines.

The launch of a new business is always very stressful . . . people were working seven days a week for three to four months prior to the launch. It's not that we asked them to, it just gets very committed and very intense. After a big launch you can normally ease off, but for us it got even worse because of the volume of business – we reached our five-year target in the first six months, with 500,000 customers and £5 billion in deposits. Nothing worked, we didn't have the capacity, and it put huge strain on all of us and it was crisis after crisis; some people did get very stressed, but it felt supportive, it didn't feel too hard.

He paused and added that he'd recently been looking at a video of the egg management team made about five years ago. He admitted, 'It was a bit of a shocker for me to see how all the management had aged in that time.' He continued: 'Within a few months, we switched to internet supported by phones rather than the other way around, bringing forward a strategy we had intended to implement over three years, but the internet was moving fast. By September 1999 we launched the credit card, and it was the fastest-growing internet credit card in the world; the pace was frenetic. It was the launch all over again.' By February 2000 egg's rate of expansion had been rapid, and it went for an IPO, Initial Public Offering, raising capital on the stock market. The following year it acquired a French internet bank. The pace hasn't slackened.

Looking back at a distinguished business career over several decades, Harris is unequivocal: 'The pace of work is getting worse, there's no doubt about that. It's the rate of change in globalisation – you're subject to competition from people who are far bigger than you and who do things you've never thought of. Wherever you look you see the global competition, and you no longer have the forms of protection because of deregulation.'

Globalisation is a notoriously large piece of baggage into which all manner of phenomena can be packed, but the most significant are information technology and deregulation, and the way they interact. They put organisations under intense pressure to remain competitive, and the bigger the potential pickings, the sharper the competition. It is that need for competitiveness which becomes the cause and justification of work intensification. For example, it was trade deregulation which opened up Saltfillas' UK market to the European company which undercut it, and egg had to fend off competitors from Europe and the United States. Transnational corporations closely measure the comparative performance of the labour forces in the different countries where they have affiliates, found the Joseph Rowntree Report on Job Insecurity and Intensification. This makes for intense intra-firm rivalry, and companies move production to cheaper labour markets.[17] These factors were profoundly unsettling for British workers, because of the ease and speed with which corporations could move production from one country to another, claimed researchers David Ladipo and Frank Wilkinson.

They also found that workers were unsettled by the 'impatience' of dominant stakeholders, and that 'managers and employees were conscious of the increasingly "contingent" commitment of their investors'. As Will Hutton puts it: 'The more liquid a financial asset, the less committed the owner must be to the long-term health of the underlying investment. If the going gets tough or conditions change the investor has already made provision for his or her escape: sell the financial asset, withdraw the short-term loan, rather than share the risk of restructuring and of managing any crisis.'[18]

The connection between the convolutions of a company's share price and hard work is not straightforward. Did the plummeting of Marconi's share price in 2001 increase its employees' workload? Or the spectacular gyrations of lastminute.com's shares affect the hours its workers put in? The fluctuations of the stock market are one of the factors reinforcing the logic of competition and efficiency which undermine any resistance and inculcate insecurity, the survive-or-die mentality which enables managers to push through forms of work intensification and to motivate high levels of effort. Business psychologist Jock Encombe argues that the impact of the stock market is intense on private sector organisations, and can't be overestimated: 'The sheer pressure to deliver the numbers is systemic, because if the share price suffers, you get taken over.'

This was a theme which emerged strongly in another company I visited. Travel Inn, a budget hotel chain which made it to the *Sunday Times* Best Companies to Work For list, is a young, rapidly growing company in the expanding services and leisure sector, where much employment is expected to be created in the next decade. It is owned by Whitbread plc, and its workforce is young – the average age is only just over thirty. I was curious to see what made this generation work hard; they hadn't lived through mass unemployment, so how did the 'survive-or-die' competition of the market bite on them?

Simon Mahon, the young general manager of Travel Inn's newly opened 165-bed hotel in Liverpool, would be the first to admit that launches are always difficult and require long hours. He had a clear sense of the kind of hotel he wanted to run, and it was proving hard to achieve the standards he wanted. Why? Because the labour costs had been slashed in the launch budget. 'I have to lower costs. There's been a cost-efficiency drive on the food and beverages side. We have to get the right team ethic. There's no slack in the system, and that gives the operator [manager] hell.'

I told him I'd noticed that there were only two people to serve in both the bar and the restaurant. As they ran from one disgruntled customer to the next, they looked panicked. Mahon, as a conscientious manager, was alarmed. So why the need for the cost efficiencies? 'It's corporate strategy to cut costs – it's what makes the company more profitable and gives the shareholders benefits so they will invest more. That's what my boss would say.'

'What would you say?' I asked.

'I'd say that's a short-term view, and that the customer will choose the company they like, and that it's the fat cats who are the ones who get the benefits.' Then he added, 'My labour budget is very tight – I manage that, I don't complain – the key is to get people trained. Two people could have managed that situation [the bar and the restaurant] if they had been trained. The cost saving was forced on me, and in the end we under-recruited so that there was no slack in the system, no allowance for any of the team leaving. We used to over-recruit by 25 per cent to allow for some slack. Training has been cut from six weeks to four weeks.'

When there was a staff shortage, managers had to help out. Mahon called over one of his deputies, Martin, to find out why he was working on his day off. 'I'm working seventy to eighty hours a week at the moment,' said Martin, 'but we're well paid – I'm on £22,000 with a bonus of perhaps another £5,000. In a few weeks it will be down to forty-five hours, but if I did that now, the hotel wouldn't gel. It's one to two months of being there, being very available, then the whole team comes together. I don't get paid for today.'

Twenty-four-year-old Keri, the head of housekeeping, is also in on her day off to cover for shortages of housekeeping staff. She has a two-year-old child, and looks exhausted. 'Today I'm cleaning rooms because we're short of staff and I don't want to put more work on my team – they're all working overtime already. I need another ten part-time staff. It's my day off today, and I'm supposed to finish at 2 p.m. At the moment I'm working six days a week because I want it to be right. Opening a hotel is very hard work. I'm enjoying it so much – it's a new challenge for me, even though I'm cleaning rooms. I don't get paid overtime, it's for my personal goal; we have audits to achieve and I don't want to let my team or the manager down by not giving 100 per cent. I get paid £18,000 plus another 25 per cent bonus.' She jokes, 'It probably works out at about £1 an hour.'

As Martin and Keri appeared at our table on their days off even Mahon seemed somewhat taken aback by their hard work, but he admitted he was not very different: 'What frightens me,' he said, 'is that I don't do anything else except work – I've no hobbies.' He said things were about to change; now they'd launched he'd have the freedom to recruit more staff, and the management team would get proper time off, but he had a keen sense of the competitive pressure on the company: 'For a short-term profit, you don't invest in hotels. If we don't get the investment we won't succeed as a company. The return on capital employed on new build is 17 per cent over three years, and there are more attractive investment options, so we have to keep up that profitability. By 2007, supply will outstrip demand for budget hotels, and we will be fighting in the most difficult marketplace – and we will be fighting with a product which is three to four years old.'

My most striking impression as I left the Travel Inn in a dusty back street of Liverpool's city centre, its new paint still gleaming, was that the brunt of the hard work fell on junior and middle management. As Les Worrall and Cary Cooper conclude in their four-year study of managers, 'The prime driver to the creation of the long working hours culture is the cumulative impact of years of cost cutting where managers are just "plain overloaded" as they pick up the tasks left behind from delayered and redundant posts.' They ask: 'In an economy where competitive pressures can only get more intense, what can we really do to combat these forces?'[19] The staff in Liverpool were putting in the long unpaid hours of overtime to compensate for the company's cuts on labour costs, but that didn't diminish their commitment; the company's bonus schemes, incentives and career progression programmes had reconciled them to the enormous effort required of them. What legitimised the company's claim on them was their understanding of the competitiveness of the market; they even seemed to find the toughness of their position exhilarating – something that the company seems to know works to its advantage: Travel Inn's induction programme is called 'Mission Innpossible'.

The Meaning of Overwork

Hard Work is Not Enough

If globalisation and its rhetoric of competition and efficiency convinces many of the need to increase their effort, what part is played by the much-quoted theme of job insecurity? What contribution does the P45 play in keeping people's noses to the grindstone? The theory runs that the unpredictable and sharp fluctuations in the global market lead to companies needing a flexible labour force – one which they can downsize without too great a cost, which they can shift to new tasks easily, and which they can increase through the use of agency, temporary and contract labour at short notice for short periods. Loyalty and hard work for a company no longer count for anything, and redundancies are an unavoidable fact of life, part of the restructuring companies continually have to implement if they are to remain competitive. The agile company has to delayer and downsize. These themes were pervasive in the media throughout the nineties: Francis Green has calculated that by the middle of that decade the phrases 'job security' or 'job insecurity' occurred on average one and a half times every day in the British press. But the media coverage didn't reflect reality: the average length of time spent in a job in Britain actually increased significantly for all types of work between 1992 and 2000, and the UK's proportion of temporary work is well below the EU average.[20]

The intense media interest reflected two trends. Firstly, British workers' remarkably high level of fear of losing their jobs. According to OECD figures, in 2001 Britain was second only to South Korea for the proportion (41 per cent) of workers 'unsure of a job even if they perform well'. Interestingly, British workers' sense of insecurity concerned their own personal position, not that of their company: the percentage saying they were worried about their company's future was well below the OECD average. What makes this such a disturbing statistic is that even if the company was successful, and they themselves were doing a good job, many British workers did not feel secure.[21]

Another international survey found that the drop in job security between 1985 and 1995 was sharper in Britain than in any other European country, falling from 70 per cent to 48 per cent.[22] There is no sign of this anxiety easing. In a 2003 study Britain topped the international insecurity league, well ahead of the US and the rest of Europe.[23] In the same year, a survey by the trade union Unifi (it represents many clerical workers, particularly in the banking sector) found that over half its members expected job cuts in the next year. There is a strong correlation between levels of insecurity and long hours: the highest rate of insecurity is found among full-time workers in the prime of their careers; managers are among the least secure.[24] This level of fear plays a considerable role in influencing Britain's overwork culture, yet its causes are far from clear. Is it the legacy of the mass unemployment in the eighties, or is it related to wider issues about Britain's sense of decline in world status, and of falling behind in the economic race?

The second trend which clearly influenced the media interest in job insecurity in the nineties was that professional and managerial jobs experienced it for the first time. The middle classes were catching up with some of the experience of the working classes in the eighties – though the levels of unemployment were not comparable. Francis Green found a decline in levels of job insecurity over the period 1986 to 2001 in the British workforce, with the exception of white-collar workers; they were the most secure in 1986 and the least secure in 1997 – bringing them into line with blue-collar workers. At the same time, workers who had been in their jobs for a long time showed an increase in insecurity which brought them into line with those who had been in their jobs a very short time. Questions about the likelihood of getting another job also improved for most workers, but not for those in professional and managerial categories.[25]

The Meaning of Overwork

The encroachment of job flexibility into the middle classes is evident in the growth of temporary work; for example, the use of short-term contracts is now common in higher education, information technology and the media. In particular, self-employment used to be dominated by construction and distribution workers, but by 1999 the proportion of the self-employed who were in business, education or the health services had nearly doubled to 29 per cent; and the self-employed have a tendency to work longer hours than average. The reality of life for the famous 'portfolio worker' juggling several work commitments (a concept which generated more media interest than actual exemplars) is usually insecurity and long hours.

These measures of job insecurity starkly reveal people's fears of losing their jobs, and the consequences if they do – such as the difficulty of finding another job, the risk of defaulting on mortgage payments and the problem of caring for dependants. But they don't tap into the range of insecurities around 'doing the job well', promotion and the increasingly precarious path of upward mobility which in managerial and professional groups can be a major motivational issue. It is this form of insecurity and uncertainty which often lies behind the syndrome of 'presenteeism' – being seen to be working late – which has grown stronger in the last fifteen years.

It is driven by several factors. Firstly, there is a much greater assessment of performance, with over 80 per cent of British workplaces now implementing some form of appraisal system, and for a third of workers pay is now linked to performance.[26] There has also been a big increase in pay assessed on team performance, which now covers more than one worker in five; peer pressure becomes a major driver of overwork as employees don't want to let their colleagues down. Secondly, flat, fluid organisations make promotion harder to achieve – the pyramid sharpens to a smaller point, the concept of the middle-class career is less clear-cut, there is no smooth progression up the corporate hierarchy, and chance plays a bigger part – being in the right place at the right time can be critical. Long hours can become a crucial determinant of success, either because they are a way of demonstrating superior commitment over rivals or because they simply increase the chances of being in the right place. Thirdly, 70 per cent of British managers are affected by major organisational restructuring every year,[27] which increases the stakes – the right office politics and you're in charge of a major project or department, play it badly and you're restructured out of a job altogether. As one banker reflected ruefully, he took his eye off the ball for a few months because he was getting married, and in the departmental restructuring he lost his job. Nearly 60 per cent of managers say they are spending far more time on organisational politics: overwork involves not just doing your job well, but making sure you still have the job. Eighty per cent of employees didn't feel they were involved in the decisions around restructuring, and nearly 50 per cent didn't feel the reasons for it were adequately explained. Its impact is destructive, with nearly half of managers reporting less loyalty and motivation as a result, and over 60 per cent reporting lower morale.[28] Restructuring may seem necessary to adapt to changing market conditions, but the fallout is devastating on the level of trust within the organisation: only one British worker in three trusts his or her boss 'a lot'.

Insecurity can become a crucial ingredient of how work is organised – for example how meetings are run, who insists on being at them, and how people use technology, particularly email. People insist on being copied into material so they stay in the know, and they get hooked on checking their email. Insecurity intensifies the desire for control, points out Yiannis Gabriel, Professor of Organisational Theory at Imperial College, London: 'It is not accidental that faith in control rises with feelings of insecurity, uncertainty and impending chaos. Among managers today such feelings are generated by volatile economies, global markets and technologies revolutionising information systems and government policies . . . Under such conditions, managers' needs for reassurance and comfort become exacerbated as insecurity becomes chronic . . . Reading popular management texts, one has the impression that the manuals are advising drivers to grip their steering wheels ever more tightly as their vehicles run out of control.'[29]

The compulsion to stay in contact can become almost obsessive, leading employees to phone in on their mobile or log on to their PCs at the weekend, anxious not to miss anything; as one person pertinently emailed, W.H. Auden said that it was only bearable to be a member of an organisation if you were indispensable. Or at least felt yourself to be indispensable.

Hard Work for Little Gain

Perhaps this insecurity can shed some light on one of the most bizarre paradoxes of Britain's overwork culture – one which has consumed hours and hours of the time of economists, business theorists and government. Britain may be working more intensively, its labour force putting in unprecedented hours, yet this hard work is not paying off: British productivity measured as GDP per hour worked is embarrassingly far behind that of other countries. Germany is 27 per cent ahead, France and the United States 29 per cent.[30] Are we wasting all that hard work in pointless meetings, phone calls and endless emails all devoted to office politics, rather than actually getting the job done? Are we spending long hours making low-value products with antiquated equipment? Are we fiddling with the paperclips, surfing the net and gossiping around the coffee machine rather than being properly managed to get on with the job? All these have been suggested in recent years to explain the paradox of Britain's overwork and its economic underperformance. The Trade Secretary Patricia Hewitt has said that poor management has a lot to answer for, while the government's training body, learndirect, found in a study that office staff spend almost three hours a day unproductively – chasing information from colleagues, surfing the net or in unnecessary meetings.[31]

Britain's productivity lag has generated more theories than any other of its economic indicators. Some argue that the cause lies in the labour force's long 'tail' of low-skilled, low-productivity labour, which in other European economies might be in the dole queue rather than employed. Other theories focus on the spatial advantages of countries such as the United States, where huge economies of scale are possible on green-field sites. Another set of theorists focuses on the importance of capital density – how much is being invested in enterprises – and Britain's low levels of capital investment. But one thing is clear, said Professor Michael Porter in his 2003 report for the Department of Trade and Industry: there are no further productivity gains to be had from employees working longer hours, or from getting more people into employment. 'Labour force utilisation' is already at a high level. The answers he suggested were a higher-skilled labour force, higher capital intensity and more effective use of technology.

There is a direct link between Britain's overwork culture and our low productivity; it can be summed up as rather than working smarter, we've ended up working harder. This has been a concern of British policy-makers for many decades; as long ago as 1968 it was pointed out in government reports that long hours through overtime had become institutionalised in British industry, and were used to compensate for low productivity and to manage the peaks and troughs of manufacturing cycles. Trade unions became complicit in a bid to boost their members' overtime earnings. Instead of investing in skills, technology and product innovation to boost productivity, companies simply push their low-skilled workforce to put more effort into a low-value process, argue economists Ewart Keep and Jonathan Payne.[32] Government policy, they believe, has only reinforced this 'low road' approach, with a weakly regulated labour market which makes it so easy to hire and fire workers that it reduces the incentive to invest in skills and technology as a strategy to reduce labour costs. This is allied to 'long-standing and persistent cultural beliefs, linked to the English class culture, that there exists a limited pool of intelligence or talent in the population to fulfil the most demanding jobs, whilst the majority are capable of little more than menial employment'. Thus both ends of the labour market are required to work very hard: the elite because there are relatively few of them, the majority because of the low value and low productivity of their labour.

Keep and Payne go on to argue that the key to unlocking higher productivity is the patient, long-term work of job redesign to ensure the optimal use of skills. That crucially involves high levels of 'semi-autonomous group working', or teams of workers largely managing themselves, and in 1998 such self-management covered only 5 per cent of British workplaces.[33] Britain has a dire record on this kind of work redesign, unlike many parts of Europe where the 'quality of working life' movement got government and employer backing in the seventies and eighties. Countries such as Italy, Germany and France pursued the principle of worker participation to ensure that work was really paying off, rather than the much more conflictual model of management, adopting specific efficiency criteria, which prevailed in Britain through the seventies and eighties. The 'humanisation of work' agenda which was pursued in Scandinavia was strangled in Britain by the country's history of poor industrial relations, with employers resisting any formal negotiation with trade unions over 'production issues', and the unions being forced to restrict their bargaining to wages and conditions. Interestingly, a TUC survey in July 2003 showed that potential members put job design and productivity as key issues for negotiation by trade unions, ahead of pay.[34] But the kind of social partnership between trade unions and employers that could bring about this kind of work reorganisation – a slow and very complex process, admit Keep and Payne – would require much stronger unions, and has lacked government support.

Research shows that people are well aware of how unproductive long hours can be. Between 1998 and 2003 there was a sharp increase in the number of workers reporting how tiredness led to mistakes, and tasks were taking longer to complete. Nearly three-quarters of long-hours workers (over forty-eight hours a week) said their work took them longer and their performance suffered.[35] While long hours are still regarded as evidence of superior commit-ment, there is research to show that, particularly in high-skill areas of the labour market where creativity and innovation are required, they damage performance. Respondents to the 'Working Lives' website had strong views on the relationship between long hours and productivity. Their experience – and many of them had worked in Europe or the US as well as Britain – was that people wasted a lot of time. Effective intense work could only be managed over a certain number of hours. Much more than thirty-two hours a week and time was wasted because of distractions and poor concen-tration. It provoked considerable frustration that advantage was gained by staying late, rather than by working productively. As one civil servant emailed:

I often feel guilty for leaving at 5.30 or 6 even though I have done a full and productive day's work, when I know colleagues will be staying on for another hour or two or three. I do not believe that because someone puts in a marathon day they are 'better' workers. In fact, I think that excessive hours make people less efficient – I think people end up thinking they have to work these hours to be seen as good workers, and so end up filling extra hours by doing work that they don't actually need to do. I think long hours can cause you to lose the ability to focus on what really needs to be done and what can wait. Sadly, to progress to a higher grade in my job, it is given that you work the mad hours.

The Meaning of Overwork

Depressingly, our overwork has been used to mask our economic underperformance. This is an option which Professor Porter believes has largely outrun its usefulness. We can't now work any harder, and any future gains in productivity will have to be found through another formula; the win–win option is that productivity and quality of working life could be two sides of the same coin, an issue to which I will return in the final chapter.

3

Putting Your Heart and Soul Into it

The two ways of measuring the demands of a job which we have considered – time and effort – have defined industrial relations since the beginning of the Industrial Revolution, but a third is a phenomenon of the last few decades: *emotional labour*. It's not just your physical stamina and analytical capabilities which are required to do a good job, but your personality and emotional skills as well. From a customer services representative in a call centre to a teacher or manager, the emotional demands of the job have immeasurably increased. Emotional labour has become one of the hardest parts of many jobs. So just why is your employer after your heart?

The demand for emotional labour is driven firstly by the growth of the service economy. Companies are increasingly competing to provide a certain type of emotional experience along with their product, be it a mobile phone or an insurance policy. Where once muscle-power was crucial to the employment contract for millions of manual workers, its modern-day equivalent is emotional empathy and the ability to strike up a rapport with another human being *quickly*. Employers believe customers will stay loyal, and will sometimes pay a premium, for a certain kind of interaction – they want to be treated as individuals, with a personalised service in a mass consumer market driven by technology. The standards are exacting: employees are instructed to provide service with personality, 'naturalness', spontaneity and warmth; qualities which they must, paradoxically, provide consistently.

Another kind of emotional labour is also in increasing demand. It is a response to the changing structure of organisations. The clearly defined hierarchical bureaucracies which served industrial society well in the nineteenth and twentieth centuries have been outstripped by the pace of change; only much flatter, more fluid organisations can adapt and continuously re-adapt in different formulations of networks. But as the lines of authority become less clear, much more falls to the individual employee to negotiate, influence and persuade. This is often called the 'relationship economy', and what makes it particularly hard work is that it requires skills of empathy, intuition, persuasion, even manipulation, for which there is little preparation in an educational system focused exclusively on analytical rather than emotional skills.

Speak As If You're Smiling

The phrase 'emotional labour' was first coined in 1983 by the American sociologist Arlie Russell Hochschild in her study of how flight attendants were trained to provide their customers with a particular emotional experience.[1] The concept has spawned a large academic literature analysing the emotional demands of the service economy on the workforce. Call centres, one of the fastest-growing sources of employment in Britain, represent perhaps the most intensive form of emotional labour. Nearly half a million employees are handling around 125 million calls a month in centres which have clustered in areas of high unemployment such as around Glasgow, Tyneside, South Wales and South Yorkshire.

Projecting warmth on the telephone is a skill which Claire and Tracey, in an Orange call centre in North Shields, Tyneside, have perfected. Both in their early twenties, they are paid to talk – all day. My conversation with Claire is punctuated every few sentences by her incantation, 'Hello, this is Claire, how may I help you?' She says it with the same tone of friendly helpfulness every time, only to then explain to the customer that the system is down and she can't do anything. Nothing rattles her, nothing alters her wording or the tone of her voice; it is entirely consistent. Ironically, what is less consistent on this particular afternoon is the technology; but Claire continues to give the cheerful, good-natured emotional interaction which is expected of her.

They work on the site of an old colliery, but there are few clues to that now. The land has been levelled apart from one hump in the distance which is the last slagheap, now grassed over. The pit was called the 'Rising Sun', oddly echoing Orange's famous slogan, 'The future's bright, the future's Orange'. Both speak to an optimistic aspiration of a dawning new future. In the past it would have been men working here; now over half the workforce is women. They drive in – it's twenty minutes from Newcastle – to sit at a desk all day answering the phone.

The key thing, Claire explains, is: 'You have to take control of the call. A lot of customers go mad if you don't know what you're doing, and the calls escalate [have to be referred to the supervisor], so you have to be confident all the time. Some customers can be very patronising, and if you don't seem like you know what you're doing, the call will escalate.'

On Claire's computer screen, a series of little squares indicate if there are calls waiting, as well as telling her how long she has been on her current call; she usually has no more than eight seconds between calls. If a call has been difficult, there are only eight seconds in which to take a deep breath and compose her voice into the expected tone of friendliness. All the time she's managing her emotional demeanour, she's flicking through a wide range of information on the screen, which she uses to answer customer queries. Later, the head of Claire's section, experienced in call-centre work, acknowledges that it has become much more technically complex than it used to be. It looks very hard work to me, yet Claire much prefers it to working in a shop, her previous job: 'I don't mind talking, I could talk all day. Usually I can cut off after a call, I'm very easy-going. But a really complicated call is sometimes still going through my head.'

The system is down for several hours that afternoon. What is striking is how on the one hand Claire is dealing with very rigid systems set down by company procedure and the vagaries of the computer system, while on the other she is expected to convey a sense of naturalness and her own personality. It's a tricky combination, and she is frequently apologising for things which are beyond her control. No matter how many times she repeats exactly the same response, she must make it sound 'warm', 'sincere' and 'natural'.

Tom is twenty-four, and has been a customer service representative (CSR) here for two years, which counts as experienced in an industry plagued by high turnover. While I listen in, he answers the call of an elderly gentleman who isn't sure how to explain what the problem is with his mobile phone. He meanders and frequently goes off on long explanations which appear to have little to do with his query. Tom gently coaxes him back to the point and tries to intuit what he really wants from him. It's not an easy task, and it requires considerable patience – which Tom seems to have in abundance. His easy manner doesn't falter for a moment, and gradually he manages to establish what he can do to help. As he talks, he's flicking through computer screens, bringing up the customer's account details and information about the products he needs.

All the while, there's a ticker board above the CSRs' heads showing the number of calls waiting to be answered. They are distributed by the ACD – automatic call distributor – a computerised telephone-handling system which identifies the CSR who has been waiting longest and sends the call to his or her workstation. In most call centres, calls are expected to be dealt with in a specified period of time, although Orange is unusually relaxed on this, believing that too tight a target compromises quality. In other call centres, operators are reprimanded for not meeting the target call duration.

John, another CSR, spends seventeen minutes on one of his calls, advising a customer with great patience and enthusiasm on which mobile phone to buy. Again and again the customer asks questions, and John seems to relish the opportunity to dig out the tiniest detail on the potential purchase. Without a pause, another customer comes through with a complicated enquiry which John also goes out of his way to help answer, only to find that the line has gone dead after he puts her on hold. He calls her back in case she got cut off, but she doesn't answer her phone. He shrugs it off – he'd been trying to save her money.

Do the customers ever bother him, I ask. He smiles, then admits, 'The customer wants the moon on a stick . . . they treat you like a work monkey.' It's as if he's not supposed to say things like that, but having said it, it comes out with real passion. 'Customers don't treat you like you're a human being. [But] if you see things from their point of view it's easier, and I'm better than I used to be. You need resilience, but I do get worked up. I do raise my voice.'

While John admitted that he sometimes gets upset, Claire seemed at some fundamental level disengaged from what she was doing. There was something robotic about her level of fluency as she switched back and forth between talking to me and answering the phone. What makes the job so demanding is that this intensity of emotional labour goes on for several hours, with little let-up. What the call-centre manager wants is a steady stream of work, and technology, in the form of the ACD system, offers them the possibility of achieving that.

The level of monitoring in a call centre is intense. Alison, the head of a 'community' of teams (about two hundred CSRs) at Orange, can see with a glance at her computer screen what everyone is doing. A CSR's name flashes into red the *second* he or she is late back from a break. Everything is monitored: the length of calls, the time spent on 'off-call work' and the number of calls put on hold. All the figures are collated and sent back to CSRs – those that fall below the targets are highlighted as 'NI'(needs improvement), while those which exceed the target are 'HE' (highly effective). Every second of their time is accounted for.

There are sweatshop call centres where the profit margins are so tight that operators are under continual pressure to meet tight deadlines, forced to stick to strictly scripted interactions, and yet still to manage some cheerfulness and good humour. What all call centres drill into their employees is to 'speak as if you are smiling', and 'as if you have been waiting for this particular call'. This is a job where you're not allowed an off day – or even an off moment. If a customer is difficult or rude, the call handler must not respond aggressively. He or she certainly can't betray any irritation or frustration during the next call which is instantly routed through to them. While call handlers are expected to provide the customer with a certain pleasurable emotional exchange, they must also continually repress their own emotions to ensure a standardised service. The equation of providing empathy to another while denying it to oneself is complex. A five-minute call to a call centre represents a profoundly unbalanced human relationship. It is an interaction in which the possibility of reciprocity has been shrunk – by technology and the tyranny of efficient time-use – to the smallest possible component, perhaps no more than a 'thank you'.

Empathy has become big business, according to consultants Harding & Yorke, who specialise in what they describe as an 'empathy audit'. They claim to be able to measure every aspect of the emotional interaction between customer and company. If a company wants its employees to sound warmer or more natural, they turn to the likes of Bob Hughes at Harding & Yorke.

I'm intrigued by the idea that something as subjective and spontaneous as human communication can be measured so minutely and then prescribed for employees, and Hughes offers to explain why his company has been called in by the likes of Toyota, Standard Life and Vodafone. He has snippets of recorded call-handler interactions which he plays on his laptop. In one, the handler is confused and uncertain, and the customer ends up hanging up. That could cost the company a customer, points out Hughes, adding that customer loyalty is the biggest predictor of profitability. Delight your customers and they'll be back; empathy makes money, he argues.

The taped clips are the kind of raw material which Harding & Yorke analyse; they put as many as five hundred questions to the call-centre client about every aspect of the call handler. The client is asked to analyse exhaustively their own emotional response to each part of the interaction, answering questions such as: How much confidence did the call handler inspire in me? How personalised does their language feel? How sincere are they, or did they sound perfunctory? How well did I feel they were listening to me? On the basis of the answers to these questions the call handler is given a score.

Quality emotional interactions are the hardest things to short-circuit, claims Hughes. People are extraordinarily sensitive at recognising emotional cues, so 'Sincerity is a big thing for us,' he adds, claiming, 'If one person has been told to smile and a second person has been made – by a joke, for example – to smile, we could measure the difference.'

The call handler's voice is minutely analysed for pace, volume and timbre to ensure the right 'mood'. Timbre is a function of breathing, and if there is any anxiety the ensuing adrenaline surge can constrict the diaphragm, which raises the timbre. So Harding & Yorke train people to breathe properly. The final aim is to achieve 'emotional resolution' as well as practical resolution of the customer's call, and that, explains Bob, is about 'making the customer feel great'. He quotes management guru Tom Peters: 'It doesn't matter how good you are, the only thing which matters is how good does your customer *think* you are.' Bob believes it's instinctive to be empathetic, so his consultancy's job is to 'liberate people's natural behaviour'. To top it all, Bob claims empathy is efficient: it's a win–win formula, because empathy means the employee works out more quickly what the customer really wants.

Empathy, defined by *The Oxford English Dictionary* as 'the power of identifying oneself mentally with (and so fully comprehending) a person', has become an important skill in the labour market, and it is changing the employability status of individuals. This intrigues social theorist André Gorz, who argues that while the assembly line represented 'the total and entirely repressive domination of the worker's personality', what is now required is the 'total mobilisation of that personality'. He writes that 'technical knowledge and professional skills are only of value when combined with a particular state of mind, an unlimited openness to adjustment, change, the unforeseen'.[2]

At the Orange call centre in North Shields, the manager told me they never recruited someone for their technical skills. What they were looking for was a particular personality: cheerful, outgoing, flexible, good-natured, adaptable – because these were the characteristics which they couldn't train. It is an approach shared by B&Q, the DIY retail chain which uses an automated telephone personality test to recruit employees with the right kind of emotional characteristics; applicants have to press their telephone keypad to answer questions such as, 'I prefer to have my closest relationships outside work rather than with a colleague.' In December 2002 B&Q's Human Resources Director explained to the *Financial Times* that 'We wanted a psychological underpinning to the entire culture –

the same description of cultural fit across the entire population [of the company] – including management.'[3] Identifying the right personalities has become a big industry, with a turnover of £20 million a year; over 70 per cent of companies in the FTSE 100 now use psychometric testing. In this labour market women and young people are favoured, while the shy, the reserved and those who find it hard to adapt to change are disadvantaged.

Gorz goes on to claim: 'What this represents is an end to the impersonal relationship in which the employee sold labour to the employer regardless of personality, a return to the pre-capitalist relations of personal submission as described by Marx.' That submission does not depend on rules and coercion – you can't force someone to be 'warm' and 'natural' on the telephone. The required attributes derive from the worker's 'entire ability to think and act'. The 'power battle' is no longer played out in the workplace, says Gorz, but shifts 'upstream': 'The battle lines of that conflict will be everywhere where information, language, modes of life, tastes and fashions are produced . . . in other words, everywhere the subjectivity and "identity" of individuals, their values, their images of themselves and the world are being continually structured, manufactured and shaped.'[4] In other words, the conflicts over power and autonomy which always characterise working lives now no longer take place in the factory, call centre or office, but in the wider cultural life of the country, which promotes the required norms for the twenty-first-century workplace. For example, when a human resources director gives out instructions that staff are to 'be themselves and be natural' with customers, the staff's understanding of self or naturalness can be drawn from a disparate range of pop psychology, television, magazines and friends.

These required emotional characteristics are in continual conflict with the pressure to be efficient; a conflict which is symptomatic of many forms of service work with low profit margins. There's an inherent contradiction in this, because contrary to Bob Hughes' claim, empathy is not always efficient: the confused old lady who can't use her mobile might take up twenty minutes if a call handler is too empathetic. The old lady may even get canny and try to reach the same call handler every evening, in a bid to alleviate her loneliness – it happens – and just how empathetic should the response be? The empathetic employee is caught in a tension between the organisation's drive to be efficient and competitive, and meeting the consumer's desire for satisfaction. Balancing the two is no mean feat, given the often unrealisable promise of consumer culture that 'we can have whatever we want whenever we want it': the 'enchanting myth of customer sovereignty'.[5] Often the failure to cope with this tension is placed on the shoulders of the individual employee, rather than acknowledged as a contradiction of the position they've been placed in.

Furthermore, the emotional labour may require some degree of deference on the part of the employee. Bowing is taught to workers at the Imperial Hotel in Tokyo because 'Guests wish to experience an appropriate feeling of prestige or superiority, purely by virtue of their using what is commonly evaluated as a deluxe enterprise.'[6] The culture of the hotel industry is about an illusion of old-fashioned servility and ingratiating hierarchy. The flipside of the catchphrase 'the customer is always right' is the put-upon employee who is required not only to repress his or her own emotions (irritation, frustration), but also to accept responsibility, which results in the endless and meaningless apologies of service culture. The egalitarian aspirations of Western democratic countries do not seep into the interface between employee and consumer in the service economy. The result is a mismatch between the values of the workplace and the values of consumer culture: in the former, employees are expected to repress their own emotional responses; in the latter, they are encouraged to give them full rein.

Inevitably, the mismatch is most acute amongst the lowest-paid: they are required to provide emotional experiences which they

could never afford to receive themselves. In a culture which privi-
leges the expression of emotion and rejects traditional forms of
emotional self-management – such as the British stiff upper lip –
the mismatch becomes even more acute: on the one hand, the
consumer can become more demanding, while on the other, the
employee has to control his or her own culturally legitimised
emotions.

One study quoted the instructions given to clerical staff at
Harvard University, who were advised to 'Think of yourself as a
trash can. Take everyone's little bits of anger all day, put it inside
you, and at the end of the day, just pour it into the dumpster on
your way out of the door.'[7] In Hochschild's seminal study, flight
attendants were told to think of passengers as guests, children, or
people who have just received traumatic news – similar analogies
are used in training British call-centre staff. This kind of cognitive
restructuring of employees' responses is required to pamper the
customer's every whim. Such self-control can be very hard work, as
management theorist Irena Grugulis points out: 'Expressing warmth
towards and establishing rapport with customers may provide a
genuine source of pleasure for workers. Yet in practice, emotions
are incorporated into organisations within strict limits. Emotion
work does not necessarily legitimise the expression of human feelings in a way that supports the development of healthy individuals,
instead it offers these feelings for sale. Work is not redesigned
to accommodate the employees' emotions, rather employees are
redesigned to fit what is deemed necessary at work.'[8]

There is a world of difference between the waitress who chooses
to smile, quip with her customers and be good-natured, and the
one whose behaviour has been minutely prescribed by a training
manual. The former has some autonomy over her own feelings;
the latter has been forced to open up more aspects of herself to
commodification. Research into a call centre for a British airline
concluded: 'Service sector employers are increasingly demanding

that their employees deep act, work on and change their feelings to match the display required by the labour process.'[9] Employees are left to manage the dilemmas of authenticity, integrity and their sense of their own natural, spontaneous personality, which all spill into their private lives. Perhaps this reinforces the low self-esteem often associated with women and the low-wage service economy; perhaps it also contributes to the high turnover of call-centre staff – often 25 per cent or more a year.

This alienation from the individual's own emotions was Hochschild's concern: 'When the product – the thing to be engineered, mass produced, and subjected to speed-up and slowdown – is a smile, a feeling, or a relationship, it comes to belong more to the organisation and less to the self. And so, in the country that most publicly celebrated the individual, more people privately wonder, without tracing the question to its deepest social root: "What do I really feel?"'[10]

Perhaps you're wondering what all the fuss is about. What does it matter if the call handler has to talk as if she is smiling? What does it matter if staff are instructed to smile – has being made to smile ever hurt anyone? This is a fascinating aspect of this form of hard work – how it is dismissed, belittled, or just *happens* without being remarked on: 'The truly remarkable feature of emotion work is its sheer ordinariness, the extent to which it has permeated most forms of work and to which it is deemed natural.'[11]

Two reasons explain the uncritical acceptance of this kind of hard work. The first is that it is largely done by women: 54 per cent of service sector jobs in Britain are held by women, and 89 per cent of the jobs held by women are in the service sector.[12] Whatever is regarded as women's work has historically been underpaid and undervalued compared with men's work. That structural inequality has been extended to many of the emotionally demanding service jobs created in the last few decades. Women are regarded as being better at managing their own emotions while serving the emotional needs of others; these are skills which they have brought to bear in the building of family and community life, and which until now had little market value.

Secondly, a historical legacy of rational materialism still values the solid, measurable and tangible over the immeasurable and intangible. That makes us better at treating heart disease than afflictions of the heart such as depression and anxiety; the former is declining, the latter are increasing. There is still a cultural stoicism which belittles emotion: 'Sticks and stones may break my bones, but words can never hurt me.' But how can you think of yourself as a 'trash can' all day, and then go home with the satisfaction of having done a good job? How do you gain the sense of self-worth which properly comes with paid employment if you're being paid to be servile?

While we've learnt that certain forms of labour are inimical to good health – coalmining often led to lung disease, for example – we have yet to begin to think that perhaps some forms of emotional labour fall into the same category. Many people compartmentalise human interactions, applying completely different etiquettes to each: they are generous and solicitous to friends, but switch to being rude to the customer services representative, demanding of the waitress, and ignoring the cleaner and the dustbin men. 'Blank them out' is the most common attitude extended towards those who serve. In some ways this is an even more cruel denial of a human being than a patronising hierarchy in which at least 'everyone had their place'. Underlying this indifference is the erosion of human reciprocity – a sense about what we owe each other – which is symptomatic of a culture which puts so much emphasis on the individual.

Increasingly, policy-makers focus on 'self-esteem' as a critical element in how to break the cycle of poverty and deprivation entrenched in some neighbourhoods. It's an issue which Charles

Leadbeater takes up in his book *Up the Down Escalator* (2002). He quotes Robert William Fogel, the Nobel Prize-winning economist: 'The *modernist* egalitarian agenda was based on material redistribution. The critical aspect of a *postmodern* egalitarian agenda is not the distribution of money income, or food, or shelter, or consumer durables. Although there are still glaring inadequacies in the distribution of material commodities that must be addressed, the most intractable maldistributions in rich countries such as the United States are in the realm of spiritual and immaterial assets.' Leadbeater points out that 'Self-esteem cannot be redistributed in the way income can,' and goes on to claim that 'Assets of the spirit [in Fogel's words] have to be personally produced; they cannot be delivered by the state.' But self-esteem is not a personal achievement; it is the product of a set of social relations, and it is the state which orders many of them. What is missing from the analysis is how the emotional labour of low-paid jobs in the service sector reinforces that low self-esteem.

The contradictions of the growing emotional economy are increasingly an issue for the public sector. The welfare state has wrestled with different forms of emotional labour – in health, education and social services – for many decades, but now the demands are increasing. For example, teachers are having to cope with much higher levels of behavioural problems and children with special needs (between 1993 and 2003 their proportion nearly doubled from 11.6 per cent to 19.2 per cent in primary schools, and from 9.6 per cent to 16.5 per cent in secondary[13]). In higher education, lecturers can be allocated as little as five minutes to assess a student's work.

In other areas of the welfare state such as health, some of the historic methods to contain the intensity of emotional labour are now crumbling. Nowhere is emotional labour more demanding than in a hospital, where issues of life and death generate huge amounts of fear. Doctors developed a form of emotional detachment as part of the professionalisation of their work in the nineteenth century, and usually delegated the emotional labour to female nurses. Part of the impetus behind the highly bureaucratic procedures adopted in the mid-twentieth century was the desire to reduce anxiety levels. Isabel Menzies wrote a groundbreaking paper in 1959 analysing how nurses' emotions were managed:[14] for example, a single nurse would be allocated a particular task, such as taking temperatures or providing bedpans, for all the patients on a ward, thus reducing continuous one-on-one contact with individual patients with whom close relationships might have developed.

These methods of emotional management are being dismantled in response to patient pressure for continuity of care. There is a growing insistence on the part of recipients of the service to be treated as individuals rather than as 'just a number'. In an individualistic society, the consumer wants to be recognised, and for the service to be personalised; he or she wants the emotional interaction they can buy in the private sector. As a result there has been a shift in nursing practices, so that each nurse has a particular responsibility for a small number of patients, and is expected to develop a relationship with them. The consultancy Harding & Yorke has even been called in to do training for the Royal College of Nursing, and has been commissioned to carry out an empathy audit for an NHS hospital prosthetics department.

Doctors are now expected to communicate sensitively with their patients, and are trained to do so. Old habits of deference and respect for professionals have given way to a new assertiveness. In many cases this is clearly a welcome development, but it can also generate inflated demands which can be difficult to meet: how many times, for example, does a doctor have to explain a complex course of treatment, and to how many relatives?

Mike Travis, a stocky one-time docker in Liverpool, has been a paediatric nurse for twenty years, and he is in no doubt that the emotional demands of the work have increased. He cites two reasons: 'We now have family-centred care, which actively encourages the workforce to become intimately involved in the child and the family. It's good for the quality of care, there's better continuity; but it can have very negative consequences for nurses because of a much greater degree of emotional involvement. The other reason is that when I first started training, the children weren't as sick. Now in oncology [treatment of cancer] and with the refinement of drug regimes, your contact is a lot longer. Twenty years ago, these children would have died. Also, the throughput in hospital is quicker – your contact with them is only at very vulnerable times.'

Mike does a lot of work as a trade union rep in the north-west, and he's come to the conclusion that most nurses suffer at some point from 'emotional burnout': 'Everyone does. There've been times in my career when I've been exhausted by the work. You have to accept that if people say they've not been, they're denying it. It's very easy to lose the boundary between home and work – nurses have very high divorce rates.'

Barbara Tassa, a sister in charge of a fracture clinic in Birmingham, feels that the pressure to keep up the throughput of patients is 'soul-destroying': 'Nurses managing units are having to get through their daily work as quickly as possible, and they don't have time to interact with patients and relatives. It's soul-destroying if you come into nursing to make a difference to people's lives; it's very frustrating when you can't do it.'

The work is more demanding, agrees Professor Pam Smith, who lectures in nursing. While on the one hand the job has become more specialised and skilled, the emotional demands are as exacting as ever: 'What hasn't changed is the inner expectations of what nurses think they do and what the public thinks nurses do. That "relationship work" has intensified; people talk more about emotions and feelings, and they see nurses – and nurses see themselves – as having counselling roles. Nurses are having to do it all – and nurse. The speed-up of throughput of patients with a greater emphasis on day cases means there is a shorter time to get to know people. The NHS has been trying to improve throughput without factoring in the relationships which have to be built in a much shorter amount of contact time.'

Mike Travis summed up the conflict: 'On the one hand, they [hospital management] encourage your relationship with families, while on the other they manage you in a very businesslike way. How do you balance these two things out? It's not unusual that an organisation sends out very mixed messages – it's not clear itself – and the more distant the manager, the more difficult the conflict for the nurses.'

Whether in the hospital or the call centre, it is the individual employee who is left to resolve the contradiction between the human relationship and the organisation's understanding of efficiency.

'The Relationship Economy'

Sue had just taken a sabbatical of several months to take stock of her work when she emailed:

It's not the hours but what goes on in those hours – the tremendous drain on my emotional and mental energy. In the evening, 50 per cent of my mind is consciously thinking about work and 50 per cent subconsciously thinking about work. It often just won't go out of my head – sometimes I wake in the morning with a solution to a problem and my mind must have been working on it while I was sleeping.

A senior media executive, she dismisses outright any suggestion that the hours of her job is the problem; what she struggles with is the intensity of the work, particularly its emotional intensity, which leaves her completely drained:

> I've thought about the job my bosses did ten or fifteen years ago, and there's no comparison with what I'm doing now. It's the speed of change: my boss would have had a very predictable job which didn't change for years at a time, certainly didn't change from month to month. It was clear who did what and what were the lines of responsibility. I'm in a fast and unpredictable environment, and it's not clear who's responsible for what. Nor do the old silo structures work: I have to collaborate across the organisation, so there is constant pressure on top of my day job to build relationships, and to try to influence and persuade people. Sometimes you don't have the authority – and even if you do have the authority, it's not always understood that you do. In the old days, you had authority and you said, 'Do this,' but that doesn't work now. That's why I come home absolutely wrecked.

This form of work intensification erodes the traditional boundaries between people's personal and public lives. Once they were carefully policed, and any crossover from office life to home was carefully managed – such as on the rare occasion when the boss might invite a favoured junior to bring his wife round for dinner, for example – while the reverse flow of home life into the office was discouraged. Now the workplace culture has been personalised; along with the often appreciated relaxation of reserve and formality comes a wealth of complex emotional relationships to negotiate. Often these relationships can be intense: in over 50 per cent of all British workplaces the workforce numbers between twenty-five and forty-nine.

This is the relationship economy. It replaces the bureaucratic and hierarchical organisations which developed in industrial economies in the late nineteenth century in order to manage complex and large challenges, and which aimed to achieve a degree of impartiality and to reduce the risk of error by following set procedures. It left little room for autonomy. But such is now the speed and unpredictability of change that organisations like this are too slow and cumbersome to respond, and work processes are usually outdated by the time they are implemented. Since the 1980s, organisational restructuring – as discussed in Chapter 2 – has become a permanent feature across the private and public sectors, affecting 70 per cent of all managers every year.[15] Management hierarchies have been flattened in a bid to make organisations more agile, quicker to adapt to change, with more responsibility being placed on individuals to take the initiative. In addition, the mass of information is such that it can only be handled effectively by a team which communicates and collaborates well. The structure of teamwork and increased autonomy in highly skilled sectors can blur who's ultimately in charge. This requires an intensification of relationships – everything is fluid, everything is up for grabs, and your survival is achieved by constantly reaffirming the personal contacts which ensure your position. There is much less 'command and control'-type management, and the successful manager has to build consensus, persuade and influence people. Over 70 per cent of managers questioned in the four-year Quality of Working Life study on managerial work singled out greater demand for their 'inter-personal skills', and 60 per cent said they were spending more time than before on office politics.[16]

As Sue remarks, 'It's not clear who's responsible for what. I've had to learn how to make relationships quickly. For managers, it's an important skill to know how to make friends – as important as reading a balance sheet.'

Susan Rice, Chief Executive of Lloyds TSB in Scotland, believes that the 'single most important skill' for managers is the ability to listen, and that they often lack it: 'Managers need to hear from a lot of staff, because decisions now are made differently. You have to listen to make good decisions, and people have to have had their input so that they'll take the decisions away and carry them out for you. People have to be engaged in making the decision. You also have to listen to what people are doing in other parts of the organisation, so that you can offer them a proposition which they'll go for – and you can get what you want. It's probably like negotiating. You have to be aware of where people are coming from, and don't expect them to be subservient.'

In service companies, where the staff are required to put in a lot of emotional labour, the system of managing them has to incorporate a higher degree of emotional awareness, claims Keith Astill, Head of Corporate Personnel of the building society Nationwide. He describes an extraordinary shift which the organisation implemented in the whole way it was managed: 'We went from numbers to feelings. That was a brave step. Our management of performance now rests on three aspects: the achievement of tasks and objectives, employees' attitudes, and the development and growth of the individual. Before, we'd focus on the technical side – how many sales, and so on. Now we've shifted to more emotional management: How supportive are the line managers? How are they developing as a team leader, and how are they developing their self-awareness?'

Where once supervisors sat down with a print-out of statistics, now they ask how the employee is *feeling*. It's a different language, and it revolutionises the relationships we have in the workplace. Employees can no longer rely on clearly defined hierarchies of responsibility to carry out their work – now it often comes down to the quality of the relationships built up in a network of contacts inside and outside the workplace. The boss can no longer fall back on 'positional authority' – 'Do what I say, I'm the boss.' Information is so dispersed and accessible that the boss often cannot claim superior knowledge. Alan Little, a consultant with the international human resources consultancy Hay Group, argues that work is now much more emotionally demanding:

People used to understand line-reporting relationships, but now decision-making goes on in all sorts of groups in a network. Managing those kinds of dynamics which tug in different ways is very demanding. The behaviour which is the most important and effective in this workplace requires emotional intelligence, influencing and negotiation skills as well as the ability to take multiple perspectives.

A lot of management is implicitly about taking control, but now we need a completely different set of skills. Sometimes the key person in a decision-making network is not the most senior. Resilience and adaptability to change all come from emotional maturity, and these are now crucial work skills.

This makes for new problems in the handling of work relationships with colleagues. They are less formal, more personal, and that can make much more complex the power dynamic of the relationship with the boss. 'There's increased informality, and the barriers are coming down in a physical sense, so that the manager now has to create their own barriers or they are just swamped. I continually see managers who are giving of themselves, and all their emotional energy is sucked out,' says Neil Paterson, also a consultant at Hay Group. 'Managers have to think through their "emotional positioning", whereas before hierarchies used to manage that kind of distance.'

Mike Harris, of the internet bank egg, agrees that there is now a lot of hard emotional work to be done in organisations:

We ask employees to bring their humanness to work. Most people hang up their personalities at the door on the way into their office. [But] we want your humanness and with that comes your creativity, commitment and personality. We also get the emotion – the anger for example, and we've been prepared to put up with that because it's the corollary of bringing the personality to work. The only time when we've got into trouble here is when we've forgotten that deal . . . when we've forgotten the emotions. There was an occasion when the car keys and the mobiles were taken off people [when they were made redundant] before they could even phone their wives. It was a new boss, and this incident reverberated around the whole organisation like an atomic bomb. It took a long time to get over that. We forgot that the people we were making redundant were human beings. We should have gone out with them and had a party and handled things in a more humane way. This kind of humanness doesn't mean you can't take very hard rational decisions, but you must not ignore the human fallout.

The defining characteristic of the relationship economy is ambiguity, and that can require immense skill to navigate, as Lucy Kellaway has characterised in her *Financial Times* management column:

I know how to talk to friends. I know how to talk to authority figures. But I don't know how to talk to people in authority who seem like friends. Twenty or thirty years ago, you knew where you were. In those days, your boss's door was always closed. You were summoned for an interview from time to time, you addressed him with respect, and followed orders. Now the boss's door is always open – if he is old-fashioned enough to have a door at all. You chat to each other in an easy colloquial way; someone observing the conversation might not even be able to spot which of you held the power. Yet the reality is the same as ever. The boss is still the boss and can fire you or promote you. The hierarchy is still there, only you can't see it, you keep tripping over it by mistake.

As Kellaway also points out, the demands on the boss become near impossible: 'The successful boss has to be both engaging and authoritative. He must continuously adjust his behaviour and tone of voice depending on who he is talking to, and on the situation.'

The boss used to expect obedience, hopefully also respect, but he or she now has to combine a wide range of skills, from those of a diplomat to those of a friend – skills of persuasion, tact, diplomacy, leadership, even of being 'likeable' and, worst of all, funny: David Brent, the infamous boss in the television comedy series *The Office*, wanted above all to be seen as a 'good laugh'. Once, the boss was tucked away in his own office, beyond a secretary, behind a closed door and a large desk; now the walls of his or her office are of glass, or are non-existent. One manager of a local authority housing department described how he sits in an open-plan office only a few metres from his team; after dressing down someone in an annual appraisal for poor performance, he then had to sit down near them and join in the banter about football; for neither party was there any spatial separation with which to negotiate the power relationship

Relationships can't be left entirely to chance, such is their importance for business success. In rapidly changing organisations trust runs short; hence the mushrooming of an industry of organisational psychologists devoted to the 'relationship economy', in which consultants encourage team bonding, personal awareness and personal growth to ensure smoothly functioning relationships. Work intensification leaves less time for socialising between colleagues, so companies compensate by subsidising or sponsoring events outside working hours. AWG, formerly Anglia Water, proudly boasts that 'Friendship is part of our corporate culture,' while Unilever admits it recruits graduates whom it believes will become friends.[17]

The intelligent organisation, aware of the potential for dysfunction in this relationship economy, now invests considerable resources in the personal growth of employees. Once this was the private domain of the individual; now it's the employers' business. The lessons of Daniel Goleman's 1999 bestseller *Working with Emotional Intelligence* have hit home. The successful manager requires characteristics such as self-awareness, self-control and the capacity for 'deep listening', the flexibility to be both decisive and receptive to new ideas. In a bureaucratic organisation, the scope for an individual's emotional disposition was deliberately restricted; now it is vital that a manager understands the dynamics between people and recognises how their own emotional make-up predisposes them to handle a particular situation.

The result can be a shift of psychological energy, points out psychotherapist Professor Andrew Samuels: 'We lose sight of a relationship with ourselves at home because there is so much focus there on relationships with others. So people pursue this inner journey at work more than at home; at work the language is about self-development. In assessments and appraisals, there's a lot about your goals. It doesn't represent the classic understanding of the inner journey, but it carries some of that burden. For example, when someone says, "My work means everything to me. I come alive at work," which is true of a privileged minority – the energy for personal growth is implicated in the workplace and the management consultant has picked up on this shift towards looking for salvation at work.'

This revolution in the nature of organisations has had a huge impact on women's employment prospects. The emotional skills women have practised for generations in the home are now in demand in the labour market. Human resources consultant Adrian Rickard suggests that this 'feminisation of the workplace' requires 'men to acquire traditional female qualities'. Frequently, experts and managers concede that the crucial skills of networking, consensus-building and shrewd assessment of individuals seem to come more easily to women than to men. Neil Paterson argues that a new set of skills is required of the manager: less of the task-oriented, problem-solving mentality, and more that of the facilitator and co-ordinator of a team – a job more in the background and less glory-seeking. In short, a job women have been doing for a very long time. As Rickard points out, the implications of this for the way in which boys are socialised for work are significant.

Of all the aspects of overwork, the emotional labour of the

relationship economy is one of the most intractable. The demand for it will continue to expand, as will the stress it generates. The challenge for employers is to give proper recognition of the particular demands it makes on employees in terms of their emotional skill and energy – neither of which can be measured by time actually spent in the office.

Part Two

The Slavedrivers:
Who's Making us Work so Hard?

4

Missionary Management

In the early sixties an American psychologist, Abraham Maslow, left his university post and headed west to a company in Del Mar, in southern California, in a radical new departure in his career. He had pioneered concepts such as self-actualisation and the hierarchy of needs, and radically redrawn a framework of human motivation and human potential. Now he would turn his mind to a totally new territory – business and management. He kept a journal of his summer in the Californian factory, and eventually it was published under the unpronounceable title of *Eupsychian Management*. Not surprisingly with a title like that, it never reached any bestseller list, nor did it make for Maslow the millions acquired by subsequent business gurus who have adopted and popularised his ideas, which are now commonplace in corporate boardrooms all over the United States and Britain. But it was Maslow, in a hot Californian summer in 1962, who first dreamt of a new way to manage people which would make them into a 'better type of human being'. He set a grand and glorious goal: 'Proper management of the work lives of human beings, of the way in which they earn their living, can improve them and improve the world and in this sense be a utopian or revolutionary technique.'[1] It was through the properly managed company, Maslow argued, that the individual could find personal growth and achieve the ultimate aim of human existence – 'self-actualisation'. The 'only real path [to personal salvation is] via hard work and total commitment to doing well the job that fate or personal destiny calls you to do, or any important job that "calls for" doing'. Work was, Maslow continued, the route to happiness: 'This business of self-actualisation via a commitment to an important job and to worthwhile work could also be said, then, to be the path to human happiness.'[2]

This was a way of recasting the work ethic by fusing it with the growing preoccupation of the sixties' New Age movement with self-development and personal potential; put simply, it was through work that one 'found oneself'. It reformulated the concept of commitment; it was no longer enough to do a good job – nothing short of total dedication, of setting oneself to achieve the impossible and to exceed every expectation, was enough. The task for management was to nurture and stimulate this kind of heroic self-realisation. That required devising a company culture 'so that the goals of the individual merge with the goals of the organisation'.

In one of Maslow's essays in *Eupsychian Management* he listed thirty-six assumptions which should underlie 'enlightened management' (the very use of the word 'assumption' rather than 'principle' or 'rule' shows how this method of management would mask potential conflict by claiming to be implicit). Here are some of them:

> *Assume in all your people the impulse to achieve.*
> *Assume there is no dominance–subordination hierarchy.*
> *Assume that everyone will have the same managerial objectives and will identify with them.*
> *Assume that everyone can enjoy good teamwork – not enough attention has been given to the pleasures of being in a love community with which one can identify.*
> *Assume that people can take it . . . the strain should not be constant but people can benefit from being stretched and strained and challenged.*

Assume that people are improvable.

Assume that everyone prefers to feel important, needed, useful.

Assume that everyone prefers or even needs to love their boss.

Assume that everyone wants responsibility, prefers to be a prime mover rather than a passive helper.

Assume that we all prefer meaningful work, a system of values, of understanding the world and of making sense of it.

Assume that no matter how menial the chore it can become meaningful by participation in a meaningful or important or loved goal.

Assume that the person is courageous enough for enlightened processes, i.e. he has stress-tolerance, knows creative insecurity and can endure anxiety.[3]

Maslow's challenge to management was astonishingly ahead of its time; only in the late eighties and early nineties did his ideas begin to take form as organisations sought to reformulate the 'psychological contract' with their workforce. In the new contract they no longer offered security, there was no such thing as a 'job for life', nor could they ask employees for loyalty; but they wanted harder work than ever. What companies were increasingly aware of was that employees' commitment made a significant difference to the bottom line. For knowledge-based companies, their biggest asset is their employees; it used to be that companies had about 80 per cent of their assets in buildings, plant, land and stock, and 20 per cent in employees; now the proportions have reversed. It's not just a cliché that a company is its people: increasingly, a company's value lies in immaterial assets such as employees and how the organisation works. As John Micklethwait and Adrian Wooldridge put it in their 1997 book *The Witch Doctors: What the Management Gurus are Saying, Why it Matters and How to Make Sense of it* : 'Now firms realise that their most important asset is knowledge, [which] is so much more difficult to manage than capital: fixed in the heads of pesky employees rather than stored in the bank and infuriatingly volatile and short-lived to boot.' Never has 'the ghost in the machine', as early management theorists described motivation, been so critical to a company's performance and valuation.

Over the last couple of decades the aim in many companies seeking to motivate their staff has been to devise a work culture which people would *like*, would find fun, and which offered the kind of personal development and individual affirmation people needed. The result was the emergence in the early nineties of the 'employer brand', as the marketing department was pulled into human resources meetings to assist in the task of 'selling' the brand to the 'internal customer'. Employees were no longer expected to be loyal to the boss, but *committed to the brand values* (the shift of wording from 'loyalty' to 'commitment' underlines the end of reciprocity). The brand values, of course, were devised with an eye on what would go down well with the prospective audience, the workforce. The aim was to 'align the employees with the brand', which meant recruiting people who reflected, or could be moulded to reflect, the brand values. As one human resources director put it, he wanted the company's brand values in his employees' heads at all times and in everything they did at work. The organisation wanted the right 'psychological fit' between employee and company culture. As a psychologist put it in the Chartered Institute of Personnel and Development's magazine, *People Management*, 'The organisation and the human resources function in particular needs to articulate not just how it wants people to act differently, but how it wants them to think and feel differently too. Then it needs to set about finding people who will do, think and feel those things. It needs to change those who don't, and it needs to focus on the power, influence and obstacles that smooth or roughen the path of change.'[4]

What this can amount to is an unprecedented invasiveness as management practices reach after parts of the employee's personality which have hitherto been considered private in order to unlock the required commitment, high performance and overwork.

Richard Barrett of the World Bank says: 'The only way to develop long-lasting commitment is to tap into an individual's mental and spiritual motivations. Our mental needs are met in the realm of personal and professional growth. Our spiritual needs are met when we find meaning in our work; when what we do actually makes a difference; and when we are able to be of service. This is the realm of spiritual growth.'

Depending on your point of view, either this reformulation of the psychological contract licenses a re-engineering of human personality to suit the ends of the corporation, or the company is simply taking on the roles of other declining social institutions by meeting employees' need for purpose, identification and personal affirmation. In one survey 46 per cent of men and 37 per cent of women said they were looking for a job which would provide meaning;[5] David Boyle in his book *Authenticity: Brands, Fakes, Spin and the Lust for Real Life* (2003) comments that 'Most people can't bear to devote their lives to companies whose only purpose is to make a profit. They need a higher purpose.'

To try to resolve where the balance lay between these two views, I visited three companies, all well known for their strong 'brand cultures'. Two of them – Microsoft and Asda – are past winners of the *Sunday Times* Best Company to Work For title, and their own employees rated them highly. The third, Orange, developed a distinctive brand culture in its pioneering days; in the course of two visits, two years apart, I gathered some idea of how it had weathered the vicissitudes of a turbulent market. Microsoft and Asda (which is owned by the American Wal-Mart chain) have been influenced strongly by their US parent companies, though both stoutly insist on key elements being home-grown: they represent the British version of the American 'absorptive corporation'. In all three, the brand culture is regarded as critical to motivate the kind of commitment, emotional labour (as described in Chapter 3) and hard work considered essential to the companies' commercial success.

The Slavedrivers: Who's Making us Work so Hard?

Picture of Perfection

The bus ride from Reading station to the computer giant Microsoft's UK headquarters is only twenty minutes, but it seems like a passage to another world from the shabby terraced streets of Reading to the swathes of landscaped lawn of the Thames Valley Business Park. In front of Microsoft there's a nature reserve bordering a lake on which a fountain plays, and on summer afternoons the company offers free ice creams and picnic rugs to its employees. Inside the airy atrium of the American corporation's most successful subsidiary (an annual turnover of £17 billion) is one of four cafés in the complex. Employees – including the chief executive – sit in armchairs in open-neck shirts for meetings, and waiters stroll over to offer drinks. There's a quiet, purposeful hum more akin to a café than an office. Microsoft workers have little reason to leave the office during daylight hours: there's a dry cleaner's, a crèche, a financial adviser, and a well-being centre with qualified nurses on hand. Groceries are delivered to your car, and the canteen offers such good breakfasts that employees plan their team meetings at 8.30 a.m. to take place there.

Perhaps this is the sort of utopia Abe Maslow had in mind. Certainly, Microsoft UK is proud of having put a great deal of effort into providing exactly the right conditions in which to cultivate the most commitment. Kay Winsper, a senior human resources manager, even has the job title 'Head of Great Companies', and is responsible for nothing less than the 'physical, emotional and intellectual well-being' of employees. It probably helps that Microsoft is a young company – founded in 1990 – so there has been no gear-grinding adaptation of an old corporate culture: it's had a green-field site both literally and metaphorically. In 2003 Microsoft was awarded the *Sunday Times* title 'Best UK Company to Work For', and such is the level of interest from other companies that it is holding open days to spread the word. According to the *Sunday*

Times' survey, 93 per cent of Microsoft UK's employees are proud to come to work, and as Kay Winsper adds, 'They put phenomenal energy into their jobs.'

One of the first things Kay wants to talk about is Microsoft's 'strength finder' programme. This assesses employees' personalities to find their top five strengths, so they can focus on them. She shows me a wall chart which illustrates how identifying your strengths leads to good work, which in turn leads to customer satisfaction, which leads to profit increases, and finally stock-price increases. It is a perfect illustration of the merging of individual and organisational goals. Employees' personal development at Microsoft UK is perfectly attuned to raising the company's share price.

The problem is that Microsoft UK just can't find the staff, complains Steve Harvey, Director of People and Culture, over a delicious lunch in the company canteen. He explains: 'We've had 13,000 applications for jobs in the last nine months, and we hired fourteen. We're having to target individuals now – sniping to pick out the good ones. We look for change agents, the best and the brightest.'

Everything that can be outsourced at Microsoft UK has been; what's left is a hard-core team of 1,595 'change agents'. Fifty-five per cent of employees are under thirty-five, and fewer than 1 per cent are over fifty-five; the ratio of men to women is 74:26. People work there for an average of seven years at senior levels, and only three and a half years at junior levels. When I challenge Mr Harvey that the company is creaming off the years of peak energy and drive of the top talent, he agrees: 'These are people who are doing what they love,' adding, 'There has to be "clear contracting", and the employee and employer have to understand each other. It's implicit in the culture that there is no job for life.'

He refers several times to 'clear contracting', and insists it is about 'putting people back in control of their lives': 'So many people in the technology sector come in and hand over their soul. You could work all day long here . . . I want people here to know why they are here. If you hand over your soul, any corporation will use it. I don't want it, I don't want to take over their lives.'

What he does want is exemplary dedication for a short period of time; any longer and it's probably not sustainable, as employees lose momentum, or family commitments compete for their time. Microsoft's culture of 'all or nothing' doesn't really work part-time – there are only twenty-three part-timers amongst the Reading workforce. Mr Harvey becomes emphatic over the question of work–life balance: 'What a stupid question! We hire very driven people who try to balance work–life over a life. They take the long-term picture. The difficulties come when you try to balance work–life on a daily or weekly basis.'

I ask how that fits in with being a parent, and he responds by referring me to the company's two-day 'Personal Excellence Programme', which inculcates a form of corporate philosophy in employees: 'We try to teach choices and consequences – if you choose to have a family or play golf, you have to be honest about what kind of job you can do and what responsibilities you can manage. We're educating people to make those choices, and loads of jobs are very demanding and very challenging. Women look at how big those big jobs are, and take a choice.' That explains the 80:20 per cent split of men to women at the senior levels, he argues, but insists that the 'senior ladies are getting through'. The average age of employees is thirty-four, and significantly, most of those I met had no children.

According to Mr Harvey, it's a good two-way deal: employees know the score, and are paid handsomely (average salary is around £65,000, and there are stock-option schemes and flexible pensions), and in return the company gets their hard work. But he knows what the critics say; he muses that a temp working for him had accused him of exploiting his employees, saying that Microsoft's was a culture in which 'no one ever took their foot off the gas'. His comment was: 'We challenge people to make choices.'

The 'change agents' Microsoft UK wants to employ are not just clever – in fact cleverness is quite secondary, insists Harvey. Far more important is the right kind of personality. He sums this up as 'very driven, very adaptable, and passionate'. I suspect it's the combination of drive and adaptability that is the most tricky to find in prospective employees: one is a characteristic of focus, determination and single-mindedness, the other is more commonly associated with flexibility, compromise and pragmatism. Add a requirement for unbridled enthusiasm to the mix, and one begins to see why Mr Harvey has a recruitment problem. 'If you aren't adaptable, it'll kill you here,' he admits.

The problem is the 're-orgs', or re-organisations, which seem to be going on almost continuously. In the past five months, three hundred positions in the company have been 'touched' (as Harvey puts it), and 16 per cent of employees have moved jobs. Management is 'always keeping an eye on the bottom 5 per cent – constantly testing them and asking, is it time for them to move on?' he explained, adding, 'If you're a great Microsoft employee, it shouldn't bother you. If you're talented, there's always opportunities coming up.' Harvey smiled, leaned back in his chair and added happily, 'It's lovely. There's constant pressure to perform. You know where you're going in life, it's up to you how hard you push yourself.'

The most striking characteristic of Microsoft's work culture is the emphasis on the individual. A poster on the wall sums it up: a motorbike boot standing next to a clog stamped with the Microsoft logo. Underneath are the words: 'All Microsoft employees are different, the one thing they do have in common is their individuality.' Harvey said he wanted to know what made each employee tick. This focus on the individual and how he or she negotiates the 'choices' offered by Microsoft is reinforced not only by the Personal Excellence Programme, but also by their extensive mentoring scheme. Everyone in Microsoft can choose an internal 'mentor', and meet them as frequently or infrequently as they like. At more senior levels, employees are entitled to the services of both an external and an internal mentor. Around 65 per cent of the workforce is involved in the mentoring at any one time.

Given the level of constant restructuring, many employees are almost permanently thinking about what job they might like or might be able to do next. The mentor can help them plot their career, at the same time reinforcing Microsoft's values: the company handbook says one of the qualities needed by a mentor is to 'overtly aim to live the values in day-to-day concrete behaviours'. Among the duties of being a mentor is 'passing on corporate wisdom and knowledge and to equip people to become more self-managing, a crucial skill in the future world of work . . . the mentor's role is to help the mentee reach their *picture of perfection* – for their role, their career, their team or Microsoft as a whole' (my italics).

According to the handbook, people want three things from work: money, meaning and magic. It draws a distinction between 'salary work' and 'soul work', and states that, through the mentoring scheme, Microsoft aims to increase the latter: 'Talented people are crying out to spend time with individuals who can help them focus on their purpose in their private and professional lives.' From the comments of mentees included in the handbook, the connection to hard work is evident:

> 'Having the opportunity to have a mentor . . . makes me feel like I'm a valuable asset to the company and ensure that I work hard to maintain that perception.'
> 'After a mentoring session I feel focused and driven to achieve my personal and professional goals.'
> 'With the re-org coming up, I want to ensure I am making my best possible contribution to Microsoft and playing to my strengths.'

Making claims to recognise employees' individuality is an effective tool of human resources: it pre-empts the potential formation of any countervailing collective identity, such as that of a trade union. It goes without saying that the individuality Microsoft celebrates is within strict, corporate-defined limits: you can wear clogs to work, play snooker for three hours a day and eat all the ice creams you like, but woe betide anyone who fails to show the right degree of enthusiasm – *passion* is the ubiquitous word – for technology and for Microsoft, or who fails to put in the hard work which is regarded as standard in Thames Valley.

A lot is expected of employees, and none of those I interviewed was in any doubt that that meant hard work. 'It takes three to four months to get your head around the culture. People are so busy, I thought they were unfriendly – they are constantly trying to cram more and more into their day, and rushing around. They've always got full diaries. It's great. We are a busy organisation, there's always a lot of pull on our time. But because it's fun and rewarding, you don't mind doing more. You want to see it through to completion,' said twenty-nine-year-old Chris Bartlett, a Business Productivity Advisor. He joked: 'People do say it's like the Moonies at Microsoft.'

He smiled, then resumed his earlier train of thought. 'The reward is that we're making a positive difference to how people live their lives and do their work ... We're helping people to do things better, faster and more efficiently – if we aren't, we might as well pack up and go home.' It's not the money which keeps him at Microsoft: he says he could get better-paid jobs elsewhere. 'I made a conscious decision that I wanted to be on the bus and that I wanted to be near the driver. I have a passion for technology and all those brand values.'

Bartlett says his mentor has been helping him to find his 'soul work' – the job which will make him jump out of bed in the morning – because 'If work doesn't make you feel really good, why do it?' His mentor helps him work out 'what I'm about as a person, making myself feel better and making others feel better. I want people around here to enjoy their jobs at Microsoft.'

Kathy Isherwood is forty, and sees things a little differently. She manages a busy team on a customer technical support desk. It's pressured, demanding work, and Microsoft expects high standards: the customer must be made to 'feel delighted and that we've been waiting for their call'. Kathy is hugely enthusiastic about the degree of autonomy she has in her job, and praises the Microsoft culture. She's clearly very dedicated; as she talks, I notice that whenever I ask her a question she thinks not of her own situation, but of her team's. She tells me how she took on a team which 'had lost its way', and how she 'healed them'; she says several times, 'My people come first,' and when I press her, she explains, 'I need to be there for my people.' She commented fondly that they were all so different they were like 'dolly mixtures', and with some satisfaction concluded that, during re-orgs, 'I've been the point of stability for my team.' Probably a very good manager, she reminded me of a proud mother talking of her large brood of thriving children.

But one thing she was very clear about was that, although while she was in the office Microsoft of course came first, it was most definitely 'part of my life, not the whole of my life'. This was not the case for some of her colleagues, she added, suddenly becoming animated: 'There's a lot of people here who get into trouble. They are addicted to Microsoft. They're in denial, but they live, eat and breathe Microsoft. It's their world. The thing is, they choose to throw themselves into something. They *need* to be addicted. If it wasn't Microsoft, it would be something else: they need to prove themselves. They are so absorbed by what they're doing – like Rembrandt – there's no start, no end to what they're doing.'

Is that Microsoft's fault?

'Sometimes Microsoft could be more responsible and help that person to understand they are addicted. I make my team take lunch, but a lot of people here work and work. It's a bit lame when Microsoft says it's their choice. If you have an alcoholic in the house, you don't put a bottle of gin by the bed.'

But she took a very clear-eyed view of the labour market: 'There's no job for life, it's hard out there. You need to have the right skills, and people work very hard. We're a commodity, and they'll get everything out of you. If you offer Microsoft your soul and your life – and people here want to please, they need to feel valued, because Microsoft employs high achievers who want to be the top of the tree – they'll take everything that's offered. I've found people in the loo sobbing, exhausted and overstretched. People are frightened of getting a bad review. You're only as good as your last project. There's tremendous pressure to perform, but that's because of today's business environment, there's nothing Microsoft can do about that.'

Kathy's exoneration of Microsoft from responsibility was echoed by other employees. The frequent internal communication reinforces the sense of a market environment where the wolves are baying for blood. There is never a let-up in the competitive pressures. If that is the case for Microsoft, the world's biggest multinational, how much more true is it for the lesser fry? Microsoft has created a utopia available to an elite for a short period of their lives. It's an extremely clever, utterly internally coherent sealed community, divorced from its geographical context and, it would seem, from any other social context.

Microsoft UK is exceptional on one particular point: it is very successfully doing what many other British companies are increasingly attempting to do. Its model of the high-performance, high-commitment workforce is the goal towards which hundreds of other highly skilled, so-called knowledge companies are fumbling. You can see why – it works (very hard), and it's immensely profitable. Microsoft UK is at the bleeding edge of technology, motivating highly skilled workers in a competitive labour market. But how does a company succeed in motivating the lowest skilled?

The Slavedrivers: Who's Making us Work so Hard?

Miles of Smiles

From the staff canteen at Asda on the York ringroad, one has a superb bird's-eye view of the entire store: a vast emporium of neatly stacked shelves beneath a ceiling of brightly coloured banners announcing special offers. On the corridor on the way to the canteen is a detailed breakdown of the store's key performance indicators over the previous week, giving sales measured against targets, profitability and staff absences, in pages and pages of statistics, including a category called 'Go the Extra Mile', under which the York store had failed to score any points in the previous week. (At least these indicators weren't pasted on the inside of the toilet door, as a researcher discovered in another supermarket.)

Like all Asda stores, the one at York is continually monitored by mystery shoppers on every aspect of its performance, from points as mundane as whether the tins are stacked correctly on the shelves to whether the checkout girl smiled throughout her three-and-a-half-hour shift, and whether the shopper felt the warmth of the greeter. The manager receives these audit figures every day, with the store ranked against other stores in its geographical region as well as nationally. The smile above the 'Happy to Help' badge can't slip for a moment without it being tracked on Asda's computer systems. The corridor from the staff changing rooms to the shop-floor passes these noticeboards, and on the staircase there's a full-length mirror and above it a big sign reading: 'Are you ready for the Asda stage?'

David Smith, head of HR at Asda's headquarters in Leeds, promised me I would feel the warmth immediately I entered the store: 'Our store is a community. Staff are encouraged to chat to each other, and the managers to get to know the staff. How can you treat people with respect unless you understand them? You can feel the warmth in our stores. We have regular customer focus groups, and stringent mystery shoppers providing quality information to measure what it feels like.'

The mystery shoppers measure the friendliness of each interaction with staff, the eye contact, and the use of the customer's name at the checkout. The 'colleagues', as staff are known, are exhorted to exhibit 'miles of smiles'. 'It's got to be a *real* smile,' says Smith. 'We don't just take anyone – a degree of gregariousness, that's the most important recruitment characteristic. You can make people more gregarious – we can draw out the gregarious side. We do have a sense that people in the Asda family live the values – it's gregarious, off the wall, a bit wacky, flexible, family-minded, genuinely interested in people, respect for the individual, informal. That's what makes the business go – we've gone into personality, a family and a community feel. Society is more isolationist – solitary lives, single households – so people look for interactions in a retailer. We have elderly people who come to our store every day, and we set out to meet that need.'

I asked him if that meant he employed more staff. He quickly rejected that. 'It's not that we employ more people. We have to be efficient. It's the quality of the interaction.' He pauses. He's wearing the same 'Happy to Help' name badge as a shelf-stacker. 'Life is much more than what people get paid day to day. Instead, it's "What does the boss think of me? And what do the colleagues think of me?" Maslow was an absolute genius. Once people are warm and fed, they want to be fulfilled.'

Asda has taken this last point very seriously; it (rather complacently) admits it doesn't pay its 133,000 UK workforce particularly well – a basic £5.07 per hour – but it lavishes them with 'Bursting with Pride' and 'Thank You' certificates. There are 'listening groups' and 'huddles' and 'colleagues circles' to hear their views and tell them about how the store is doing and to encourage a sense of 'ownership', as Smith puts it. There are so many forms of competition within Asda, from Oscars awarded to colleagues for work 'above and beyond the call of duty' to various leagues such as the 'Fantasy Store' and the 'Horror Store', that I lost track.

Back at York, Owen Hickley has just arrived as the new general manager from the store he set up in Dewsbury. He's been at the company for twenty-three years, and has worked his way up from storeman to running the six hundred staff at York. He's a true believer, full of sincerity and devotion to Asda and his colleagues. He didn't flinch from pulling everyone into line when he started out in Dewsbury: 'We took on three to four hundred people, and we recruited people purely on attitude. I took a dozen of the management to a lovely hotel and put them through their paces and we watched them doing the Wal-Mart Chant – if they couldn't throw themselves into something like that, how could they serve? I wanted people who were not just good, but great. It's a bit American, and I was a bit sceptical at first, but I find it quite natural now. It's a good leveller. It's the way you measure whether people are with you.'

He was proud of the larks they'd had at Dewsbury, and the fundraising they'd done. He described a breast cancer awareness day which the store had got involved in; every member of staff either dyed their hair pink or wore some pink clothing: 'Everyone joined in, it was a great cause. But there were two dissenters who forgot. I told them to go home. I told them, "You're not in the team." They knew what was the right or wrong behaviour, and they went off, bought pink shirts and came back.'

Hickley had gained a reputation in Asda for the number of schemes he'd invented to reward staff, from free cinema tickets to a week of free 'Stuff your Face' lunches in the canteen. 'We're trained to look for what people are doing right. Asda is the best possible company in the world to work for – there's a wow factor. It makes you feel ten feet tall. There's a contract: you'll never walk on my shopfloor unless you're dressed properly and shaved properly. I'll send you home because you're not one of the team.

We want it inch perfect, every tin facing in the right direction, and that's really hard. It's much harder managing like this than by "tell and do". One manager I hired was excellent on the figures, but he was cold, and I pulled him in and said, "I'm going to have to let you go unless you change. You're not taking the people with you. You have to be observant, intuitive and pick up on how they feel. Do they feel a million dollars?" I ask employees to choose their attitude. You can do that, you know. You can choose to feel happy or sad. All these initiatives and incentives don't work unless you believe in them passionately and buy into the vision.' Hickley was a huge success in Dewsbury: his absence levels were the lowest in the country, and the store rated highly in the national audits. Teams from Wal-Mart, Asda's American owner, even visited to hear how he did it. He's a rising star in Asda management.

But talking to some 'colleagues' late on a Thursday afternoon in the York store canteen, I heard a different story. Did I just chance upon some rare grumpy dissidents, or was it a truer picture? Maggie, Kath and Jean (not their real names) had little to say about Asda's culture. What they wanted to talk about was the pay: it was terrible. 'I might as well be a cleaner for this money. For what we do, balancing all the till receipts, we'd get £3 more an hour at other places,' said Kath, her face tired and strained. 'I should have gone a long time ago.'

Kath is on what she calls an 'old-world contract' of a lower than usual hourly rate, but which pays double time for her regular Sunday shift. Her biggest complaint is that she was paid better in the past, before the company phased out supervisors. She's still doing the same job, with some managerial duties, but she's no longer paid for the level of responsibility she has. She's doing a forty-three-hour week for about £185 take-home pay. She's taken on a second job in a pub six evenings a week to keep up with the payments on a new car and the mortgage – giving her a working week of about sixty-seven hours.

But Kath is still there at Asda after more than twenty years, despite all her complaints. There must be something about the place, I say, if she's stayed so long? 'I've made quite a lot of money on the shares, and I'd lose some of that,' she concedes. 'I like my job, I'm left to get on with it. The managers do actually speak to you now – before, they didn't. It's a much more comfortable atmosphere. The quarterly meetings, when they tell you how the store is doing and what's going on in the next three months, are good fun. You come out with a positive attitude.' Then she remembers another thing which irks her: 'They've cut the number of staff in our office, so I have to work harder to get through all the work.'

Jean's story was similar. 'I've worked here for more than ten years, and we're so understaffed. It's much worse than it used to be – we're rushed off our feet. You do make an effort. They've cut back on the staff, down to a minimum, and I go home really stressed.' What had kept her – and Maggie – at Asda was the flexible hours; they both work part-time, which fits in with the rest of their lives. But Jean admitted she'd finally had enough, and was looking for another job.

As for Asda's prided distinctive culture, it has made little impression on these three employees: 'All the league tables – there are so many scores, I don't bother, but there's a lot of goodwill to charities and social events, things like that.'

'They tried the Wal-Mart Chant once here.'

'The "Asda stage" notice above the mirror is a bit cheesy, I just check my eyeliner.'

'You cringe when you watch the videos at quarterly meetings.'

Jean, Maggie and Kath had a much more clear-eyed attitude to their employer than did either their store manager or Asda's head of human resources. They saw right through the claims of 'Respecting the Individual' (emblazoned in the atrium of the company headquarters), and wanted to know why that didn't translate into better pay. On the other hand, Asda must be doing something right, or such long-term employees in a tight labour market like York would have moved on; Asda claims its staff turnover rates are 10 per cent below the retail industry average of around 35 per cent. Offering very flexible part-time work accounts for some of this, but another is in the culture: Asda offers its staff more autonomy than some of its competitors, and they appreciate the lack of formality and the approachability of the management. While Jean, Maggie and Kath may have been diffident about it with me, some of the morale-raising has evidently worked. Asda's achievement is considerable: it doesn't pay its shopfloor staff particularly well, and is working them harder than ever, with constant demands to perform – yet it succeeds in keeping them.

Living and Breathing the Brand

Take another brand, the mobile telephone company Orange, whose call centre was described in Chapter 3. I first visited and interviewed Orange employees in 2001, and returned two years later after the company had gone through a rocky time in a fiercely competitive market. In 2001 it was still riding high as one of the most successful brands of the late nineties. Its advertising was beautiful and humorous: it associated technology with being human, funky and warm-hearted. Its human resources policies were a combination of high tech and New Age: *feng shui* call centres, aromatherapy and headsets. It even produced aromatherapy sprays named after its brand values, so employees could spray on some 'Integrity', some 'Fun' or some 'Honesty'. A bag labelled 'Boost' containing all the fragrances had been given to each employee in the North Shields call centre (they were not, however, allowed to take them home).

In 2001 Nicole Louis, Orange's former head of brand communications, summed up the commitment of employees as something that 'can't be bought with bonuses, it can't be incentivised. They fall in love with the brand. I did. It's like a relationship.' For Sharon

Young, then head of call centres on North Tyneside, the brand means a different type of call centre altogether: 'We asked [employees] how they wanted to sit, and we try to create a community environment with units of twelve people. Call centres are traditionally open-plan, vast and impersonal, but our teams go for lunch and breaks together to build up rapport. It's a big challenge in a call centre – staff don't feel important. But we don't hot desk, and we encourage a sense of belonging so that people feel, "I'm not just a number, this is my home."' The response from employees in 2001 was enthusiastic. They liked the sociability of the job and the approachability of the management. One told me that people changed after working for a while in Orange: they became more friendly and relaxed. As at Asda, the pay has never been good, and in August 2002 it had to be increased to match the industry average in the region.

Some of the old enthusiasm was still there in 2003, even after a bout of redundancies and restructuring which had made everyone in the call centre feel insecure. Julie, a supervisor, commented, 'In previous call centres where I've worked it was like pigs in a pen, but here the team is all together in a community. Some of these people have worked together for quite a while. It's like a little family: if someone's stuck, someone else is happy to help out.'

In spite of the knocks, people were still being won over: 'On Valentine's Day, there was a heart-shaped chocolate on everyone's desk. I thought, no one has ever done that before. It sounds very small and trivial, until you come in and find it there,' said one employee. Little gestures make people feel appreciated, but as the same employee brusquely commented, 'No one is that naive to take on all the brand stuff.'

That's not what the management think, either at the call centre or in the London headquarters. As at Asda, my impression was that the people to whom the brand values and culture really matter are management. Simon Cartwright is Orange's head of human resources, and readily admits to working long hours and at weekends. In fact, he takes his mobile phone away on holiday with him, and jokes that his wife sometimes resorts to hiding it. But, he insists, it's all fun. 'I passionately believe it should be fun to work here. People tend to work long hours at Orange, but the relationships and the atmosphere can be fun. We're in a sector where there's immense competitive pressure, and our culture is hard-working and driven. Hans Snook [the departed founder of Orange] left this legacy that "Being good is not good enough." Once we achieve a goal we set the bar higher, and people are driven by that.'

He said he wanted employees to 'live and breathe the brand'. Did he, I asked. 'I feel proud to work at Orange. I'm proud of what Orange stands for in the marketplace. I'm passionate about the business, and I care about the people and what we do. I get frustrated when I see us behaving in a way that isn't Orange.' Later, he added, 'I see my values as aligned with Orange values. I don't hold myself up to being a saint, but I try to incorporate the brand values into everything I do.' Then he laughed. 'It's beginning to sound like a cult.'

I pressed him on how he 'incorporated the brand values' (one of which is specifically about trust, after all) into making people redundant. 'It doesn't undermine my faith in the brand, because I rationalise it. You can deal with the employees you're losing in a way that's consistent with the brand values. You have to be open and empathetic, and don't keep people waiting. If we have to let someone go, it's our mistake. I'd do more than say sorry. I'd take them through the rationale: "We not only feel sorry, we feel concerned. We built this [the organisation], the world has changed, we weren't flexible enough. Orange was at fault, not uniquely so." It's very difficult – the economic cycles of the world are sharper and shorter, and to avoid those, societies and individuals have to be more flexible.'

The Slavedrivers: Who's Making us Work so Hard?

What's in the New Psychological Contract?

Jack Welch, the legendary Chief Executive of the US corporation General Electric, said that 'Any company trying to compete . . . must figure out a way to engage the mind of every employee.' His words are up on the walls of Microsoft's office, and it's a lesson that all these three companies are trying to implement.

In earlier stages of industrialisation, employers could rely on a combination of material need and discipline to exact hard work. That kind of command-and-control labour relations doesn't work with the highly skilled who want autonomy and whose work is such that their contribution cannot be specified and ordered; for example, a manager of a computer programming team won't know as much of the technical detail as will those who work under him. Nor can the kind of emotional labour expected at Asda or Orange be ordered: you can't yell at someone to put warmth into their smile, or personality into their telephone voice. As one researcher put it, 'You need their [the employees'] commitment, not their obedience.'[6] Competitive pressures drive the need to raise the quality of the service or increase productivity; both require employees' discretionary effort.

In return for wanting more from employees, the company offers more – not more money, and no longer much job security of course. Instead it offers to meet a range of emotional needs. This was summed up in a working paper by two consultants from Hay Group:

Getting engaged performance is not just about investing financially in employees through pay and benefit increases. It is about striking a new contract in which the organisation invests emotionally in its workforce. In exchange, employees make a similar emotional investment, pouring their 'discretionary effort' into their work and delivering superior performance. The new contract says, 'We'll make your job (and life) more meaningful. You give us your hearts and minds.'[7]

The paper goes on to quote the comment of an American corporate executive: 'It's imperative that leaders give people meaning in their work because passionate employees get better results. If leaders can't give people passion about their work, employees will find it somewhere else.'

A well-developed brand culture firstly offers to meet the employee's need to be recognised as an individual – the anonymity of the factory-floor assembly line won't deliver high discretionary effort. It requires emotional investment: if you want people to work hard, you have to spend a lot of management time on them, coaching them, singling them out for praise, encouraging them, appraising them in 'one to one's', and then devise all manner of recognition events to 'celebrate the successes'. Management is required to do a lot of stroking, which makes the job of middle managers more complex and more emotionally demanding, as both Kathy Isherwood at Microsoft and Owen Hickley at Asda indicated. Tom Peters pointed it out in his 1982 business bestseller *In Search of Excellence*: 'We like to think of ourselves as winners. The lesson that the excellent companies have to teach is that there is no reason why we can't design systems that continually reinforce this notion; most of their people are made to feel that they are winners.' He was articulating a long tradition of American management theory going back to Elton Mayo in the 1930s, who argued that social rewards such as consultation and recognition were more important than economic incentives in winning the co-operation of the workforce.

Secondly, the company's brand culture offers to meet the need to participate in a purpose greater than the pursuit of one's own interest. Companies put great effort into identifying and exalting their 'mission' and encouraging staff to subscribe to it. One phrase which employees and companies alike frequently come up with is 'making a difference'; behind its banality lies an appeal to a sense of agency, of personal impact on the world. Meeting this need is one of the main drivers behind the corporate social responsibility agenda: employees need to feel their labour is doing more good than just increasing the company's share price, and employers cater for that need by setting up voluntary schemes for their staffs, such as helping out in local schools.

This spills over into the third need the brand culture offers to meet: the need for meaning. This marks another development in the expansion of the work ethic. Work has always provided identity and belonging; what's new is that it now also offers to provide purpose and meaning. It used to be religious institutions, political parties and the state which met such needs; now, *faute de mieux*, they are channelled into work. Gurnek Bains, a business psychologist at the London-based YCS Ltd consultancy, refers to Abraham Maslow and his famous hierarchy of needs to explain this corporate philosophising: 'At the bottom are the most basic such as the need for food and security, but as these are fulfilled, we seek other needs and the top need is the need for meaning. In a wealthy society, most people's material needs have been met, and the need for meaning becomes the most important; rather than work being a transactional relationship for money, more and more people are looking for emotional engagement in work and a sense of purpose. Companies have always been about the generation of profit, but people can't get excited about that. One way to give meaning is to make the brand important, and try to get people to buy in emotionally. In large urban societies, work is the only way to connect you to society in a meaningful way and recognisable brands meet a basic need to connect.'

American sociologist Joanne Ciulla is critical of how employers are expanding the work ethic, and comments in her book *The Working Life* (2000) how one 'consequence of this loaded meaning of work is that we put our happiness in the hands of the market and our employers ... earning a decent living is not enough, we want something more ... and this challenges employers to find ways to motivate people to satisfy a variety of abstract desires and needs such as self-development and self-fulfilment. Managers are charged with the task of "making meaning" and have tried new ways of persuading employees to invest more of themselves in their work than the job required . . . words such as "quality", "commitment" and "teamwork" all attempt to control and change the meaning of work in an organisation.'

Three companies hardly amounts to a representative sample, but what was striking in Microsoft, Asda and Orange was that the higher they were in the pecking order, the more excited the managers were about their brand. After all, it was probably they who had spent a lot of time devising it and thinking about how to communicate it, and they are certainly expected to subscribe passionately to it. The brand business – because it *is* a multi-million-pound business, with innumerable consultancies – belongs to a generation that grew up in the sixties and seventies believing they had to fight for a great cause, and found by the eighties and nineties nothing but disillusionment after Vietnam and the failure of communism. Business gurus from Tom Peters to Gary Hamel, with some help from Charles Handy, spotted an opening for the corporation: there was a vacuum of spiritual purpose amongst the 'hungry spirits' and 'empty raincoats', as Handy called them in the titles of two of his books. A huge reserve of energy and commitment could be tapped by a corporation which offered its management a chance to make, as Peters put it in *In Search of Excellence*, not just money, but *meaning* for people, because 'We desperately need meaning in our lives and will sacrifice a great deal to institutions that will provide meaning for us.'

'Meaning-making' was exactly what that generation had experienced in the protest movements of the sixties and seventies; they simply applied that experience and that reforming energy to corporate life. They used their egalitarianism to flatten corporate hierarchies and put everyone on first-name terms, while doing little to alter the bigger picture of dramatically-increasing inequality through the last decades of the twentieth century. Gary Hamel, another business guru to capitalise on this baby-boomer generation's angst, melds the language of sixties protest and corporate capitalism, and offered companies such as the doomed American energy corporation Enron a blueprint for the 'business activist' to 'lead the revolution', urging them to 'first break all the rules'.

While the brand cultures which managers devise may or may not have a positive effect on their workforce, they are significant for their own levels of motivation. Those institutions which offer them the opportunity to 'make meaning' get a lot of time and energy in return, as Peters had promised. This goes a long way towards explaining why the harried senior executive willingly forgoes the freedom of his own time, and accepts the trade-off of invasive work for the pleasures of being needed, and involved in something meaningful. The trade-off can be punitive, argues André Gorz in a passionate description of how the corporate brand culture entraps the willing slave in a self-reinforcing logic:

> In a disintegrating society, in which the quest for identity and the pursuit of social integration are continually being frustrated, the corporate culture and the corporate loyalty inculcated by the firm offer the young workers a substitute for membership of the wider society, a refuge from the sense of insecurity. The firm offers them the kind of security [which] monastic orders, sects and work communities provide. It asks them to give up everything – to give up any other form of allegiance, personal interests and even their personal lives – in order to give themselves body and soul to the company, which in exchange will provide them with an identity, a place, a personality and a job they can be proud of. They become members of a 'big family', and the relationship to the company and to the corporate work collective becomes the only social bond; it absorbs all their energy and mobilises their whole person, thus storing up the danger for them of a total loss

of self-worth ... if they lose the confidence of the company and that is earned by indefinitely improving their performance.[8]

Gorz's analogy with monasticism – it's one which the business guru Charles Handy also uses for the managerial elite – echoes the re-emergence of a spiritual language in people's everyday lives. It isn't in the church they never visit, but in the office and on the shopfloor that they hear of 'soul work', 'vocation' and the 'corporate soul'. Jack Welch said people 'wanted to be rewarded in their pocket and their soul'. Work is where we now most often hear of sacrifice. Books with titles like *Corporate Religion* and *Leading with Soul* are no longer on the wacky fringes of business literature, but are symptomatic of an American-driven phenomenon which recognises that the 'super-performance' companies require from employees involves a process of transformation of potential, of self-discovery and self-realisation and transcendence of limitations, which springs directly from the New Age spiritual experiences of the sixties. Doing a job well is no longer enough; 'stretch targets' deliberately push the boundaries of the possible; there are no limits to the expectations. 'The giant within' must be awakened, claims Anthony Robbins, one of the business gurus, along with Stephen Covey, who has made millions out of this genre of business spirituality.

Simultaneously, the corporation speaks the language of a religious institution – 'meaning' – and, confusingly, the language of love. 'Passion' has slipped from bedroom to boardroom, and spread like a contagion throughout management-speak; the word carries connotations of both emotional intimacy and strength of purpose. The language used to articulate brand values is elastically stretched to accommodate contradictions and confusions in evocative phrases intended to obfuscate – to window-dress – the sometimes brutal workings of the organisation, as well as to inspire. Employees are subjected to mission statements, vision statements, brand values, all of which are designed to capture their hearts, minds and souls.

Employees, in a deceptively egalitarian spirit (not borne out by the pay structure) are known as 'colleagues' in Asda, or 'partners' in Starbucks; 'human resources' – itself a comparatively recent replacement for the earlier 'personnel department' – has taken on pleasantly democratic overtones as the 'people department'; and companies are very fond indeed of instituting 'communities' in place of departments, while 'positions', not people, are made redundant. Two of the most ubiquitous and fraudulent words are 'empowerment' and 'ownership'; companies claim they want their employees to be 'empowered' and to 'own' their jobs; as the currency of these words has spread in the United States, American companies have been downsized, and inequalities over pay have grown. You may 'own' your job, but you're unlikely to own much else on some of the wages low-paid Americans earn; they may not own their home or most of their belongings (bought on credit), but they are expected to lavish on 'their' job all the time, energy and responsibility which ownership requires.

Is this an Orwellian, ideologically motivated use of words to conceal the truth, asked Deborah Cameron, Professor of Languages at the University of London, in an elegant analysis in the *New Statesman* in 2001: 'The problem . . . is not so much that it represents reality inaccurately or dishonestly, but that it does not set out to be a representation of anything at all. When organisations proclaim they are "pursuing excellence" . . . they want us not to believe the words, but to applaud the sentiments behind them. Their claims are not primarily "veracity claims" ("What I am telling you is a fact") but "sincerity claims" ("What I am telling you comes from the heart").'[9]

There are large swathes of the British workforce which are impervious to, or even downright cynical about, the brands for which they work. They have a pragmatic view of their job and what it requires of them, and realise that this may on occasion include their paying lip service to the brand values. To Lucy Kellaway, a seasoned observer of management fads in her column in the *Financial Times*, brand cultures are not to be taken too seriously, they are simply a set of conforming principles in the organisation, a way of measuring enthusiasm. The reason management imbibes them particularly deeply is because they become enmeshed in office politics: everyone wants to outdo each other in their admiration of the imperial new clothes. Believing in the brand becomes part of your tool kit for climbing the greasy pole. One manager admitted to me that at her company 'everyone had become paranoid about being off-brand'.

It's possible to see how much the brand culture rubs off on even the most sceptical employee. Joanne Ciulla sums up the dangers of these management practices: 'First, scientific management sought to capture the body, then human relations sought to capture the heart, now consultants want to tap into the soul . . . what they offer is therapy and spirituality lite . . . [which] makes you feel good, but does not address problems of power, conflict and autonomy.'[10] The greatest success of the 'employer brand' concept has been to mask the declining power of workers, for whom pay inequality has increased, job security evaporated and pensions are increasingly precarious. Yet employees, seduced by a culture of approachable, friendly managers, told me they didn't need a union – they could always go and talk to their boss.

At the same time, workers are encouraged to channel more of their lives through work – not just their time and energy during working hours, but their social life and their volunteering and fundraising. Work is taking on the roles once played by other institutions in our lives, and the potential for abuse is clear. A company designs ever more exacting performance targets, with the tantalising carrot of accolades and pay increases to manipulate ever more feverish commitment. The core workforce finds itself hooked into a self-reinforcing cycle of emotional dependency: the increasing demands of their jobs deprive them of the possibility of developing the relationships and interests which would enable them to break their dependency. The greater the dependency, the greater the fear of going cold turkey – through losing the job or even changing the lifestyle. 'Of all the institutions in society, why let one of the more precarious ones supply our social, spiritual and psychological needs? It doesn't make sense to put such a large portion of our lives into the unsteady hands of employers,' concludes Ciulla.

Life is work, work is life for the willing slaves who hand over such large chunks of themselves to their employer in return for the paycheque. The price is heavy in the loss of privacy, the loss of autonomy over the innermost workings of one's emotions, and the compromising of authenticity. The logical conclusion, unless challenged, is capitalism at its most inhuman – the commodification of human beings.

Government, the Hard Taskmaster

Inspections are very time-consuming, and we now have at least one most months. For example, an inspection team today asked for twenty pieces of information. I had one person working full-time for an inspection for a year – that process doesn't contribute to improving the service. Some of the inspection is about numbers, a lot of it is leadership, vision or partnership; often if we get a bad inspection report, it's simply because we didn't prepare well enough for it. When you get a bad inspection, then you have to go to more meetings and fill in more forms, but if you get a good one, you don't.

I spend about 25 per cent of my time on bids and inspections. What's frustrating is that the difference between success and failure in providing a service is not that great – that 25 per cent of my time could make a huge difference, that's where achieving excellence lies. We've just had four people in for two weeks on an inspection, and they missed the main problem we have. In the end, I had to tell them: they had our rent collection down as excellent, one of the best in the area, but we had accidentally used an outdated set of guidelines. Calculated according to the new guidelines, our rent collection was almost the worst.

We had two inspections recently, including one for the Audit Commission. They used different sets of indicators, and under one we were the worst, and under the other we were the best. In yet another inspection, the whole council dropped to the bottom and we got zero star rating because of three things we did badly on – the satisfaction survey, on general leadership, and worst of all on child protection. The fact that the housing department was doing well got lost in all of that. I have to put so much energy into just keeping people calm.

This government has never left us to get on with it – every day I get forms to fill in. We have to fill in loads of forms with things we are going to do, but we aren't going to be able to do any of it, because all the money is already committed, so it's all junk. Still, it's much better. People in local government used to be lazy – they had tea breaks. I remember I had to talk to the switchboard operators for half an hour in the morning to be sure of getting an external line, and it would take me six weeks just to get a letter signed.

Tim, a senior local government manager in housing, 2003.

What Tim describes is an absurd, Kafkaesque charade of public administration. A generation of political battles over the future of the public sector has led to a deterioration in morale and working conditions. Long hours, work intensification and stress are endemic among the country's five million public sector workers. Underfunding and a flawed reform process have been major factors behind the deterioration of public sector working conditions in the last two decades. Professor Francis Green argues that the sharpest job intensification in the nineties was in the education sector. Top of the stress league are jobs in education, health and local government. This chapter focuses on how the pressure for reform has hit the middle management struggling to implement it, and how public sector professionals have been subjected to new forms of accountability and scrutiny to raise productivity.

The problem of public sector overwork goes back to the eighties, when budget cuts overstretched resources and resulted in growing public impatience at the inadequate standard of service. According to an analysis by Anatole Kaletsky and Robin Marris in *The Times* in 2001 (based on OECD figures), British public servants work longer hours, and have more patients and more pupils to attend to, than their counterparts in Europe. They blamed an 'over-zealous application of Thatcherite managerial philosophy. To treat more patients with fewer staff is, by definition, to raise productivity and this had become a criterion for success. Since the 1980s the Treasury had been freezing public sector pay bills, but allowing individual wages to rise, provided staff levels were cut. The result had been a factory-style emphasis on productivity. It eventually won the grudging acquiescence of professional bodies and unions, as it allowed their members' wages to keep rising, albeit at the cost of overwork, overcrowding and queues.'[1]

Since the early nineties, successive waves of reform have overlaid these working conditions with an unprecedented degree of central government interference. Tim's complaints are echoed in a raft of reports on low morale in the public sector, such as the King's Fund report on health professionals (2002), which identified over-centralisation as a key issue; initiatives failed to 'join up' with the services provided, leaving staff to spend considerable time on tasks which yielded few improvements.[2] A specialist registrar said: 'We are expected to steer by directions from the Department of Health – that's been a big problem. They talk about local decisions for local situations, but then they say you must do a, b, c, d, e. They allocate you money and they tell you how to spend it. You're not allowed to be creative to suit your local population, and that's a big demotivator.'

The overworked public servant has become a recurrent theme of newspaper headlines. The report of the inquiry into the tragic death in 2000 of the little girl Victoria Climbié, published in January 2003, painted a picture of an overstretched social services department which, in the plethora of government interventions, had lost sight of the people it was intended to serve; as Martin Willis of the

School of Public Policy at the University of Birmingham pointed out in a letter to the *Guardian*, 'Targets drive managers to focus on procedures rather than whether children are safe. High social service star ratings are achieved by authorities which ensure that most children are taken off the child protection register ... the pressure is to get the numbers down ... [and] to allocate [child protection cases] even when this creates an impossible workload. Failure to achieve these targets results in naming and shaming, more bureaucratic reporting, low morale and staff leaving.'

A motion at the 2003 conference of the professional body, the Association of First Division Civil Servants, complained of an overload of 'initiative-itis', which is leading to unacceptable pressures on staff and a worsening of the long-hours culture. NHS managers are 'punch drunk' with changes, commented the health inspectorate, the Commission for Health Improvement, in 2003, so that they downgrade improvements to patient care in order to be able to meet government targets on finance and waiting times.[3] The pace of government reform had caused such pressure, said the commission's chair, that it was becoming difficult to persuade people to take up senior posts in NHS trusts.

What infuriates employees is the twisting of the system to meet centrally dictated targets. A former NHS consultant told the Audit Commission that the last straw was 'when a manager turns round and tells me that the only way we will get listened to is by creating a waiting list, because that is the only thing that politicians and managers understand, and I have worked all my life to ensure that there isn't a waiting list'.[4]

The central government interference generates a blizzard of paperwork. A further education lecturer, Diana Whelham, told the *Guardian* in an interview how it gets in the way of doing her job: 'My college is due an inspection in April, so I will be spending more time than usual working [extra] at home. Inspection is a really stressful time for all teachers because we have to fit even more paperwork into our already very busy schedules. We are also observed and graded on our performance in the classroom. I think most further education lecturers feel there are just not enough hours in the day to do the job properly these days. Unfortunately, the increased stress and tiredness make it more and more likely that I will change the direction of my career into an area where I will feel more valued generally. Most FE lecturers work very hard. Their jobs, like many public sector workers' jobs, have been made more difficult by the increase in paperwork. This means they have less time to deal with student problems and the development of their skills. On the other hand, we are constantly being pushed to improve examination results. We are caught in the middle, and it is often the students who suffer.'[5]

The paperwork had contributed to a rise in sick leave and stress in her office, said Sarah Nazran, a probation service manager in Keighley, West Yorkshire. 'National standards have since been introduced which define levels of contact with offenders, and I welcome being able to show that I'm meeting these standards. But they also place higher expectations on us, and we're not given the adequate tools or resources to deal with them. I feel inundated by bureaucracy. For every court report I write I could be filling in up to ten forms. The people who implement policy don't seem to know what we do. They send us email requests for another form to be filled in, but we are never consulted as to how that will affect us. The critical issue is that we are now required to spend increasing amounts of time inputting data into computers. When I first joined, I spent a lot of time face to face with offenders. Now that time has become restricted.'[6]

Concerned at the proliferation of the 'measurement culture', the Public Administration Select Committee in 2002 heard evidence spanning the entire public sector, and published its report in 2003.[7] Whether they worked for local authorities, the health service or in education, the theme was similar as public servants described intolerable pressure to respond to centrally dictated interventions. Councillor John Bees of Bristol City Council told the committee: 'We had the inspectors in, I think it was a team of seventeen, for a fortnight, and it was a bloody awful experience and really did run the organisation ragged. There was very little feedback between the inspectors and ourselves . . . You can get into the cycle where [it's] bullying . . . they will turn up on your doorstep every six or nine or twelve months and you will spend an enormous amount of officers' time and politicians' time in trying to cope with that particular inspection and make that inspection, hopefully, view the service in a better way, and that can be enormously demoralising for the staff who are working in the organisation. It is almost as though the cycle is bound to be downwards.'[8]

The Tyranny of Targets

Within two years of arriving in power in May 1997, Tony Blair's Labour government had set a staggering total of about 8,500 targets[9] – it isn't possible to be more precise, because government departments didn't even keep track of their own targets. They ranged from the wonderfully grand and vague ('Halve world poverty by 2015', 'Improve the quality of life worldwide') to the magnificently minute: the Health Secretary even had a target to ensure that carpets in NHS hospitals are 'of an even appearance without flattened pile'. Almost every measurable entity within the compass of the five-million-strong public sector workforce is now subject to a target – a target that we, the general public, have been told about. We even know that the National Maritime Museum has a target to reduce the number of reams of photocopier paper by 3,000 within three years: stationery was once a matter for the privacy of office politics, but now it is conducted in the full glare of an alternately indifferent and bemused public.

What makes the preoccupation with targets even more bizarre

is that a good proportion of them are missed. According to a Liberal Democrat analysis of the government's own figures, 42 per cent of the targets set for the 1998–2002 spending review period were missed. The Home Office in particular struggled with its 197 targets, failing to meet eighty-six of them (44 per cent), and had to drop a target to deport 30,000 asylum seekers because it was unrealistic. But Tony Blair was unapologetic about the proliferation of targets, and insisted they would stay: 'They were in part constructed as a rod for our own back in order to make sure that we were as bold and ambitious as we could be.'[10]

But the rod falls heaviest on those held responsible for meeting the targets – the managers and professionals running the public sector. Their complaint is that this new politics of accountability and transparent government restricts their professional autonomy and frequently distorts the process of administration – even to the self-defeating point of undermining the quality of the service. As Dr Ian Bogle, the then Chairman of the British Medical Association, commented, 'You can't win with targets. The professions are sick to death of being shackled in this way and feeling that their clinical priorities are being undermined by targets. The professionals should decide without always having a government target from Whitehall skewing what they are doing locally.'[11] One human resources consultant who does a lot of work in the public sector quipped that 'Targets are like guns, dangerous in the wrong hands.'

Some of the most dramatic instances of distortion have been in the health service. The government decreed that 90 per cent of accident and emergency patients must be seen within four hours, and set the week beginning 23 March 2003 for a national audit of waiting times. As that date loomed it triggered chaos in hospitals around the country, with departments recruiting locums, offering staff bonuses and double shifts just for the audit period, as well as cancelling surgery to ensure there were beds available for patients transferring from A&E.[12] John Heyworth, president of the British

Association for Accident and Emergency Medicine, said, 'There is a feeling of panic out there at the moment. All sorts of quick-term fixes are being tried. Money appears to be no object, with staff being recruited and paid whatever necessary for the measuring period.'[13]

Various ruses were used to massage the figures. For example, it would seem quite straightforward to measure the time from when patients arrive in A&E to when they leave, but no: some hospitals 'stop the clock' when a *decision* to admit has been made, and the time the patient then spends on a trolley waiting for a bed is not counted. Another trick is to keep ambulances waiting outside A&E departments because they are 'full'; the clock only starts when the patient is unloaded. At one hospital, six ambulances at a time were waiting. Targets for ambulance response times have prompted similar ruses over when to start the clock.[14]

Targets can even put lives at risk. One set by central government is that all suspected cancer patients must be seen within two weeks; but lung cancer does not usually require urgent treatment, and the pressure to meet that target reduces resources for other chest patients, such as cystic fibrosis sufferers, who have a high morbidity rate and can deteriorate very rapidly.[15]

The figures produced to meet targets get fiddled. A spot-check of forty-one NHS trusts in March 2003 found that only three were reporting figures on waiting lists accurately. Three hospitals were deliberately misreporting, and one of them had been massaging the figures on a regular basis for several years. In nineteen hospitals there were reporting errors, and in another fifteen there were weaknesses in the system of reporting.

In the education sector, allegations of abuse of the system culminated in March 2003 in a primary school head teacher, Alan Mercer, being jailed for three months for forging test papers for his eleven-year-old pupils. He felt under intense pressure to raise standards at the school, South Borough primary in Maidstone, Kent. Investigations revealed that he had also fiddled the tests at his previous school. The Qualifications and Curriculum Authority (QCA) has received complaints of teachers telling children the answers in tests, rubbing out the wrong answers, even working through the whole test with the class question by question. Teachers circulate tips on how to improve results, such as opening the papers early and working out the maths problems using different figures, or sitting less able children next to more able so that they can copy. One primary school teacher wrote in the *Guardian*:

> I am an experienced teacher who has gathered testimony from children in several areas of England showing that cheating by schools in the SATS [Standard Assessment Tests] exams for outgoing primary pupils is widespread. Most of those children do not realise that teachers – who test their own class behind closed doors – are doing anything wrong. The teachers are under enormous pressure to meet targets, and there is also an emotional urge to help their 'own' children. If school league tables are to be published on the basis of SAT scores, the results must be fair – otherwise honest schools are penalised. Some teachers and parents have complained to the local education authorities and the exam watchdog (the Qualifications and Curriculum Authority) but the authorities do nothing to tighten the system because they are trying to satisfy government targets.

Studies by Durham University and the National Foundation for Educational Research question the whole basis of the government's much-vaunted improvements in primary education, reporting that children's better achievement as measured by SATs is evidence only of cramming and widespread cheating.[16] The head of Ofsted, the Office of Standards in Education, David Bell, acknowledged in 2003 that there had been 'an excessive or myopic focus on targets' which could damage children's education; the harder the targets, the more likely they would be 'treated with cynicism or defeatism'.[17]

A pamphlet published in 2003 by the thinktank Demos commented: 'Government has begun to acknowledge that the quantity of formal testing now undertaken, the cumulative effect of almost a generation of reform, may be having a negative effect on learners and teachers.'[18]

The frequent complaint is that the culture of targets and inspections is too often an elaborate game in which targets are set, performance is geared to meet them, yet the actual quality of the service doesn't improve. 'Many felt that the content of their work was increasingly driven not by what matters but by what could be measured,' commented an Audit Commission report in 2002. Given that large amounts of money and an increase in institutional autonomy are the reward for improved performance, public sector managers and professionals often have little choice but to play the game or lose out. They find themselves caught up in rituals of accountability which often bear little relation to what motivates them to do their job in the first place – such as pride in the quality of service, or the chance to make a difference to people's lives. 'Many current and ex-staff do not feel that they have the space, the resources or the autonomy they need to make this difference in practice. They feel that they are working in an environment in which levels of bureaucracy, paperwork and externally imposed targets are diverting them from what they see as the core of their work – time spent with people,' concluded the Audit Commission.[19]

One probation officer kept a list of the official reports, strategy papers and circulars he was expected to read – it came to a grand total of 24,000 pages a year.[20] A head teacher counted the letters in her in-tray after her Christmas holiday – there were 134 which needed a reply and/or action. The scale of the inspection regime is awe-inspiring. In just one year, 2000–01, registration and inspection units carried out 57,000 social services and health-related inspections on 32,400 establishments – 44,500 on social services and

12,500 on health establishments – at a cost of £64 million.[21] In July 2003 the Public Administration Select Committee urged 'root and branch reform' of the government's system of performance measurement. Its report criticised 'arbitrary' target-setting and argued that 'demoralisation and resentment' were common among public sector employees.[22]

Bureaucracy and paperwork are cited as the biggest cause of stress, and exacerbate the recruitment crisis in the public sector, said the Audit Commission report on recruitment and retention in 2002. Lack of resources came second, followed closely by 'workload/ hours' for over 60 per cent of public sector employees surveyed. 'Not valued by government' and the 'pace of change' were factors for over 50 per cent, while 'not valued by the public' affected nearly 40 per cent. Pay ranked eighth out of eleven issues which prompted people to leave the sector. What workers most detested about the bureaucracy was that they believed it had little purpose: 'In the end I just used to dread going to work because when I got there, from start to finish, there would be people in my ear, meeting after meeting . . . and then I ended up having to stay after work to finish protocols and guidelines,' said a former NHS nurse, while a former teacher commented: 'The downside is the paperwork, which you feel nobody is going to look at. I am not against paperwork if I feel that it is going to progress me or my pupils, but I would say that with a good 80 per cent of it, that doesn't happen.'[23]

Restructuring has hit the public sector hard. A survey for the trade union Unison found that 54 per cent of those in local government and 51 per cent of those in the health service had gone through major organisational change in the previous year. The survey quoted a former teacher who complained: 'I think another problem with teaching has been one initiative after another initiative. You just get one thing in place and you change to something else, then you get that settled in and you change to something else. It could be paperwork, it could be assessments, targets, profiling, mentoring, National Curriculum, and so it goes on.' A former emergency services employee echoed this view when he told the Audit Commission: 'They would come out with some pea-brained scheme ... and put it into operation, and then eighteen months later somebody would come out with another one, and another two years later someone would come out with something else ... they would reinvent the wheel and it would go round and around again.'[24]

Central government intrusion becomes an additional hurdle – any improvement in the service is *despite*, rather than *because of*, the targets and inspections which eat into the valuable time and attention needed. The intrusion is also resented because it strikes at the heart of what it means to be a professional – the autonomy implicit in the expression 'professional judgement': a staggering 82 per cent of those leaving the public sector for the private sector felt that they had more autonomy in their new jobs.[25] Many professionals in the public sector have come to the painful conclusion that they now have two tasks: they do their job, and then they have to prove they've done it.

The battle to reform public services has cast a long shadow over the politics of the Labour administration. It is now widely accepted inside and outside government that many of the mechanisms it has put in place to raise standards in health, education, local government and the criminal justice system have led to a deterioration in the working lives of millions of public servants. The implications for recruitment, retention and the ultimate objective of improving services have begun to hit home. As a Cabinet Office performance and innovation unit report warned in January 2001, 'Delivery of public services always depends on the actions of people who cannot be directly controlled by central government, departments and agencies. Although short-term results can be achieved through direction, in the long run, it is more effective to motivate and empower ... Excessively direct methods of government that appear to treat front-line deliverers as unable to think for themselves, untrustworthy or incompetent, undermine the very motivation and adaptability on which real-world success depends.'[26]

To meet government targets, the NHS needs 35,000 more nurses, midwives and health visitors, and 15,000 more consultants and family doctors, by 2008, while the DfES needs 10,000 more teachers and 20,000 non-teaching staff by 2006. But the availability of workers to meet the demand is at its lowest point since 1987, and demographic trends mean that fewer young people are entering the workforce. Already, vacancies are reported across all jobs in the public sector in all parts of the country, with the most acute problems being in London and the south-east. Demand is outstripping supply of new recruits, but the most worrying statistic of all is the demographic timebomb ticking away under the public sector: 27 per cent of public sector workers are now over fifty. Their fast-approaching retirement within the next decade will coincide with rising expectations from the electorate for a better standard of service.[27]

It is the prospect of this recruitment crisis which is beginning to curb government, the hard taskmaster; one senior government thinker advised that there should be a moratorium on any more NHS reform to give the service time to consolidate. It is also prompting some soul-searching on how Labour came to preside over this deterioration of morale – the same government adviser admitted that the lack of an 'institutional philosophy' has been its biggest failing. But considerable damage has been done by Labour's earlier, more confrontational approach, such as when Prime Minister Tony Blair famously declared that he bore 'scars on his back' from his battles to reform the public sector. For the millions of public servants caught in the tension between efficiency and quality of service, between the rising expectations of a consumer culture and the continuing restrictions on resources, public sector reform has been a recipe for overwork.

Reinventing Government

Just how did Labour manage to squander the goodwill of so many of its natural allies and cast itself in the role of hard taskmaster? The answer to that question lies in the aftermath of the 1992 election defeat, when an increasingly influential group of thinkers in the party feared that a decade of neo-liberalism had succeeded in irretrievably undermining the legitimacy of a big welfare state funded by tax increases. No party would ever be elected on a tax-and-spend manifesto, argued those who would go on to formulate the 'Third Way' in the mid-nineties. A profound distrust of government's use of taxpayers' money had taken root in the electorate, and despite a decade of booming consumer aspirations which had left public sector provision of services such as health and education lamentably lagging, the electorate were unwilling to dig into their pockets to fund the improvements they desired. By the mid-nineties, Labour believed that the great challenge of government would be to save and justify the entire rationale of a welfare state. A sense of desperate urgency has underpinned public sector reform for nearly a decade since; as a report for the Institute of Public Policy Research put it at the beginning of Labour's second term, 'If in five years' time, after a period of strong funding, citizens feel that services are still failing, there could be a backlash. Those opposed to collective provision would find it easier to argue that public services are an anachronism: blunt, inefficient, restrictive of choice. If the case for universal public services cannot be won now, it could be lost forever.'[28]

In the mid-nineties, Labour Party strategies were influenced by two trends. Firstly, they were fascinated by a new model of public administration gaining credibility amongst American Democrats which might be able to achieve a better standard of services without costing the earth. *Reinventing Government* (1992) by the American government advisers David Osborne and Ted Gaebler was arguably one of the most influential books on government of the nineties on both sides of the Atlantic. Osborne and Gaebler's analysis was that the state was in crisis: few Americans believed it offered value for money, and few wanted to work for it, yet the political debate was caught in the old conflict between either higher taxes or tax cuts. They argued that the old bureaucratic model of government was bankrupt: 'It delivered the basic, no-frills, one-size-fits-all services people needed and expected during the industrial era: roads, highways, sewers, schools.' That had worked in the past, 'in an age of hierarchy, when only those at the top of the pyramid had enough information to make informed decisions', but now institutions had to be extremely flexible and adaptable, 'responsive to their customers, offering choices of non-standardised services; [to] lead by persuasion and incentives rather than commands; [to] give their employees a sense of meaning and control, even ownership. It demands institutions that empower citizens rather than simply serving them.'[29]

The answer, they proposed, was for government to institute competition between service providers, to measure performance, and to redefine the client as a customer, by offering the kind of choices available to the consumer in other areas of life: a choice of schools, hospitals and doctors. Authority would be decentralised, and all sectors – public, private and voluntary – would be mobilised to tackle social problems. Cost control and financial transparency would ensure value for money, and better systems of accountability would ensure a high quality of service. It was a combination of devolving power, but at the same time setting the objectives and strengthening the audit mechanisms to monitor whether they had been achieved. What made this model so seductive was that it promised better government without having to increase taxes: it seemed like the magic bullet for Labour's conundrum of how to save the welfare state.

The second trend which influenced Labour's public sector reform was the growth of the 'audit society'. The rapid development of technology enabled information to be gathered and analysed in ways that hadn't been possible before. In the public services this information could serve several functions. It could be used to spur competition – for example, through school league tables. It could also be used to promote public trust: if the electorate could be persuaded that their taxes were improving services, they'd be prepared to stump up more money. That placed a huge emphasis on what information was gathered and how it was communicated – or 'spun' – to the public. The hope was that greater transparency and information could resolve what philosopher Onora O'Neill called a 'culture of suspicion' towards public sector professionals in her 2002 Reith Lectures, 'A Question of Trust'.

Both trends converged on the issue of central government setting targets and measuring their achievement: this was the aspect which Labour adopted with enthusiasm as soon as it came to power, extending the Conservatives' experiments with the audit society to new lengths. In primary school education, the 'command and control' model of central government was even stretched to cover the fine detail of teaching methods and timetabling. But Labour showed little inclination for the other part of the *Reinventing Government* equation – decentralisation. Tim, the senior housing officer quoted at the beginning of this chapter, has one comment to make on *Reinventing Government*: 'It was the good idea which New Labour has never actually implemented – if only they would decentralise and leave us to get on with it.' But the 'control freak' label applied to Tony Blair's first government was not without reason; it wanted improvements fast. Besides, the interventionist instincts of even a reformed socialist party run deep, and the audit culture was grafted onto the paternalistic, bureaucratic structures of a centralised welfare state.

Over the last few years, the flaws of the audit culture have become increasingly apparent. Some were a consequence of that fatal graft;

others are inherent in the audit process, which never fulfilled its rationalist promise of pure objectivity. What the enthusiasts were not prepared to acknowledge was that an audit is never going to be neutral. It distorts what it sets out to measure, particularly in such complex areas as health and education. The audit process itself is shaped by the political context, which 'tends not to generate clear objectives against which effectiveness can be judged', according to one analysis of the audit culture.[30] It is politics which determines what should be measured and what constitutes success; for example, are hospital waiting lists always the right way to chart the progress of investment in the NHS? Another example, which was a particular irritant for Tim in his housing department, are the anti-social-behaviour orders brought in as part of a well-publicised 1999 government 'crackdown on anti-social behaviour' designed to appease a right-wing tabloid press. They made little practical sense to him, since the bans they imposed on unruly families were far more expensive to enforce than the much simpler option of eviction. The political context can lead to a rhetorical fudge in which public servants are left to deal with contradictory or conflicting targets. This was a point picked up in July 2003 by the House of Commons Public Administration Select Committee in its report 'On Target? Government by Measurement', which accused government of a 'lack of clarity' and 'failure to give a clear sense of direction'.

The audit process itself begins to shape the priorities of the service it is allegedly verifying: 'The efficiency and effectiveness of organisations is not so much verified as constructed around the audit process itself,' as Professor Michael Power puts it in his sharp critique, *The Audit Society: Rituals of Verification* (1997). Who conducts the audit and according to what measures, become crucial determinants of who has power within an organisation as old systems of accountability are swept aside; in many parts of the NHS the audits have become the battleground for a fierce war between managers and clinicians.

There is also the impact on morale of how the audit culture interacts with the media, which seizes on the negative, giving prominence to failures. A sense of public esteem used to be an important reward of the job of a public servant, but no longer; the political focus on public sector reform exacerbates the sense of being under scrutiny – and of being found wanting. 'Naming and shaming' must be one of the most destructive aspects of the audit culture. The demands on senior executives can be immense, as Helen Oakley, Assistant Director of Social Services, Stoke on Trent, told the *Guardian*'s 'Common Good' series in March 2001: 'I love my job . . . but I'm continually shattered as the pace of change since May 1997 has been phenomenal. Public sector services are under immense scrutiny and this, too, has its tensions. On the one hand it is really good that people are debating the value of health, education and social services; on the other, the pressures to perform to a political agenda and to rising public expectations are enormous.'[31]

The pressure can be overwhelming, as Robert Crawford told the media when he resigned as Chief Executive of Scottish Enterprise in 2003. He said the public scrutiny was 'brutal' after leaks in the media of the agency not meeting its targets, 'not only for myself but more importantly for the staff. The strains of the last five months have taken their toll. We do need to be careful in the UK about how public servants are treated. Stakeholders have a right to be critical, but that criticism has to be judicious and fair or people will not go into public sector jobs like this.'[32]

Not even a £200,000 salary could console the well-regarded Crawford for working in 'a goldfish bowl' of 'constant daily scrutiny', so it's not surprising that teachers in a school which has been condemned as 'failing' by Ofsted get disheartened by the hostility of the local paper, or nurses get upset at being tarred with incompetence because of an inspection report on their hospital. The audit culture, and how the information it generated was used by government, brought the public service into the heart of a battle between government and the media over spin: were waiting list targets to be believed or not? In the process, the work and careers of public servants could be publicly denigrated. The Audit Commission (ironically, the institution which has done more than any other to implement the audit society) concluded in its report 'Recruitment and Retention' that 'a strong measure of "value" for public sector workers is the public image of their job or profession. Many workers perceive this to be negative and, in extreme cases, are reluctant to admit what they do for a living.' It concluded that 'overall, people felt that they were much more likely to be blamed, pitied or misunderstood, than respected as competent professionals'. It sounds like a case of the poacher turned gamekeeper as the report pleads for a shift in the tone of the national conversation to boost the status of public servants: 'Our analysis suggests that in the public sector, the psychological contract is part of a wider, unwritten contract with government, citizens and the media. To create a real sense for public sector staff that they are rewarded and valued, their financial reward must be "felt fair", their work experience must be rewarding, and their wish to be viewed as competent professionals, rather than as objects of pity or blame, must be realised.'[33]

Michael Power identifies four serious defects of the audit society: it can increase pointless information in an 'inspection overload'; it can lead to a decline in organisational trust as everyone becomes anxious, inhibited and preoccupied with how they are seen by others; new games are generated to demonstrate quality, and performance declines; finally, there is an overcommitment to create politically acceptable images of control – put simply, politicians have to be able to demonstrate that the great organs of state are responsive to their initiatives, that they have an effect. This last is often not easy, and it is rarely, if ever, quick. Unlike much change in our culture, which is rapidly accelerating, the process of institutional reform and change has not kept pace, and is even slower because it has to deal with increased complexity. Professor Power provocatively asks in his conclusion whether 'the audit explosion [is] the product of an institutionalised delusion, a refusal to confront the politically uncomfortable policy reality of loss of control, and the creation of ritualised cover-up as a response?'[34]

A Question of Trust

For many public servants caught up in the pointless charade of that 'ritualised cover-up' it presents an acute crisis in their sense of pride and the worth of their work. They are well aware that its implementation has been a response to a crisis of trust in their own professionalism. As Michael Power puts it, 'Many of the audit-related changes which have taken place in the public sector in recent years reflect institutionalised distrust in the capacity of teachers, social workers and university lecturers to self-regulate the quality of their services.'[35] But that crisis of trust in public servants, which the audit culture was intended to ease, has only been aggravated. As John Clarke and Janet Newman summed it up in *The Managerial State* (1997):

> In the place of the presumptions of trust associated with old public service ethics, the relationships of public service have been increasingly formalised through contractual mechanisms, monitoring and both financial and performance audits ... The widely perceived crisis in standards in public life and the range of inquiries and investigations which have resulted ... are the consequences of a political ideology which has consistently insisted that 'public servants' are not to be trusted by the public.[36]

The paradox is that the very systems put in place to buttress failing public trust become in themselves distrusted. The pressures bearing down on individual public sector employees are such that the system is abused, and hence no longer trusted. 'Assumptions of distrust sustaining audit processes may be self-fulfilling as auditees adapt their behaviour in response to the audit process,' comments Power.

The failure of the audit culture to reverse the decline in trust in the public service was the subject on which Onora O'Neill chose to concentrate in her 2002 Reith Lectures. She gained widespread public support for her defence of professionals when she attacked the audit explosion for making their job much more difficult, and for overlooking how the most crucial aspect of their work is often quite simply beyond any method of measurement. 'The new accountability is widely experienced not just as changing, but I think as distorting, the proper aims of professional practice, and indeed as damaging professional pride and integrity,' declared O'Neill. She went on to ask if the accountability revolution was working. Why wasn't it increasing levels of public trust, and 'Might we therefore be setting up the wrong sorts of accountability?' She warned of the danger of 'a culture of suspicion, low morale [which] may ultimately lead to professional cynicism, and then we would have grounds for public mistrust', and argued that current methods of accountability 'damage rather than repair trust'.[37]

What she recommended was 'fewer fantasies about total control' and leaving institutions some degree of self-governance, accountable to outsiders with 'sufficient time and experience to assess the evidence'. She insists that 'real accountability' requires 'substantive and knowledgeable independent judgement'. This was perceived as a clarion call for a return to the professional's self-regulation. O'Neill rightly identifies a delusion at the centre of government, a fantasy of micro-control. But the decline in trust is not only about a crisis in the role of the state, it is also about a profound shift in the attitude of the public. Three elements have transformed the individual's expectations of the public sector professional: the end of deference, the information revolution, and the rise of 'consumer sovereignty' – a sense of entitlement to 'whatever you want whenever you want it'. All three make the nineteenth-century understanding of the role of the professional unsustainable.

Deference was part of how professional status evolved as a way of guarding and regulating a body of knowledge – whether of medicine or the law. The profession developed self-regulation over training, entry and practice. In return for submitting to such regulation, the professional's status conferred authority and autonomy. Clients or patients were expected to defer to his or her expertise, and that deference was used to manage the relationship. Doctors didn't have to explain themselves, and the patient's role was passive. This type of relationship echoed a hierarchical society in which class determined deference: the teacher, the policeman and the local doctor were figures of respect in the community. That deference has crumbled at the same time as there has been an increase in economic inequality and crime. Frequently it is public servants who are caught at the interface, as the head teacher of a Leeds primary school comments: 'This is the second-poorest ward in the country, and sometimes it is horrible taking on so much aggression. Many people have low self-esteem, and they attack me first. I have to tell them I am not the enemy, I am trying to help. I feel a victim of bullying sometimes.'[38]

One in three doctors told a BMA survey in 2003 that they had experienced violence and verbal abuse in the past year. A paramedic in the London ambulance service, Ken Murphy, described the violence towards staff: 'People used to call an ambulance for help. Now, if you turn up they see your uniform and they abuse you and attack you. We all wear stab-proof vests now. They know you carry drugs on an ambulance, so sometimes they try and steal them. I've been attacked – I think the guy was high on drugs. I ended up with a black eye and my glasses smashed.'[39]

The information revolution has transformed attitudes towards professionals by making all sorts of knowledge much more accessible. Patients arriving in the doctor's surgery now have access to the latest medical papers on their complaint; for an unusual condition, they can often be better informed than the doctor. A few hours on Google and they might have turned up research on a rare skin condition from an Australian university or from Brazil. Knowledge has become global, and its rapid circulation has eroded the way in which professions used to guard their expertise. Such is the quantity of information available, it is beyond the capability of one individual doctor to keep abreast of it all. The balance of power between professional and client has been transformed.

Attitudes towards public service have also been influenced by one of the most pervasive sentiments of consumer culture. Almost every advertisement reinforces the notion that we are *entitled* to a particular product; consumer culture offers the powerful seduction of making all our dreams come true – the magical tropical holiday, the transformation of our home with a new kitchen, the transformation of our skin with a new cream. Our expectations are inflated, and we are offered an enormous range of choices. It is in the exercising of those choices that we most commonly understand personal freedom and personal agency – our sense of our ability to control our environment. These principles of a consumer culture are being rapidly transferred to the public sector. This means that choice – of school, hospital, doctor – becomes an important political goal, even though it may be expensive (by generating overcapacity in schools and hospitals), and it inflates our expectations of and entitlement to public services without also inflating our willingness to pay for them.

Labour has made a point of emphasising this shift from citizen to consumer. Almost every speech Tony Blair has made about public sector reform uses the word 'consumer'. For example, in February 2002 he said: 'Reform means redesigning public services around the consumer, giving people the services they today expect – services that put them first, that are prompt, convenient, responsive and of the highest quality. For example, they want hospital appointments booked to suit the patient, not the hospital . . . Fulfilling consumers' expectations is different now for doctors whose patients have discussed their symptoms in internet chatrooms or called NHS Direct. It's different for teachers, talking to parents who have researched local schools' exam results on the web.'[40]

There are undoubtedly some huge advantages to these challenges to the traditional authority of professionals, which was open to abuse when it disempowered the recipient of the service, or when professional groups sought to protect their own interests at the cost of those receiving the service. The reform of the public sector has aimed to curtail that power – whether it was of the consultants or of the trade unions that dominated local government services. The question is, at what point has the pendulum swung too far? How can Tony Blair rightly call for services which put the client 'first' without a serious deterioration in the quality of the working lives of those providing that service? He certainly can't claim that it could be achieved without enormous investment, and this is perhaps where the concept of the consumer is most pernicious in the context of the public sector: it raises expectations which cannot be fulfilled without an increase in taxation of a level which is regarded as politically unacceptable. It is public servants who are left to straddle the gap between expectation and reality. Put concretely, it's the nurse on the end of the phone of NHS Direct who gets an earful from an angry patient kept waiting for two hours who expects a standard of service similar to that offered by his bank's call centre. Or it's the teacher who has to explain why a child cannot be given extra tuition for lack of resources.

This was the issue that Elizabeth Lindley, a clinical scientist in renal care in Leeds, described: 'We have awkward customers in dialysis, as you would in any job that served the public. My perception is that we've had more threatening behaviour from patients than we used to. It's only a small percentage . . . But I think that in the past patients were relieved to have a chance to live after their

142

kidneys had failed, whereas our new "blame" culture means that some of them feel that someone should have stopped their kidneys failing in the first place.'[41] A head of libraries in Essex working sixty hours a week admitted, 'It's not easy, I don't think it ever has been, but it has been getting tougher ... The public expect us to continuously improve and deliver more for the same or less. Increasingly it is less about being a public servant and more about being a public entrepreneur.'[42]

Consumer sovereignty exists only for those with a large bank balance; but the welfare state does not choose its customers, and is firmly wedded to the principle of equality. Delivering high quality in services which are extremely expensive such as health and education as well as offering choice is a Nirvana which Labour has dangerously conjured up. There is growing concern that this was the wrong direction in which to point public sector reform; at a research seminar at Number 10 in January 2003 it was reported that policy experts were concerned that citizens had become 'like adolescents, impossible to govern and overdemanding'.[43]

This may all seem a long way from the issue of overwork, but these questions directly affect the psychological contract of those working in the public sector. The role of the state and the nature of the relationship between government and citizen profoundly affect the sense of purpose and meaning of the five million people employed in the public sector. All the evidence suggests widespread confusion and uncertainty. The old public service ethos is challenged by a new rhetoric of 'social entrepreneurship', and the stability of the old bureaucratic structures is challenged by the constant invocation by politicians of the need for innovation, flexibility and continuous change. No wonder thousands of highly skilled public servants are voting with their feet, taking early retirement or switching careers. A quality of working life agenda would start with government putting its own house in order.

Part Three

Why Do We Do it?

6

You're on Your Own

Job satisfaction fell in Britain throughout the nineties. We were unhappy about the nature of our work, the size of our workload, our boss, our pay, and that we weren't allowed to use our own initiative. Nearly 60 per cent of British workers think management will always try to get the better of employees if given the chance.[1] The unhappiest workers of all are those in their thirties and forties and those with university degrees, and what they are most unhappy about is their hours. Between 1992 and 2000, the number of men satisfied with their hours at work dropped from 35 per cent to 20 per cent, and the number of women fell from 51 per cent to 29 per cent. The largest falls were at both ends of the occupational grading – the highest- and the lowest-paid – and were most severe amongst the over-fifties (from 54 per cent to 26 per cent).[2] The conclusion of researchers Michael White and Stephen Hill is that there has been a 'very substantial change over time' which has led to a 'marked apparent deterioration in people's experience of work'.[3]

But for all the grumbling, and the fact that the vast majority are working harder than ever, there has been little collective protest about Britain's overwork culture. It hasn't swelled the ranks of the trade union movement – on the contrary, union membership has continued its long-term decline. More of us are in paid work than ever before in Britain; the employment activity rate has risen to 74.5 per cent, just below the post-war peak of 75.7 per cent, and the government has set a target for it to rise even further, to 75 per cent. Women are spending more time than ever in paid employment, and now represent 45 per cent of the country's workforce.

So why do we manage only the private litanies of complaint? Why aren't we demanding a better deal, a life worth living in return for our pay packet? Why aren't we insisting that time and energy are crucial ingredients of freedom, and that work is depriving us of both? Some people are in jobs too precarious to allow such workplace radicalism, but why aren't those with the strongest bargaining power in the labour market – the white-collar sweatshop labourers who have been hit so hard in the nineties – fighting back?

Are we suckers for punishment, or are we just seduced by a paycheque and a rising standard of living? Are we a nation of wimps, bullied by the Thatcherite onslaught on the trade unions, who now, cowed, march dutifully into our offices without complaint? Or a nation of masochists who cheerfully put up with the destruction our work wreaks on the rest of our lives? Why is it that so many of us have got caught in the overwork trap, to the detriment of our health and our families? Just how much is our complicity in the overwork culture driven by necessity, or by greed, or by a work ethic which has spun out of control?

The simplest explanation for people working hard is that they need the money. There is a link between long hours and low pay, as we saw in Chapter 1, but in fact long hours are not primarily a problem of the poor: the average working week for the lowest-paid is around twenty-seven hours.[4] The introduction of the minimum wage has even led to reduced hours, as employers try to save costs by reducing the working week. Long hours are most commonly now a problem of affluence, not poverty; the evidence is that the higher the salary, the longer the hours.

More widespread is the use of overtime pay to increase a basic wage among the skilled working class and the self-employed such as window cleaners, plumbers and electricians. Here, the proportion of long-hours workers almost matches that among white-collar workers: 30 per cent of process, plant and machine operatives work over fifty hours a week, as do 20 per cent of other 'elementary occupations' and skilled trades. It is estimated that 1.6 million workers get overtime pay for their forty-eight-hour-plus week.[5]

According to a study of long-hours workers in December 2001, just over 70 per cent of those in skilled and semi-skilled trades and factory workers do it for the overtime pay, while those in white-collar jobs, from clerical up to professional and managerial levels, say heavy workload is the main reason for working long hours. A fifth of those in these groups say their long hours are due to their enjoying the job so much.[6]

The overwork culture demands a greater effort from the workforce, and in many workplaces job intensification has been introduced with sweeteners to employees in the form of pay and productivity deals. Earnings have been rising steadily for several decades, which reflects the increasing wealth of the country. But the way in which the cake is being shared out has become vastly more unequal in the last two decades. At the bottom levels of the labour market, the work may be much tougher, but the pay packet as a proportion of average earnings has shrunk significantly. Pay inequality has yawned wide: between 1979 and 1998–99 the incomes of the poorest 10 per cent of employees rose by 6 per cent in real terms, whereas those of the top 10 per cent of earners rose by 82 per cent. Mean incomes rose by 55 per cent in real terms.[7] Boardroom pay increased by 23 per cent in just one year, in 2002, compared to an increase of only 3 per cent in average earnings.[8] Because the rise in earnings at the top end has been so sharp it has pulled the average earnings figure up, so that a majority of full-time employees now fall below the average. There's little evidence that this deepening inequality has been stemmed under Labour; Income Data Services pointed out in May 2003 that while the introduction of the minimum wage has 'done something to boost the position of the lower paid ... it has had little impact on the growth in overall earnings inequality'. In spring 2002 14.4 per cent of workers over the age of twenty-two were earning less than £5 an hour, while 17.6 per cent of all jobs paid less than £5.10 – that's nearly one job in five.[9] The result is that there were more individuals with incomes below 60 per cent of the median (the official measure of poverty) in 1999–2000 than in 1994–95, up from eleven to 11.7 million.[10]

One of the things that make the position of these lowest-paid shocking is that for them, the overwork does not pay. We have seen develop a whole new form of degradation and humiliation at work in which people are required to work very hard, yet still aren't paid enough to provide a decent standard of living, and are forced to depend on the state benefit of the Working Tax Credit. While the preoccupation of the eighties was the terrible scourge of un-employment, more widespread now is the plight of the 'working poor' whose overwork does not earn them a living wage. The jour-nalist Barbara Ehrenreich described this phenomenon in the United States; she took poorly paid jobs in several American cities to write her book *Nickel and Dimed* (2002): 'I grew up hearing over and over, to the point of tedium, that "hard work" was the secret of success ... no one ever said you could work hard – harder than you ever thought possible – and still find yourself sinking ever deeper into poverty and debt.' The delinking of hard work and self-sufficiency is an uncomfortable reality of the labour market on both sides of the Atlantic, and it is one that Labour has largely reinforced, despite the introduction of the minimum wage. It has simply reconfigured the dependency culture from unemployment benefit to Working Tax Credit, which is a means of subsidising cheap labour.

Some of those working the longest hours – the professional and managerial groups – have seen an increase in their standard of living, even if the growth in their income is well below that of the top 10 per cent of earners. Between 1991 and 2002, managerial pay increased by 70.8 per cent, and professional pay by 59.9 per cent;[11] both well above the 32 per cent increase in retail prices. This accelerating inequality, whereby some do fine and others fall further behind, has been characterised as the 'winner-takes-all culture', and becomes a driver of the overwork culture. A 2001 study for the American National Bureau of Economic Research concluded that it is wage differentials that motivate America's overwork culture.[12] Robert Reich, the US Secretary for Labor under President Clinton, refines the concept and how it drives overwork: 'It's not the winner-takes-all economy, because the top 5 per cent also do very well, and then the top 20 per cent are doing well, the middle hasn't changed much and the bottom has deteriorated . . . It's just that the spaces between these points have expanded . . . as the income ladder lengthens, people on the top rungs earn far more and run the risk of losing far more, which spurs hard work; people at the bottom have to work harder to have a decent level of income . . . where the disparities are wider, people work harder.'[13]

These widening gaps in the ladder have been an important factor in pushing women into the labour market. In lower-income families, as relative male earnings have declined, the importance of women's incomes has increased – they're no longer a bit of pin money on the side, but an essential contribution to the family budget. Thus, while pay at the lower end of the labour market may not have kept pace with median earnings, some of that inequality has been offset by women taking on paid work in dual-earner families. For example, a family will struggle on one wage of £12,000, but the pressure eases when that income is doubled in a dual-earner family.[14]

In studies of why women work, over 60 per cent cite money reasons first, and for 40 per cent of those with a partner who works, her wages help pay for essentials.[15] One study claims that as many as one in five working women now earn more than their partners.[16] In higher-skilled occupations, this rises to 41 per cent of women living with or married to a partner who are the main breadwinners, while a further 33 per cent earn the same as their partner.[17] Women have made significant inroads into men's traditional breadwinning role for the family. Furthermore, in a job market which feels insecure, the family spreads its risk by having two breadwinners.

The widening steps on the ladder which Reich describes have increased both the accompanying rewards and costs – and at the top of the labour market these have grown exponentially: you get paid huge amounts for working extremely hard. Reich points out that the 'choice' of whether to put in the effort required or not becomes more and more difficult: 'You don't have to scale the wall (put in all that effort and time), but the consequence of not doing so is harsher and the reward for doing so is sweeter than you ever encountered before.' As the rewards from the job grow, so do the multiplying opportunities on which to spend those rewards in a consumer culture. At the same time, the costs of opting out of this 'hard work, hard spend' are also higher in an increasingly unequal society with a minimal welfare state safety net. Cut down on the hard work and not only is a range of consumer experiences beyond reach, but you struggle to afford a home and a decent education for your children.

This presents a particular conundrum for 'Middle England'. Among the broad swathe of the English middle classes – now defined more widely than ever – the last two generations have grown accustomed to rising prosperity and the expectation that they will be better off than their parents were. They bought their council houses, visited countries their parents had never seen, and gave their children experiences they had never had. But what they did not reckon with was that the price for this would carry on rising. The precarious balancing act on a particular rung of the ladder, or the climb up to the next rung, now requires a greater degree of effort or talent or both in the workplace – and often from both partners.

This *stagflation* of Middle England – running harder to stay in the same place – is one of the factors behind the overwork ethic. The rising price of standing still is evident in the cost of providing one's children with a good-quality education (either in fees or housing in a suitable school catchment area), saving up for a decent pension and buying one's home. Even the core of the traditional middle class, in professional occupations such as GPs and teachers, struggle to realise such aspirations in many parts of the country. As property prices have soared, home-buyers are taking on bigger mortgages; between 1996 and 2002 the advance to income ratio rose from 1.99 to 2.34.[18] This also helps explain why, over the last decade, Middle England's children have been prepared to work harder when they arrive in the labour market. They have the task of maintaining the social status they were born into, often saddled with university debts and trying to buy into an inflationary housing market, in an awkward mismatch of aspirations and earning potential. This stagflation could deteriorate even further as the crisis over pensions unfolds, the ratio of earnings to property prices continues to deteriorate, the expense of a university education soars and the older generation's wealth is poured into their own care.

Stagflation also affects social mobility into the middle classes. The bottleneck has become tighter as the prospects for promotion shrink at lower managerial levels in sectors such as retail, hotels and leisure. In the bid to make it to the next level up, the competition can be intense, and long hours become an essential way to differentiate oneself from rivals; for those now in their thirties, the experience is much more demanding than it was for their parents, who were the first generation to benefit from the expansion of higher education and white-collar work. Studies of social mobility in the UK show a decline in recent decades.[19]

This powerfully drives a sense of grievance in Middle England that they don't enjoy the 'just deserts' of their labour; they compare their own position with the increasing wealth of the top end of the labour market, and measure the relative decline. The resentment is evident in the aggressive paranoia seen in the *Daily Mail* and targeted at anyone who can be claimed to be enjoying 'unjust deserts', be they asylum seekers, welfare scroungers or lone parents. In a strange parallel experience to that of the lowest-paid, Middle England is struggling with the delinking of hard work and success. As Professor Yiannis Gabriel puts it, success is 'no longer the product of hard work, achievement and heroism as it was for the Puritans; instead success is brought by the magic of "being discovered", which involves luck, self-presentation, image and finding oneself in the right place at the right time'. This is how 'presenteeism' becomes a form of modern-day superstition, characterised by the thought that 'If I stay late, I might just be in the right place at the right time for the ever-elusive career breakthrough which will bring me to the promised land of security – of both income and reputation.'

The markers of success in an unequal society move beyond many people's reach; there is an escalator of aspiration. It is no longer sufficient to work hard, you also need luck – winning the lottery, or a scarce promotion – to achieve the recognised symbols of success. Overwork may be a prerequisite of success, but it is no longer sufficient in itself.

How to Spend it

If someone complains about having to work too hard, sooner or later they'll say that they have 'no choice'. Probe a little further, and what becomes clear is that for much of the workforce living well above the poverty line, the connection between pay and overwork is about aspiration to particular patterns of consumption. This is murky territory, where one person's 'needs' are 'desires' to another. Are mobile phones, foreign holidays and DVD players luxuries or necessities of contemporary living? The perceived lack of choice may be the consequence of a series of choices – the bigger house, the new car, the rising debt – which trap people into carrying on working very hard. Consumer debt has rocketed in the last decade, with the British splashing out with their credit cards (borrowing three times more than they did ten years ago[20]) and using their homes as cash machines (loans secured against homes surged by a staggering 40 per cent in 2002 alone[21]). The ratio of household debt to disposable income grew steadily throughout the nineties, from 90 per cent in 1990 to 107 per cent at the end of 2001.[22] As many as six million households are struggling to pay their debts, a sharp increase of 47 per cent between 1996 and 2003, according to a study by the Citizens Advice Bureau.[23]

This is where those campaigning on the work–life-balance agenda become moralistic, and the onus shifts to the individual's moral fibre to resist the seductions of consumer culture. The American economist Juliet Schor followed her 1991 bestseller *The Overworked American* with *The Overspent American* in 1998; to her mind it is the rising aspirations of consumer culture which drive the hard work. She argues that we now compare ourselves not with the Joneses but with the celebrities who dominate the media, and that this spurs on the overwork in the vain hope of bringing the designer labels and lavish lifestyle within reach. She urges America to downshift to a simpler way of life.

This sounds very wholesome and healthy, but such moral judgements neglect the powerful role consumerism plays in the majority of people's lives. Consumerism cannot be boiled down to a moral failing; it has become the arena where we develop our sense of self, and experience a sense of freedom. It has become the very definition of the good life – we know who we are through our patterns of consumption: our choice of brands, our leisure habits, and so on.

Why Do We Do it?

Consumption has replaced work as the core principle governing our identity, argues sociologist Zygmunt Bauman: 'The same central role which was played by work, by job, occupation, profession, in modern society, is now performed in contemporary society by consumer choice . . . The former was the linchpin which connected life-experience – the self-identity problem, life–work, life–business . . . social integration.'[24]

Bauman goes on to argue that our aspirations to freedom, autonomy and fulfilment are now channelled into consumption, and are thus diverted away from conditions in the workplace. He traces this back to the earliest stages of industrialisation, when the power conflicts were gradually channelled into one issue – the fight over pay – and the existing power structures of work and the distribution of the wealth it created were tacitly accepted: 'Increasingly, it was the ability to win a greater share of the surplus that came to be seen as the definitive way to restore that human dignity which was lost when the craftsmen turned into factory hands.'

Once we have shifted the craving for freedom into the sphere of consumption, conflicts over work are transmuted into consumer fantasies: 'Frustrations and unhappiness could then be directed towards buying rather than political protests against working conditions,' writes Sharon Beder in *Selling the Work Ethic* (2000). Vance Packard argued in *The Status Seekers* in 1959 that consumer goods as status symbols had replaced promotion at work as a measure of personal advancement, while Barbara Ehrenreich wrote in *Fear of Falling* (1989) that the American middle classes have turned to consumption to compensate for their disappointments at work: the jobs they wanted to do didn't offer enough money: 'The would-be social worker turned banker . . . must compensate for abandoned dreams . . . Consumerism picks up where the work ethic left off . . . Shopping malls, debt and the advertising industry whip everyone, even moody teenagers, into obedient workers and customers.' Furthermore, consumerism offers an illusion of equality, in what commentator Roland Marchand called 'the democracy of goods'; Americans looked to 'similarities in consumption styles rather than to political power or control of wealth as evidence of significant equality'.[25] Consumerism, rather than religion, becomes 'the opiate of the masses'; it is addictive because it reinforces the problems it promises to ease. And it deflects aspirations to freedom and autonomy away from the workplace.

Through consumerism we find our sense of dignity: you put up with the bullying boss and salve your wounded pride by treating yourself to a pedicure at the weekend. As Sharon Beder comments, 'It is only as purchasers that we are treated with the courtesy worthy of a human being.' This is how the overwork culture interconnects with the drive to consume. The harder you work, the longer and the more intense your hours, the more pressure you experience, the more intense is the drive to *repair, console, restore,* and *find periodic escape* through consumerism. As one senior NHS manager said, as she described a hugely demanding work schedule, the odd weekend in New York had become essential for her sanity. We've placed the solutions and the adjustments to the problems of the workplace in our private consumption patterns: in millions of dreams featuring the perfect aestheticisation of our homes and gardens as places of retreat and restoration; in the perfect getaway, the holiday as far removed from our daily life as we can possibly find. The fantasy is all about retreat and escape. Overwork and consumerism feed off each other.

For those on low wages, this interrelationship is the cruellest of jokes: their hard work brings little dignity, and their low wages deprive them of the consumer experiences which might. They end up with the worst of both worlds, consigned to the role of providing others with the experiences they themselves cannot afford – the pedicure, for example, or cleaning the hotel room after that weekend break. They are outcasts from the consumer rituals of social inclusion (such as shopping) and the symbols of status (such as brands) which delineate self-worth. Their only value to society is their labour, and that counts for very little because it receives so little financial recognition. Low-paid hard work is a double dose of public humiliation.

What we have lost to a very great degree is the possibility of resistance, confrontation or reform – of taking the struggle for freedom back into the workplace. Many of the private sector jobs worst hit by long hours and rising stress have a low rate of trade union membership. The number of workplaces with high union density and well-established collective bargaining fell from 47 per cent in 1980 to only 17 per cent in 1998.[26] Two-thirds of all workplaces have no union presence at all.[27]

The British workforce have largely lost faith in trade unionism, the consequence of nearly two decades of a series of spectacular union defeats and a legislative programme by the Conservative government to restrict their influence. Their old power bases in public utilities, heavy industry and manufacturing were vastly reduced. The British Social Attitudes survey asked non-union members in 1998 what difference a union would make to their workplace: only 18 per cent said it would make it better, and a staggering 65 per cent said it would make no difference. For many workers, unions have little relevance to their workplace struggles. Several times in the course of interviews, workers (often women and often in new service industries) would themselves volunteer their distrust of unions, and their irrelevance; they could take their grievances, they claimed, to the boss. The informal approachability of recent management styles has helped to sideline unions.

The highest union density is now in white-collar jobs, particularly in health and education, where long hours are endemic; yet the unions have largely failed to resist the deterioration of working conditions in the public sector. There have been exceptions to this generalisation: for example, in January 2003 teachers won a national agreement to reduce work intensification. Some of the issues outlined in Chapter 5 have been crucial in undermining the legitimacy of protest and resistance; both the Conservatives and Labour emphasised the principle of consumer choice as a way of combating the 'producer interest'. Overworked public servants routinely now accept government injunctions that the consumer's interest must come first, and struggle to articulate their own interests in opposition: the common refrain is, 'Of course, the needs of the patient/pupil/client must come first, but . . .' But the interests of the provider and the recipient are tightly interwoven, neither can be prioritised over the other without a cost: the rested, happy teacher or nurse will do a better job.

What has crippled the unions in resisting intensification is the rhetoric of 'survive or die' much used by management in the nineties: the company will go bust unless everyone works harder. The fact that the number of jobs in British manufacturing fell by 450,000 between 1993 and 2003 means that no worker can take that as an idle threat. It gives a new incentive for management to tell their workers how the company is doing. Information has become a tool of management; there are always threats to flag up in an intensely competitive economy. In the public sector the threat has now become 'survive or be privatised', and it leaves a workforce anxious and fearful for their jobs.

You're on Your Own: New Work Ethics

Pay and the lure of consumption may spur overwork for the bulk of people on the factory floor and at their desks, but they lose their force at the two poles of the labour market. Over the last decades of the twentieth century it became a real issue to policy-makers and business to keep these two ends of the labour market working as hard as ever. At the top you don't need more money, and education can make you less interested in consumer status symbols; so how do you ensure those employees keep working hard? In the mid-seventies there were growing fears that the hedonism of consumer culture would erode the Protestant work ethic, the underpinning of capitalism. But the work ethic was reformulated, as we saw in Chapter 4, as the route to personal fulfilment, identity and happiness. This ensured that those least motivated by consumerism – either because of wealth or because of education – would still work just as hard, if not harder. Meanwhile, at the other end of the labour market, there were growing concerns by the middle of the eighties on both sides of the Atlantic that the poorest were never going to get much money to participate in the consumer fantasies, so they would have little incentive to get off benefits and into work. One work ethic was used to seduce people into falling in love with work, the other to cajole people into work: the carrot for some, the stick for the others.

The result was the welfare-to-work policies of the nineties, in which the work ethic was inflated to become part of the contractual basis of citizenship: state provision of benefit was no longer an entitlement by birth, but part of a contract in return for employment. Work was elevated as the primary means of social integration – sometimes the rhetoric veered dangerously towards claiming it was the sole means. At the same time, old Victorian themes of work as the route to self-improvement and personal advancement were resurrected. All of which was true only some of the time, and skewed this chorus of rhetoric to focus on the value and benefits of work, to the exclusion of the essential unpaid labour of care and relationship in families, friendships and neighbourhoods.

The Stick

The work ethic has always had an important place in Labour Party thinking, for obvious historical reasons. Mass unemployment in the eighties destroyed lives and communities in Britain. Throughout the eighties and nineties Labour campaigned vigorously for job-creation policies. 'Work is central to our lives ... it is the way in which we meet needs, create wealth and distribute resources. It is a source of personal identity and individual fulfilment, social status and relationships. It is the heart of wealth and welfare,' declared John Smith's Commission for Social Justice in 1993. 'Paid work remains the best pathway out of poverty, as well as the only way in which people can hope to achieve a decent standard of living.' What followed was Labour's 'Getting Welfare to Work' proposals, in which 'dependency' looms large as such a poisonous and infectious disease that its 'impact becomes more severe with every month that passes'. The benefit system 'should offer a way out of unemployment and dependency; a hand up not just a hand-out'.

By the mid-nineties America had begun its experiment with welfare-to-work as the solution to two problems: cutting escalating benefit bills and ensuring a supply of cheap labour for the expanding service sector. The thinking was that an underclass dependent on benefit was splitting further away from the mainstream, and urgently needed the discipline, socialisation and integration provided by work; if necessary, they would have to be forced to work. Some Labour voices were sceptical about this American invention. Frank Dobson wrote in the *Financial Times* in 1993 that it was 'demeaning' for people to 'work for next to nothing'; but Tony Blair was enthusiastic: 'I quite understand the resentment of every taxpayer who has to pay £20 a week to keep three million unemployed ... work and welfare go together ... welfare must enhance duties and responsibilities and not be a substitute for them.'[28] The welfare-to-work proposals unveiled by Gordon Brown in 1995 included benefit cuts for non-participation in the New Deal for Young People. Commentators observed that 'The rhetoric, contractualism and coercion of the New Deal echoes American practice – as does New Labour's emphasis on the work ethic.'[29]

In 1998 Tony Blair made clear the full reach of his government's work ethic: 'Anyone of working age who can work should work.

Work, for those that can work, is in our view the best form of welfare. It provides financial independence, a network of contacts and dignity. So those who have in the past been excluded from job opportunities, such as lone parents or the disabled, many of whom can work and want to work, will be given the chance to do so.'[30]

Virtually all previous expressions of the work ethic in industrialised society have circumscribed its writ, allowing dignity and entitlements to those whose work is outside the paid labour market, such as women, or those who need society's support, such as the disabled. But Blair declared that 'anyone of working age' should work, and specifically included within that remit single parents and the disabled. Benefit entitlement was no longer a result of citizenship, but of contractual obligations arising out of paid work. Blair described this as 'ending the something-for-nothing approach'. The claims he made for work were overblown: it will only provide 'financial independence' if there's a living wage, and since Labour set the minimum wage so low, that is beyond the reach of many. Millions of families in low-paid work are as 'dependent' on state benefit as ever, relying on the Working Tax Credit to make ends meet.

The new work ethic was at the root of one of Labour's most bruising early battles, six months after it came to power. Getting single parents into work was seen as the cheapest way to tackle Britain's shocking record on child poverty (by the mid-nineties there were four million children living in poverty in the UK, one of the highest levels in the OECD); lone parents accounted for two-thirds of all workless households with children. Labour set a target of getting 70 per cent of lone parents into work by 2010 – up from 46 per cent, representing 230,000 lone parents moving into the labour market (by 2002 it had increased to 54 per cent).

In 1997, what horrified an unusual alliance of left-wing and traditionalist Labour MPs was the idea that single mothers caring for young children were also subject to this new work ethic. Harriet Harman, the then Secretary of State for Social Security, was charged with pushing through Parliament benefit cuts to lone parents. 'Work is not just about earning a living. It is central to independence and self-respect,' she told the House of Commons. 'Work makes the difference between a decent standard of living and never-ending benefit dependency; the difference between a cohesive society and a divided one.' When she was challenged in the Commons debate on the specific issue of whether it was a valid choice for lone parents with young children to stay at home to look after them, she dodged the question, insisting that they would now have the choice of whether to go out to work or not, and promised more childcare to help lone parents into work. The episode exposed Labour's inflation of the work ethic; it was work which generated social cohesion, in a ludicrous sleight of hand which ignored how inequality (both in and out of work) divides society. In the end, the compulsory coercive aspects were dropped from Labour's New Deal for Lone Parents and New Deal for the Disabled – though not those in the New Deal for Young People.

What underpinned Labour's welfare-to-work policies was a reconceptualisation of the welfare state 'from a safety net in times of trouble to a springboard for economic opportunity', as John Smith's Commission for Social Justice put it in 1994. The policies aimed to get people off benefit and into what were often not particularly well-paid or attractive jobs. But the virtues claimed for work by Labour – that it conferred rights, dignity, self-respect, social integration – often bear little relation to the jobs taken up by people coming off welfare. Low-paid jobs in the service sector, such as care work, catering and cleaning, are often insecure, they offer little or no prospect of promotion and little dignity. Labour's trick was to conjure up the work ethic of a bygone age – that hard work is the route to opportunity, success, a decent standard of living and dignity – in a labour market whose lower reaches have long since ceased to offer any such things. The mismatch between the promise and the reality only reinforces the humiliation.

Furthermore, the emphasis on the paid-work ethic could not but implicitly undermine the value of unpaid work such as the care of small children or the elderly. Political theorist Adrian Little argues that 'Paid-work-based views of social integration have dominated contemporary political discourse; they pander to economic liberal perceptions of individual worth and neglect a variety of bonds that hold society together which are derived as much from unpaid activities.'[31] The Labour government, for all its much-vaunted feminism, has inadvertently reinforced the low status of mothering and parenting by elevating the value of employment, a point recently acknowledged by Trade Secretary Patricia Hewitt: 'If I look back over the last six years I do think that we have given the impression that we think all mothers should be out to work, preferably full-time, as soon as their children are a few months old. We have got to move to a position where as a society and as a government, we recognise and value the unpaid work that people do within their families.'[32] But she offered nothing more than some warm rhetoric to undo the damage.

The Carrot

Meanwhile, at the opposite end of the labour market, a corporate lawyer working for a British firm works ridiculously long hours. All-nighters are not infrequent, the travel is unavoidable and the pace of work frenetic. For years his family life has been squeezed into spare moments at weekends, with disastrous consequences, and there is never enough time to sort out the accumulating resentments. But, he insists, he isn't materialistic, and it's not the money that drives him; he may earn hundreds of thousands of pounds a year as a senior partner, but he says he could quite easily give all that up.

It's easy to think he's talking rubbish, and that he can only talk about not being materialistic because he has far more money than time to spend it, but many of those who work the longest hours express similar sentiments: in one study only 14 per cent of higher-level professionals and managers said that they worked long hours for the money.[33] A woman director of a major UK company whose rise to the top has never ceased to astonish her – or her parents back home in Essex – said it was never the money that drove her. She had recently decided to cut back her career and salary, and that seemed to prove her point.

Money, and the consumer goods we can buy with it, don't tell the whole story of why some people in the high-skill, high-income bracket are working harder. They don't explain why being busy is now a status symbol, why once the upper middle class desired leisure and scorned anything that looked like trying too hard, and are now rarely separate from their mobiles or Blackberry. They look exhausted, complain of too much work, yet do nothing about reducing their workload. Money alone doesn't explain the topsy-turvy inversion whereby in America in the 1890s the poorest worked harder than the rich, but by 1991 the richest 10 per cent were working harder than the poorest.[34]

Part of this is the hangover of a period of high unemployment, when predictions of 'the end of work' made having lots of work a status symbol. But more important is the emergence of a new form of elitism in the labour market: work as vocation and work as pleasure. In a post-materialist society which places a high premium on self-expression and fulfilment,[35] to have a lot of interesting work is a status symbol. It's not just that you have a job which pays decently; you have a job which is so satisfying and fulfilling that you don't want to stop working. Kristen Lippincott, director of the Royal Observatory, Greenwich, reflected in an interview that 'We've become enamoured with deadlines. We want to feel an adrenaline rush. We believe that if we're always chasing the next deadline, we must be important. A lot of our busy-ness is a way for us to avoid thinking about what is most important. There's a difference between being busy and being productive.'[36]

In the creative, highly skilled parts of the labour market, the boundaries between work and play have been eroded: work is play, work is your hobby. Work becomes the organising principle of life. David Brooks describes this in his cult book *Bobos in Paradise* (2000), on the new American bourgeoisie: 'Work . . . is a vocation, a calling . . . employees start thinking like artists and activists, they actually work harder for the company . . . if work is a form of self-expression . . . then you never want to stop . . . Business is not about making money; it's about doing something you love. Life should be an extended hobby . . . in this way business nourishes the whole person.'[37]

Sociologist Zygmunt Bauman echoes the same theme:

The trick is no longer to limit work time to the bare minimum, so vacating more time for leisure, but on the contrary to efface altogether the line dividing vocation from avocation, job from hobby, work from recreation; to lift work itself to the rank of supreme and most satisfying entertainment. An entertaining job is a highly coveted privilege. And those privileged by it jump headlong into the opportunities of strong sensations and thrilling experience which such jobs offer. 'Workaholics' with no fixed hours of work, preoccupied with the challenges of their jobs twenty-four hours a day, seven days a week, may be found today not among the slaves, but among the elite of the lucky and successful.

Work that is rich in gratifying experience, work as self-fulfilment, work as the meaning of life, work as the core or the axis of everything that counts, as the source of pride, self-esteem, honour and deference or notoriety, in short, work as vocation *has become the privilege of the few, a distinctive mark of the elite, a way of life the rest may watch in awe, admire and contemplate at a distance.*[38]

This is a reworking of the Protestant work ethic, which Max Weber described as the subjugation of one's desires and the discipline of one's efforts in an endless quest to prove one's moral worth. Martin Luther said no Christians could ever be sure of 'the integrity of their contrition', so they were driven to work to demonstrate their moral worth. As Christianity lost its grip on the beliefs and values of the educated middle classes in the sixties, many commentators in business, politics and academia were increasingly concerned about whether people would carry on working as hard in Western industrial societies.

It was believed that both increased wealth and the values of consumer culture were also eroding the work ethic: now that people's material needs had been satisfied, perhaps they would simply not bother to turn up at the office or factory any longer. In 1971 President Nixon's Secretary of the Department of Health, Education and Welfare commissioned a report on the problem of 'blue-collar blues and white-collar woes'. There were Senate committees on the 'anger and alienation' in the workplace.[39] It was feared that the younger generation of rebellious hippies were simply not going to trudge into work from their suburban homes, and struggle up the corporate hierarchies in return for a gold watch on their retirement. What they rejected was the type characterised in Sloan Wilson's 1955 novel *The Man in the Gray Flannel Suit* as 'bright young men in gray flannel suits rushing around . . . pursuing neither ideals nor happiness – they were pursuing a routine'.[40] William Whyte's classic sociological analysis of corporate America *The Organisation Man* (1956) cast a long shadow over the United States in the sixties: 'A man so completely involved in his work that he cannot distinguish between work and the rest of his life – and he is happy he cannot.' (The quest to escape this fate has turned full circle: Whyte and David Brooks are uncannily close.)

American sociologists called this challenge to the work ethic 'the problem of work': Peter Berger said the issue was that work had lost its 'meaning'; it had also lost its significance because one's private life had become more important as 'the expression of who one really is'.[41] Another sociologist, Daniel Bell, famously articulated the problem in *The Cultural Contradictions of Capitalism* (1976), in which he described a 'disjunction between the kind of organisation and norms demanded in the economic realm, and the norms of self-realisation that are now central in the culture', and warned that capitalism was destroying the foundations on which it rested. What Bell was concerned about was that the Protestant work ethic's values of thrift, hard work, future-orientation, delayed gratification and control of the emotions and urges of the body were being eroded because 'the cultural, if not moral, justification of capitalism has become hedonism, the idea of pleasure as a way of life'.[42] If work became merely a means to a much more important end, commentators feared, the quality and pace of work, and commitment to it, would tail off. What the new generation wanted was autonomy, creativity, equality and self-expression; it didn't want hierarchy and bureaucracy.

American corporations reformulated the work ethic in the course of the seventies and eighties using the kind of management practices described in Chapter 4. Work was the means to 'self-actualisation' and happiness; it was how you found yourself – it was the path to true individualisation. This was a message perfectly attuned to its times, and a seamless fit was developed between the corporate requirement for highly motivated, highly flexible labour and individuals' requirement for a sense of self – who they were, what they were about, the challenges they had overcome and the 'difference' they had made – what sociologists call the 'project of the self'. Clever corporations could offer a narrative for their employees' lives. It was the corporation that wrote the plot, which thus included no reciprocal loyalty, no job for life, and no job at all if performance faltered; but in return it offered a glittering dream of helping to realise the individual's unknown potential, of satisfying his or her craving for control and autonomy and impact – for what's called *agency*.

These are particular preoccupations of our age. Our sense of self is bound up with our sense of control and impact. That's why a new mother will say she's 'got her old self back' when she returns to a job, where the routines give a greater degree of control than the unpredictable demands of a small baby. Agency is regarded as the most significant component of well-being;[43] it is so important that we will take on, and often claim to find enjoyable and satisfying, more stressful responsibilities if they give us a greater sense of agency. The more skilled you are, the more you expect to 'make your own mark' and 'put your own stamp on things', and you are prepared to pay a high price to do that. Appraisals, performance-related pay, bonuses – all provide material for the stories people tell about themselves, about how far they've come, how well they are doing. The concept of 'self-realisation' as developed in the therapy and New Age movements of the sixties and seventies can be trimmed down to mesh neatly with the neo-liberal labour market, comments Thomas Frank in *One Market Under God* (2001). Paid work has so successfully absorbed the 'project of the self' that it marginalises all other routes to fulfilment, such as caring or the passion of the amateur.

The cleverness of the fit between the project of the self and this work ethic is that it is self-reinforcing. There is no resting point: the project of the self is never complete, and is always riddled with anxiety and insecurities. How well am I doing? is a question whose answer, like the stock-market index, goes down as well as up. Because loyalty has been written out of the script, you're only ever as good as your last assignment. The precariousness of this sense of self requires a relentless effort just to keep steady: the corporate lawyer, the consultant, the investment banker has to work on bigger and bigger deals or run the risk of dropping down the running order – or, God forbid, dropping off it altogether. Success requires constant adaptation and reinvention of the self and its skills. This is a point taken up by Yiannis Gabriel when he compares Max Weber's famous characterisation of the 'iron cage' of industrial bureaucracies with the 'glass palace of flexible organisations' in contemporary work culture, where successes are never an equilibrium but 'temporary triumphs at the edge of the abyss'. This fuels its own rollercoaster of adrenaline and exhilaration; snatching victory – the next big deal, a big sale – from the jaws of defeat. Out of the discontinuous, episodic career 'all of us construct and reconstruct our fragile selves, moving from glass palace to glass cage, at times feeling anxiously trapped by it, at others feeling energised and appreciated, and at others depressed and despondent', says Gabriel.[44]

Such a rollercoaster ride is a classic description of addictive behaviour. What increases the stakes is that you not only have to do your job, but make sure everyone knows how well you've done it – to secure both your position and your performance-related pay. In *The Future of Success* Robert Reich comments that in flatter organisations with fewer promotion opportunities, 'the only way to promote yourself is for you to do it'. Organisations without strong hierarchies leave individuals to create (or not) their power base; Dale Carnegie's bestseller *How to Win Friends and Influence People* was published in 1937, but it is in an insecure labour market that its message reaches its apotheosis. Careers are as much about your own public relations skills as about talent: 'The goal is not to fit in or gain approval of one's peers. It's to stand out among one's peers, to dazzle and inspire potential customers ... the old organisation is vanishing, and in its place are men and women who not only believe deeply in themselves but can persuade others to believe in them. To this end a generous dose of self-esteem is more important than gregariousness, beaming self-confidence more useful than humble charm,' concludes Reich.

In 1999 Tom Peters made the subject into a book, *Brand You 50: Reinventing Work*, in which he wrote: 'Starting today you are a brand. You're every bit as much of a brand as Nike, Coke, Pepsi or the Body Shop ... [your] most important job is to be head marketer for the brand called You.' The insidiousness of Peters' comparison is that as soon as we start measuring ourselves up as brands next to Nike, we wither in significance – most of us become little more than *failed* brands. We can't match a brand's longevity. But Peters' injunctions accurately capture the strategy needed to navigate the highly skilled areas of the labour market. It's no longer enough to do a good job; you also have to do your own PR. When the *Evening Standard* reported on the case of a City analyst, Louise Barton, who tried unsuccessfully to bring a case of sexual discrimination against her employers in 2002, it concluded: 'Crowing is as much part of City success as being clever, well-informed and having a great contacts book. It's something [Barton] tells young City women to do ... especially as she thinks she's paid the price for underselling herself.'[45]

Self-promotion is a demanding task, according to the ten tips offered in *People Management* magazine in April 2003. First off: 'Network until you drop. Speak up at meetings and sit in the front row at presentations. Let people get used to the sound of your voice.' Second: 'Create messages that sound positive and inspirational.' Third: 'Make a great entrance. You get roughly three seconds to make a first impression ... Make yourself look like the right person in the right place.' Fourth: 'Walk around with an air of confidence and energy ... Never loiter or lurk.' Other tips include 'smiling with your eyes as well as your mouth', never fiddling or folding your arms and 'dressing the part'. It's a daunting list, in which every part of your body language and appearance has to be corralled into the right image.[46]

'The sale of the self makes relentless demands on one's life. It also encroaches on one's personal relationships. When the personality is for sale, all relationships turn into potential business deals,' comments Robert Reich. He compares the 'marketable self' with

William Whyte's Organisation Man, whose desire to fit in and conform meant he was 'in danger of losing his identity to the group. The market-directed person at the start of the century is in danger of selling it.'

Success demands more of you, and at the same time its definition has become more elusive and more precarious. Richard Sennett comments on this in his profound analysis of the contemporary work ethic, *The Corrosion of Character* (1998), when he describes how one of his interviewees 'felt constantly on trial, yet she never knew exactly where she stood. There were no objective measures which applied to doing a good job.' Sennett points out that in such fluid situations, 'People tend to focus on the minutiae of daily events, seeking in details some portent of meaning ... such as how the boss said hello in the morning.' The result is anxiety and insecurity – and stress. We pursue the dream of a breakthrough – of our true worth being acknowledged – which might finally make sense of our work and reconfigure the downsizing, reorganisations and new assignments into the meaningful trajectory of a career. The new work ethic has been astonishingly successful at exploiting the insecurities of employees and disciplining them to work harder than their parents or grandparents probably ever did, *and* with zero job security. The feat has been remarkable, particularly in corporate America, where hundreds of thousands of white-collar workers throughout the early to mid-nineties were made redundant, yet those same workers managed no collective protest, instead re-doubled their efforts – hours of work lengthened significantly over the same time-period – to devote most of their waking hours to those same corporations. The new work ethic tantalises the white-collar worker with the possibility of satisfactions which are just out of reach, thus heading off potential challenges to the way work is organised, and continually throwing the problem back onto the individual to resolve.

* * *

'Welfare to work' and 'work as vocation' have radically different target audiences, and tell very different tales about the contemporary labour market. One was a specific political project to cut benefit bills, the other developed over three decades; but it was the same generation of baby boomers who devised both. In Britain, Labour politicians and policy-makers, in hock themselves to a 'work as vocation' ethic, proposed work as the solution to all the country's ills – from poverty to social fragmentation. The tone of national debate is skewed towards paid work as the sole definition of success and achievement – a terrible impoverishment of our understanding of the rich diversity of human experience and how that constitutes a vibrant society. Curiously quiet are the voices demanding to know what is the price – both to individual lives and to society – of the overwork culture. Or the voices articulating how policy and culture could encourage a broader basis for human well-being and self-respect than simply a paycheque.

Part Four

The Human Cost

7

Keeping Body and Soul Together

For about one in three of all British workers, exhaustion, stress or both have become an inescapable part of their working lives. That is a shocking failure of our imagination and our will to devise a work culture which sustains human well-being rather than erodes it. A job which demands a huge proportion of an individual's energy, time and emotional resources is a job which is unsustainable; it passes the cost on to the worker in terms of their health, and to his or her partner, children, friends and community. In this section of the book I will look at who pays for the overwork culture.

Human beings have finite resources, physical and emotional, and the overwork culture eats into them. For many, the result is illness: either debilitating mental conditions such as work-related stress and depression, or life-threatening conditions such as heart disease. The health of the overworked employee is hit twice – first by working too hard, and second by not having the time to develop relationships, take exercise and pursue outside interests, all of which strengthen resilience to pressure. The cost to an increasing number of individuals is evident in the spectacular explosion in the number of days at work lost to stress, not to mention all those workers below the statistical radar, who resort to anti-depressants to keep going and whose lives are a frantic effort to cope.

There are signs all around us of how the overwork culture is encroaching: the woman who only has time to text her friends, because it's quicker than a telephone call; the son who only ever calls his mother when he's in a traffic jam because there's no other time; the child alone at home while the parent races back from work. A future beckons of a 24/7 society in which we stretch childcare to cover round-the-clock flexibility, from breakfast clubs to after-school clubs. At what point does the flexibility which employers want snap the fragile threads of interdependence on which human life is based? How is it that we have so little time – the most basic requirement of human engagement – to give each other? This is where the 'care deficit' lies:[1] we simply don't have enough time and energy to invest in relationships, which are what underpin human sustainability.

The individual worker is the first casualty of the crisis in human sustainability, but it doesn't stop there, as overwork spreads its tentacles into every part of private and public life: into the time we have for ourselves, our children, our friends or elderly parents. Ultimately this impacts on the vibrancy of the community. Do people have time to socialise? Do they have time to volunteer and to be involved in community initiatives or political parties? Democracy is only effective if people have the time and energy to participate. The overwork culture threatens human sustainability at the most micro level, that of the individual struggling to keep up with his or her workload, and at the most macro level, with the 'thinning' of our social capital – the networks of relationships in a neighbourhood. Understanding of the crisis in human sustainability now stands roughly where that of the crisis in environmental sustainability stood in the late sixties and early seventies. Our realisation is just dawning of the frailty of human interrelationships, of how much they are worth, of our crucial dependence on them for our personal well-being. It is precisely these human bonds which nurture human and social resilience and foster creativity and ingenuity – the very qualities which are so necessary if we are to accommodate and adjust to twenty-first-century social and economic change.

The analogy with the environment is apt, because both forms of sustainability – human and environmental – have no market value, they cannot be bought and sold. Both fall into the category of what economists call 'the tragedy of the commons': in an unfettered market, they are subject to its depredations without any accounting for their true value. Just as the damage to the environment has become increasingly clear, so we will see in the coming decades a growing anxiety about the erosion of human sustainability as we witness an exponential rise in depression, stress and anxiety. It is the conditions of our working lives which are one of the main causes.

Former US President Ronald Reagan famously said, 'Hard work never killed anyone, but I figure, why take the chance?' He was referring to a long tradition of the Western industrialised work ethic in which hard work is something to celebrate, and a failure to keep up with the pace is a humiliating sign of personal failure and inadequacy. It is this context which explains the degree of general indifference to the growing epidemic of work-related stress.

One in five British workers now report that they have been affected by stress, and half a million people a year report stress levels that are making them ill.[2] Work-related stress, depression and anxiety account for 13.4 million working days lost per year, more than any other work-related illness in the UK. People cite their jobs as the main cause of stress in their lives, well ahead of other worries such as money, family and health; in the Samaritans' 2003 survey 'Stressed Out', 36 per cent cited work as one of their biggest stressors.

What makes this picture even bleaker is the dramatic rate of increase: between 1990 and 2001–02 the prevalence of self-reported stress caused or made worse by work more than doubled, from 207,000 to 563,000. An estimated further 80,000 reported work-related heart disease. Almost 20 per cent of British workers categorise their work as very or extremely stressful – that represents five million workers.[3] Any other illness on this scale and growing at this pace would have caused a national outcry. We would have had mass information campaigns, prime ministerial working groups and a government task force with a handsome budget. Instead we have a debate which recycles old prejudices: isn't it just that people can't be bothered to go to work, and want a duvet day instead? How can you be sure it's work causing the stress, rather than personal problems? Stress is good for you – how else would people be motivated to get the job done? Some people just need to buck up; if others can cope in the same situation, why can't they?

There is a stubborn refusal to distinguish between the kind of pressure which can spur people on, and stress, which is debilitating. Two national characteristics conspire to inhibit understanding of stress – scepticism and stoicism. For many people, the instant response to the escalating stress epidemic tends to be either 'They're faking it,' or 'They should just get on with it and stop complaining.' This can be combined with an old British managerial adversarialism reminiscent of the seventies. As the director of an engineering company told one research project: 'The very concept of "stress" is twentieth-century rubbish. Only those who can and are willing to work constantly under extreme pressure are of any use to our organisation. Those who can't/won't should be fired. Even to ask such questions [about stress] of persons who profess to be professional managers is an insult.'[4]

These kinds of attitudes to mental illness sit oddly in a culture which has allegedly become more comfortable with emotion in recent years, and where the public display of feelings is now common for both men and women. Stress prompts a punitive judgementalism reserved for what has become the twenty-first-century sin – failing to cope. In part this is driven by a widespread view that coping is tough, and you've just got to get on with it. What is celebrated in the morality tales of our time is the person who rises to the challenge, seizes the opportunity against all the odds, and triumphs. The person who is astonished to discover abilities they never knew they had. It's a morality tale which is every bit as oppressive as – arguably more so than – the saintly self-mortification developed by the Victorians. It's told by sports-men who lecture on the business circuit for fat fees. The aim, as one consultant put it to me, is to emulate what turns soldiers into heroes. The modern morality tales are often reinforced with some selective editing of Eastern philosophical texts – a slogan on the wall of Orange's call centre in 2001 warned: 'The only thing which can hurt you is your resistance to change.' These are the mottoes used to spur us on to perform, and they leave almost no room for human frailty, for the struggle, failures and inadequacies which punctuate most working lives.

This is the kind of background against which Jane is trying to understand her own predicament. One of the first things she says to me when I visit is, 'I should be able to cope,' and that sense of compulsion only exacerbates her struggle. A fifty-four-year-old primary school teacher in Gloucester, Jane has finally reached the difficult decision that she simply can't carry on. In the past few years she's had several periods off work because of stress. Two days before we met, she handed in her resignation. The plan is to downshift: she and her partner have decided to move to a cheaper house so they won't need her salary. On the Sunday morning I visit, she's sitting in her front room surrounded by lesson plans to prepare and notes for an approaching Ofsted inspection, and she's quietly desperate. It's the end of the half-term holiday, but she hasn't noticed; she's had to work straight through without a day off.

'This morning I thought I couldn't go into school tomorrow. I'm on the highest level of anti-depressants at the moment, but I push myself to keep going. Last spring I had two weeks off, and two and a half years ago I had six weeks off – all the doctor offered was "time out", and he signs the note. I spent the time off resting, reading and walking, and as soon as I'm over the stress I stop the anti-depressants. I never do it unless I absolutely have to – when I feel like I'm on the edge. That's when the adrenaline – the fight–flight reflex – goes mad. I get quite disconnected, shaky and panicky. It can hit me at any time. If it happens in the middle of a lesson, I have to breathe deeply. It happens most days at the moment. When I'm stressed I get insomnia, which only makes it worse.'

Jane put her stress down to a wide range of causes: 'I'm quite an edgy person, so it's a combination of the workplace environment and my personality – it's in my nature to expect a lot of myself.' But after taking responsibility herself, she describes several issues at work which have contributed to the stress: 'This last week, I've had to write lesson plans in triplicate, then annual plans and termly plans and weekly plans. For what? It's all bull. I just copy it from somewhere else, and it doesn't get read. It's frustrating, and it winds me up. I used to manage my time so that I didn't have to bring work home, but that's no longer possible. It's now Sunday morning, and I'm still doing the plans – it seems insurmountable. There's a new set of teachers at the school; they're very ambitious, and they feel they have it right and I have it wrong. I often feel I'm just not clever enough. They say I'm a good teacher – it's me who doesn't think I'm good enough.'

The relentless series of government initiatives for primary education has played its role in undermining her confidence, admitted Jane, who qualified in 1972. She felt the way of teaching she had developed was undervalued. The emotional and creative skills she prided herself on went unrecognised in the emphasis on exam results in the tough school where she worked. What had particularly affected her was seeing the school's very dedicated head teacher have a nervous breakdown: 'She had given teaching her all – in time and energy. She understood the children and supported the staff, but she was too caring. She took early retirement after her breakdown. Now she'll never be the same again. I thought, I don't want to go there.'

Jane tries to look after herself to prevent the stress building up – she has reflexology and treats herself to facials – but it's hard to find time during term: there's certainly no time for reading, and rarely for friends. At home there are emotional demands on her – a difficult teenager, as well as a younger child and grandchildren. 'I get up at 5.40 a.m. just to have half an hour with a cup of tea – time on my own, the only quiet time in the day. I'm worn out with the struggle of it all.'

At the end of the interview, she's anxious and self-critical. 'Does it sound like I'm whingeing? Am I making a fuss about things? It sounds like I'm blaming everyone else. I should be able to deal with it all.'

Lee, a car-plant worker with a degree in engineering, has just returned to work after three months off with stress. He believes the stress was caused by three things: a bullying supervisor, long hours, and how the company treated him over his promotion and after a major operation in which a kidney was removed. 'I was working so many hours, and the overtime was forced on us as well as weekends. Often it was fifty or sixty hours a week. It wasn't hard work, it was just very repetitive. You work like a robot, it's so automated. I was being bullied by the team leader – there was nothing I could do right, and I was getting a lot of hassle. There was no way I could report him to anyone. He made my life hell for about eight months.'

Lee doesn't fit the stereotype of someone who might be prone to stress. He's a handsome, boyish-looking twenty-eight-year-old, recently married and very popular with his colleagues. His mobile frequently interrupts our conversation; he often helps friends out by mending their computers in his spare time. But as he talks about the supervisor, he clenches his hands and his cheerful friendliness becomes strained.

'He's a bully. I got to the point where I couldn't face anyone. I couldn't even answer the mobile. I couldn't face family or friends. It got to the point where as I was driving into work, as soon as I approached the factory I felt really sick. I even thought of driving the car into a lamp-post so I wouldn't have to go to work. I was that unhappy. It seems daft now, but it was anything so as to not have to go to work. I was getting really bad nightmares; it brought back childhood stuff from when I was ten, when two of my friends were killed. I couldn't sleep. Everything was building up and up. I was looking for a way out of it, but I didn't want to kill myself. The doctor was really helpful, and he signed me off work and gave me a prescription for Prozac. I had counselling as well, and that showed me just how angry I was. I'm still not 100 per cent, but I went back to work. I saw my team leader for the first time today – he's been off with stress too, and he's been demoted. There's no way I could work with him again. I've always seen myself as relatively laid-back before all this.'

Stress has risen across the board in all occupations, and is now cited by 36 per cent of professionals, 34 per cent of managers and 22 per cent of skilled workers. Three of the ten occupations with the highest rates of stress are in education, and five in the top twenty:[5] Jane has plenty of company for her predicament. Forty-one per cent of those who work in education report a high level of stress, well ahead of any other occupational category (for nursing the figure is 31.5 per cent, and for management 27.8 per cent).[6]

Professor Michael Rose of Bath University researched stress for the Economic Social Research Council, and concluded that the education system 'arguably lies at the core of the national stress problem'.[7] Working in the public sector increases your chances of stress: nearly 40 per cent of the NHS's workforce report stress, as do 30 per cent of employees in local government. In comparison, the private sector is doing much better, with only 21 per cent of workers reporting stress. You have a higher chance of stress if you have a degree, and are divorced, separated or widowed.[8] Stress levels are highest for those in their forties, although they are rising fast in younger age groups: the number of 'twenty-somethings' affected by workplace stress doubled in 2001–02, according to one study.[9] Stress is twice as likely for those in full-time as in part-time employment, but there is no significant difference in incidence between the sexes, nor in geographical location.

The most striking finding of the research is that stress is often the price of success. The higher your salary, the greater chance you have of stress, while assembly-line workers, cleaners and shelf-fillers are the kinds of jobs which report the lowest levels of stress. Nearly a third of people earning over £20,000 a year have high levels of stress – three times the proportion of those on salaries below £10,000.[10] Interestingly, when this high-income bracket is broken down, it's the middle-ranking managerial and technical category which suffers the highest stress levels, rather than those at the very top. The twenty-five most stressful jobs are all white-collar and mostly professional-managerial, found Professor Rose, who comments unsympathetically that 'For the most part, they are at least well compensated both financially and in terms of status for so often living on their nerve endings.' He found that these high levels of stress are not incompatible with job satisfaction – work can be stressful and enjoyable at the same time. But he also found that high levels of job satisfaction do not necessarily translate into high scores on the scale of contentment. An exciting, demanding job may be enjoyable and rewarding, but it won't necessarily make you happy. In fact, contrary to what might be expected, well-being seems to be related to *less* job satisfaction, claims Rose: 'Employees with low job satisfaction have high feel-good scores and vice versa.' Six of the ten occupations with the highest proportions of 'happy' workers were blue-collar – for example, plant operatives, bus drivers and gardeners – while security guards are close to the bottom for job satisfaction, but in the top twenty for 'feel-good'.[11]

It's a puzzling phenomenon that it is the workers in the high-status, high-income areas of the labour market, with the most bargaining power, who have failed to slow the deterioration of their working conditions, let alone improve them. It is the managerial and professional categories of the workforce that are worst affected by stress, that have traded in well-being for job satisfaction.

The problem about stress is that it cannot be alleviated simply by tinkering with a few of the worst characteristics of pressure and competition; it is a direct consequence of the 'performance culture', which expects more and more, but which offers little security in return, a culture which makes one's job a tricky feat of balancing on a high wire.

Many of those contacting me had experienced acute stress. A social worker emailed:

I think stress at work is partly about how well defended one is against such pressures. I was off work with stress for two months. I learned a lot about my own limits and how to look after myself, and now feel confident I would never get to that point again. Capitalism doesn't really have any limits on how much it is prepared to demand of people, so workers themselves need to decide where the boundaries are.

It was a point echoed by a software support co-ordinator:

I've been down the path of working every hour possible and at weekends in a bid to try and keep up with the demands of my job at the time. It finally got to me, and I ended up having to take some time off work to sort my head out. So I concluded that this couldn't go on. It didn't get me a pay rise or any recognition from my boss, just more to deal with at work and stress in my relationship with my partner. So why was I doing this if I hated it so much? I couldn't answer that – I had a big guilt complex about not being able to handle the workload, and shame about letting people down, and I had my own pride to deal with, I guess. Having taken a long hard look at myself, I realised that not everything is my fault and down to me. So I stopped, and imposed boundaries for my sanity's sake.

Stress costs British business over £400 million a year, and the Health and Safety Executive predict that the bill will continue to rise. The World Health Organisation estimates that stress will account for half of the ten most common medical problems in the world by 2020. The economic costs, and the threat of legal action, have alarmed employers and governments alike; it is these, rather than the human cost, which are driving government policy – it is the Secretary of Trade and Industry who comments on stress, not the Health Secretary. Over the last decade there has been a huge amount of research into the causes of stress, yet its incidence has continued to soar. Little has come out of the research except a burgeoning industry which offers stress consultants, stress programmes, stress counsellors, therapists and, when all that fails, lawyers to fight stress claims. This amounts to a dramatic failure of collective will either to recognise the extent of the problem or to do anything effective about it. All that is offered are sticking plasters to cover the symptoms, rather than the kind of reform of the workplace which is required to tackle the causes.

According to one major study into the causes of stress, 68 per cent of the highly stressed report work intensification as a major factor.[12] Fifty-five per cent of these said they had to work very fast in their job, and only 10 per cent said they 'often have enough time to do everything'; 33 per cent said they *never* have enough time. The highly stressed reported 'many interruptions' in their jobs, and a lot of responsibility. Long working hours are a major cause of high stress, with 34.6 per cent of the highly stressed saying that they often have to work long or unsociable hours. Unpredictable hours add to the stress, affecting 21 per cent of the highly stressed, and they are more likely to report atypical working hours, at night and on the weekends.

Finally, the study looked at a number of factors relating to workers' sense of control and autonomy in their jobs – one of the areas regarded as particularly important for stress. The study separated out what is likely to cause stress and what seems to have no effect. Falling into the first category is *pace* of work: the highly stressed have less say over their pace of work, when they can take a break and when they can take a holiday. On the other hand, having a say over one's work environment, choosing who to work with, being able to take decisions concerning one's work, having a choice about what one does at work or how one does it, surprisingly have little impact on stress levels. The kind of autonomy offered as a much-lauded characteristic of the modern workplace does not in fact reduce stress, while the loss of control over the pace of work – an endemic feature of British work intensification – is a major contributor to it.

The longest-running research on stress is the Whitehall Study of 10,308 civil servants,[13] which found that stress was related to three variables: the amount of control the employee had in the job, the demands of the job, and the degree of support from colleagues and managers. How the three interacted was where the stress resulted; for example, if the support was excellent, an employee was more likely to be able to manage high job demands, but if the support was weak, even a low-demand job could be stressful. The study identified one other source of stress – the 'effort–reward imbalance': workers are more likely to be stressed if they feel they are putting a lot of effort into the job for few rewards such as income, promotion and recognition.

The highly stressed also expect 'undesirable change' in their work situation, they are more likely to say their job security is poor, and to feel that they are unfairly treated at work. The level and pace of continuous change is singled out by Professor Cary L. Cooper of the University of Lancaster in his work with Professor Les Worrall as an increasingly important contributor to stress, leading to both a sharply increased degree of job insecurity and 'change fatigue'. Cooper found that 70 per cent of British managers are affected by major organisational restructuring every year, and 40 per cent experienced redundancy and delayering – as survivors, not victims.[14] Sixty-four per cent of those questioned in 2000 felt that morale had fallen as a result, 53 per cent that motivation had fallen, and 60 per cent that job security had deteriorated. Cooper concludes that two factors are driving the stress epidemic: 'It began with Thatcher Americanising Britain and bringing in the gung-ho macho long-hours culture. That laid the foundations for two things which are driving stress: the assumption that long hours means more efficient – all the research proves that long hours means ill health and the breakdown of relationships, and we simply don't know what it does for productivity – and secondly, job insecurity. The sources of stress are overload, constant change and its poor management and the way people are managed generally.'

The result of more pressure on organisations is an increase in bullying, another major source of stress, adds Cooper. According to his investigation for the TUC, a staggering one in four of all workers reported having been bullied in the previous six months, 47 per cent in the previous five years.[15] The bullied have a higher incidence of mental illness, but so also do those colleagues who *witness* the bullying; Cooper calls this 'passive bullying', and just like passive smoking, it can make you ill.

The Bristol Stress and Health at Work Study identified other stressors, such as inconsistency and lack of clarity. Highly stressed workers were less likely to say that the information they got from their line managers was sufficient and consistent, and were more likely to be subject to expectations which were hard to combine or even contradictory. This is a particularly significant point in explaining the dramatic increase in stress in the public sector, and was echoed in the Whitehall Study, which found that 'the need to resolve conflicting priorities' is associated with a higher risk of psychiatric disorder in both sexes.[16] The stories Peter Piranty hears in the course of his counselling for a Northamptonshire-based mental health charity which specialises in stress in the public sector confirm many of these findings. His clients come predominantly from education, the police, the NHS and social services. He attributes the sharp increase in stress in the public sector to the way in which the government's reform of public services has been implemented. What most worries him is how the pressure to meet targets, and the public scrutiny, poison some organisational cultures:

There's been a real increase in the last ten years in the blame culture as many more people are talking about bullying. [Under pressure] some organisations become unhealthy and defensive, with paranoid, persecutory cultures. It can be quite subtle, and a whole organisational culture can be bullying, so that managers say things like, 'Don't come to me with problems, come to me with solutions.' I hear appalling stories of senior teams frightened of the style of a senior officer – in any other situation it wouldn't be tolerated. I hear of rigid ways of behaviour – of defining what excellence is, and what commitment is. My conclusion is that a lot of the British workforce are very unhappy, and there's a lack of recognition of the emotional costs of the workplace.

When an organisation is driven, symptoms of stress can manifest in two ways. One is to put your nose down and deal with what you can deal with. The other is to take a lot of interest in other people's failings, which leads to inter-group rivalry and dysfunctional teams. If people are frightened of being accused of not being able to do their job, they will pick on another weak member of the team; there's macho talk of 'If you can't stand the heat, keep out of the kitchen.' The bullied person often takes on the responsibility.

The drive to increase accountability and transparency in the public sector increases the pressure, adds Piranty:

Before, you might have had a private discourse about a cock-up; now it's all very public. So many people think they know how you should do the job, and people's jobs become more difficult. Social workers, for example, are damned if they do and damned if they don't; society tasks people to make those awful judgements and then disembowels them in a very public way.

Organisations are always working to capacity, there's no reserve because it's argued that it's too wasteful. People are working at such a level that it only takes one more thing – a personal crisis or work crisis [for them to snap] – there's no reserve. Some mission statements can be really crass, for example, 'Zero tolerance of defects'. People are expected to 'strive for excellence' rather than be good enough.

A high proportion of the people coming to see us are on anti-depressants, they don't see much of their kids and they're bitterly resentful that they don't have more time at home.

Piranty says that people who are particularly vulnerable to stress are 'those who are very good at caring for others and who will put their clients first. There's a high burnout among carers, who are very good at looking after others but not so good at looking after themselves. A lot of people in the public sector are dealing with life and death – we ask them to do these jobs, but don't give them the space to recharge.'

Piranty's comments are the consequence of many of the issues discussed in Chapter 5: the breakdown of trust, the obsessive accountability, the loss of respect for the public sector, the pressure to reconcile competing priorities – to be more efficient *and* to provide a better service – which make the jobs of many public servants close to intolerable.

Every employer in the country has been forced to take stress seriously since the groundbreaking legal case of John Walker's successful claim against Northumberland County Council, for which he was awarded a settlement of £200,000 in 1994. The key to that case was that avoidance of stress was ruled part of the employer's 'duty of care' to the employee under health and safety legislation. Walker, a social worker, had a nervous breakdown because of his increased workload; his employers recognised the problem, but did nothing to improve the situation on his return to work. Thus Walker was able to argue successfully that his second nervous breakdown was foreseeable.

Another significant case was that of Barry Willans, who was the first ever individual to take a private firm, Reckitt & Colman, to court for stress-induced anxiety and depression. Derby County Court ruled that the stress was caused by the pressure to meet performance targets set for him. Willans successfully argued that he had been given increased responsibilities and reduced support staff in 1991. The court ruled that the company should have adjusted his duties or offered assistance to avoid him being placed under dangerous stress, and awarded him £55,000.[17] In another case, Thelma Conway, a social worker, was put in sole charge of a residential home in 1996 with no additional training. Despite her frequent reports to management that she was struggling, and external inspection reports recommending a more experienced manager, she was left in post for four years. Unison took her case to court, the council admitted liability and she was awarded £140,000 in compensation.[18]

Partly because of the publicity generated by such cases, injury claims for work-related stress leapt twelve-fold between 1999 and 2000, from 516 to 6,428. Stress/post-traumatic stress disorder is now the biggest 'injury' both in the number of awards made by courts and the total amount of compensation paid out, according to figures compiled for one union.[19] This dramatic increase has been slightly checked by an important Court of Appeal ruling in February 2002, which stated that the onus is on the employee to alert management to stress-related problems, otherwise employers can generally assume that he or she is up to the demands of the job. This adds a further hurdle to what was already difficult to prove, namely that the stress was foreseeable, and that it was caused by workplace pressures rather than a personal or domestic situation (of course, the reality is that the two can often interact). The emphasis on foreseeability particularly frustrates trade unions which are campaigning for a preventative approach, arguing that stress should be routinely included in risk assessments of health and safety issues.

In August 2003 the Health and Safety Executive (HSE), the government body responsible for enforcing legislation on working conditions in Britain, upped the ante and issued its first 'enforcement notice' against an NHS hospital for failing to protect its workers from stress. It told West Dorset Hospitals NHS Trust that it had to assess stress levels and introduce measures to bring them down, and that if it failed court action would follow, with the threat of fines. The HSE has launched a pilot scheme to measure and reduce stress by setting certain targets: for example, at least 85 per cent of employees must say they can cope with the demands of the job, and at least 65 per cent must say they are not subjected to unacceptable behaviour, including bullying. The TUC is pressing for these standards to be incorporated into legislation, so that employers have a duty to prevent stress arising in the first place.

Large payouts in the courts, the threat of government fines and tougher legislation have led many employers to take seriously the issue of 'resilience' – both of the organisation and of the individual. How can the organisation maintain the pace without burning out its staff and ending up with massive injury claims? (For those at senior levels in many companies, this tricky question no doubt adds considerably to their own stress levels.) The response, of course, has been to get the paperwork right – to put policies and procedures in place which will protect the organisation in a court case. Rather than questioning how they operate and the way employees' jobs are done, organisations reach for a quick fix, such as offering a confidential counselling service. But do these have any effect? One study in 1996 of nine organisations with counselling services found that they led to improvements in 'mental well-being and physical well-being ... but not in job satisfaction or sources of pressure', and that while 'counselling is aimed at helping people cope with their personal lives and work lives better', 'it does not have a measurable impact at the organisational level'. It concluded by urging that 'more potential lies in the direction of job design and organisational change'.[20]

But that is precisely what employers are most reluctant to consider; instead, they personalise the issue, and place the emphasis firmly on the individual. For example, Marks and Spencer's policy on stress states that the company 'seeks to place responsibility for managing stress with the individual and likes individuals to take some responsibility for that management', and to 'enhance the individual's ability to deal with pressure regardless of the source'.[21] Not surprisingly given that kind of approach, in 2002 nearly 80 per cent of those who said they were stressed never sought any professional help,[22] although an increasing proportion of them at least admit they need help (even if they don't get it).[23]

Hard Work Never Killed Anyone

Ronald Reagan was right to be cautious. After decades of exhaustive research, it has been proved that there is a link between stress and a whole range of medical conditions. Stress triggers hormonal and chemical defence mechanisms, and mobilises the nervous system for the 'fight or flight' response. As one study concluded: 'The process enhances one's level of arousal because the cognitive, neurological, cardiovascular and muscular systems are stimulated as the body prepares for an emergency in response to a sudden shock. The heart rate is increased ... glucose stored in glycogen in the liver is released for energy, blood supplies are redirected from the skin to the brain and skeletal muscles and the secretion of sweat increases.'[24] The theory is that this evolutionary response to danger was dissipated by fighting or running – options not available to people at work, who instead have to endure the threatening or hostile conditions. This can cause stress, which is 'characterised by emotional vulnerability, persistent negative emotions, elevated hormonal base levels, hyperactivity of the automatic nervous system so that the body never relaxes and tendencies to experience psychosomatic symptoms. Over time this state of affairs may cause illness due to wear and tear on tissues.'

Stress can promote an already existing cancer or heart disease, or it can trigger these conditions where there is an existing vulnerability. There is evidence that low control in the work environment, and the stress it can cause, is associated with an increased risk of coronary heart disease; one study found that exposing workers to stress for at least half their working lives made them 25 per cent more likely to die from a heart attack, and increased their odds of a fatal stroke by 50 per cent. It concluded that 'long-term work-related stress is worse for the heart than ageing thirty years or gaining forty pounds in weight'.[25] Another study found that men who work over sixty hours a week without regular sleep may be doubling their risk of heart attack, while those working forty-eight hours a week are doubling the risk of a serious heart condition.[26] Giving employees more variety in tasks and a stronger say in decision-making may decrease the risk, according to the HSE's Whitehall II Study of British civil servants;[27] a Finnish study found that 'people who faced a combination of high demands at work, but poor control over their job, had double the risk of death from heart disease compared with colleagues who had less stressful occupations. Workers whose job involved high demands, but had low salaries and a lack of social approval, had a risk of death from cardiovascular disease that was 2.4 times higher than those whose jobs involved low stress.'[28] That finding ominously describes the position of many public sector workers. At its worst, stress can kill.

The more common impact of stress on health is to lower immunity. The Bristol study found a much higher incidence of a wide range of medical conditions amongst those reporting high stress, from high blood pressure, nervous trouble and depression to breast cancer.[29] Those with high stress were more likely to have had backache or sciatica, indigestion, Irritable Bowel Syndrome, constipation and piles. There are strong links between stress and ulcers, and those with high stress were more likely to have difficulty sleeping, more vulnerable to coughs, sore throats and headaches, and more likely to complain of chronic tiredness. Surveys of people working long hours routinely show a high proportion reporting that they feel very tired, and this is twice as likely to affect women as men. Cumulative tiredness can result in fatigue, which is used as a medical term for the deterioration of physiological or mental faculties caused by working long hours. It can be exacerbated by the interruption of the body's own natural rhythms by night shifts. The result of mental fatigue is that the mind's reasoning powers and reactions slow down. The impact of such fatigue is keenly felt by long-hours workers, of whom 25 per cent claim that their hours have led to some physical ailment, while the same proportion say it has had a detrimental effect on their mental health. Yet ill-health didn't stop these long-hours workers: 71 per cent admitted that they had carried on working even when they felt unwell.[30]

The response to such fatigue can often make the problem worse; the 'slob-out' tendency complicates the causal link between stress and disease, because a stressful job often leads to behaviour which contributes to heart disease. You come home after a stressful day and slump on the sofa with a bottle of wine or several beers, or you smoke more; you depend on biscuits, sweet fizzy drinks or grab some chips at lunch to give you the temporary energy surge you get from sweet or fatty foods. There's less time and energy to get some exercise, or to cook a proper meal.

Stress is also closely associated with back pain – the second biggest cause of lost working days. One American study found that psychosocial job-stress factors such as mental workload, work pressure and lack of job control can contribute to musculoskeletal pain because of chronic low-level muscle tension; stress-induced overbreathing may also be a factor.[31] Another study found that a lack of pauses in muscle activity can contribute to musculoskeletal disorders; that would explain, the study argued, why their incidence is higher among women, because of their double shift of work and caring; it would also explain the increase in such disorders as a result of work intensification.[32]

Go to the GP complaining of stress, and you're most likely to end up leaving with a prescription for anti-depressants. They will help you sleep, and will help you feel more cheerful, but they will do nothing to slow the pace of your work, or ease the volume of emails or the pressure from the boss. In one survey of GPs, work-related problems were the second most common reason for surgery visits. If you don't like the idea of taking anti-depressants, there's little the GP can offer except a few minutes of sympathy. The inadequacy of conventional medicine in dealing with psycho-physiological conditions such as stress, chronic tiredness and tension is driving the boom in complementary health. In particular, people turn to complementary treatments for that most elusive of essentials required in the twenty-first-century workplace – energy. The quest to boost our energy levels has fuelled a boom in multivitamins and herbal medicines. It has driven a high street revolution in coffee shops, and revitalised the sales of energy drinks like Lucozade and given birth to new ones such as Red Bull. Our need for energy to keep 'coping' has spawned a preoccupation with well-being and a new service sector numbering thousands – it has been put at 100,000 – of therapists in Britain to maintain our physical and emotional well-being. Energy has become second in importance only to time, claim futurologists at the Henley Centre, and more important to us than money, information and space. One in four of us think that within five years, energy will be our single most important resource. Two of the four key ingredients of successful managers, claimed GE Chief Executive Jack Welch, are energy – having lots of it yourself – and being able to energise others.[33]

Dr Mosaref Ali has built his career on treating stress in his Harley Street clinic. It was Mike Harris, Chief Executive of internet bank egg, who told me about the wonders of Dr Ali and urged me to interview him. Dr Ali has built up a devoted and influential clientele, from Prince Charles to Kate Moss and Geri Halliwell. He had just returned from taking a group of chief executives hiking in the Himalayas and, not surprisingly, his calmness was palpable. The source of his appeal is not hard to understand: he offers to transform stress into vitality, promising that the body can heal itself: 'Stress and energy are very closely related; stress can give a false sense of energy, and people can be euphoric with it. They work hard and work out hard, and then need alcohol to knock them out to sleep instead of taking time to calm down the body, and that will end up burning you out. The human mind doesn't like being speeded up – it doesn't like deadlines. The brain operates in cycles inherited from nature. And the brain doesn't like multi-tasking – it wants to focus on one thing.'

The answer, explains Dr Ali, is regular neck massages to improve the blood supply to the brain, yoga for physical and emotional stress management, and a diet with a reduced yeast content. 'The men who come to me are doing more work than ever, and they feel fine. The Japanese aren't fools; they follow special diets, do Tai Chi and take rests in their workplace, and yet the intensity of their work is much higher. If you stop panicking and relax, you will do the same amount of work without tiring. I work all day and I write books in the evenings – it is possible to work very hard. The human brain doesn't like speed, but with adaptation it can work faster.' The secret, he claims, is to calm the mind; only then can it make the necessary connections. 'The chief executives I work with can do lots of work and aren't stressed.' He smiles as he adds, 'Although they may stress their staff.'

At which point I'm bustled out – there are clients waiting. But one can see exactly why Dr Ali is so successful – he seems to offer a solution within the individual's grasp: you may not be able to change deadlines and workloads, but you *can make yourself more efficient*. Ancient wisdoms can be adapted to speed up human beings: this is the kind of individualised response which fits neatly into a neo-liberal market ideology. It draws on Eastern contemplative traditions of yoga and meditation which place the emphasis on individual transformation, and questions the effectiveness of collective political or social activism. Reflexology, aromatherapy, acupuncture, massage – these alternative therapies are all booming as people seek to improve their sense of well-being and vitality.

Much of it makes sense – although trips to the Himalayas are hardly within the reach of most workers – and the complementary health movement plays an important role in raising people's understanding of their own health and how to look after themselves. But the philosophy of improving 'personal performance' also plays into the hands of employers' rationale that well-being and coping with stress are the responsibility of the individual employee. It reinforces the tendency for individuals to search for 'biographic solutions to structural contradictions', as the sociologist Ulrich Beck put it: forget the barricades, it's revolution from within that matters. This cultural preoccupation with personal salvation stymies collective reform, and places an onerous burden on the individual. It effectively reinforces the anxieties and insecurities which it offers to assuage.

Time for Oneself: All Work and No Play

If we're working harder, we have less time and less energy to fit other things into our lives. We try to *make* more time, for example by sleeping less – we sleep, on average, one and a half fewer hours per night than our ancestors at the turn of the century, which is around five hundred hours a year less than we need (no wonder we're so tired). Next, we cut out exactly those activities which reduce stress: according to research by the Mental Health Foundation, exercise is the most likely activity to be squeezed out by the demands of work (48 per cent admitted this), followed by relationships – nearly half of the employees questioned said they had had to cut the time they spent with their partners.[34] Forty-two per cent reported having slimmed down their social life, seeing less of friends, while 41 per cent cut out hobbies and entertainment. These findings are backed up by worrying trends in the long-running British Social Attitudes survey, which show that in the last two decades the amount we see of our best friends has dropped, as has our socialising with family members (who still make up the bulk of our social lives).[35] In one study, 72 per cent of British managers said they had received criticism from family or friends about their long working hours, 65 per cent said work was damaging their health, 72 per cent said it restricted their ability to get involved in community affairs, the same proportion said it affected their relationship with their partner, while 77 per cent said it affected their relationship with their children. Of these, 24 per cent said it had a 'very adverse effect on their children'. Seventy-nine per cent said it cut into their social life and leisure time; it's all work and no play.[36]

This issue prompted a lot of emails to the 'Working Lives' website. Lack of time and energy for friends and hobbies was one of the biggest causes of resentment towards employers, particularly among women (with or without children). They described the deprivation as 'having no life'. One twenty-seven-year-old female lawyer emailed:

> As I got more senior the work began accumulating, and with no idea when the work would come in and when I would be forced to stay late, I began not to make appointments to see friends, go to plays etc. because it became too frustrating to cancel all the time. But that ends up leaving a vacuum in life where friends and leisure should be. After long evenings at work, weekends when I wasn't working were needed to catch up on sleep, never mind the household chores.

Another woman emailed:

> The current work crunch means that it is absolutely impossible to combine work with any form of artistic expression. I mean that modern work rips so much energy out of you that it makes creative pursuits pretty much impossible.

A woman working in a university emailed:

> I'm not a particularly energetic person, and this limits the hours I can do. I know that I have colleagues who do much more in terms of total hours per week. Even though I have what must be a lot more free time

than some . . . I'm too tired most of the time to take advantage of it. I have not made friends in this city, which I have lived in for over five years now, and often miss meetings of the few societies I have joined due to lack of energy/pressure of work. Just writing this down makes me realise what a totally pathetic individual I must appear to be . . . For me personally I don't know what to do. I make resolutions about 'having a life', and have actually managed to cut my hours a bit over the last year . . . I still constantly feel 'stressed-up' due to not being able to get everything done (and had to deal with a major depressive episode a couple of years ago caused by overwork). What else can I do?

At its worst, leisure in the overwork culture simply becomes time for rest and recuperation before work starts again. As has been seen, the predictions of a leisure age have been strangled by the rise of a neo-liberal market capitalism which exhausts its workers. Despite all the increases in labour-saving technologies in the home, our time for leisure has increased by a pathetic twenty minutes a day between 1961 and 1995.[37] The amount of time people devote to sport has got stuck at ten minutes a day, unchanged since the 1970s despite a vast increase in access to sporting facilities for much of the population. And it's getting worse: recent figures collected by the Future Foundation show a fall in every kind of leisure activity, from socialising to sports.

The harder people work in a non-standardised 24/7 working week, the more difficult it is to find your free time overlapping with that of your friends, a point eloquently made by one plaintive email:

I have a little (hobby) band, and I write songs for it, but they ALL work so hard and so many hours that they're always knackered and never have time to make much input.

Two researchers at the Institute of Social and Economic Research at Essex University have argued that the mismatch of working time is leading to a decline of many kinds of 'associational activity', as 'the more of people's time is absorbed by paid work, the more difficulty each person will have in scheduling and matching their own leisure time. This has serious consequences both for individual satisfaction and for society as a whole.'[38] It has reduced the value of non-work time for individuals such as the songwriter in the email.

The problem is that the harder you work, the less rewarding your leisure time is likely to be, comments business psychologist Jock Encombe. He sees many senior executives under enormous pressure, and observes how they get addicted to the adrenaline, which produces 'a state of mental agitation which makes it difficult to savour and enjoy other kinds of experiences'. After the thrill of a challenging big project, the details of everyday life can seem mundane. As the demands multiply on people, there's an 'increasing depletion of life outside work, because they have less time to build family and social capital and develop other interests'. The less investment in other areas of life, the less rewarding they become; the cycle becomes self-reinforcing, leading to a single focus on work, described by Charles Handy as a form of 'modern monasticism'. Everything else is subordinated to the one central purpose of life.

Overwork also hits communities, and the social capital – the networks of relationships – which sustains them. Ray emailed to describe how his work for a multinational based in the north-east left him little time for his other activities as a parish councillor and chair of the local rail-user group:

> It's very difficult to get people of working age involved in things such as school governors, cubs, guides. The local amateur dramatic society is likely to fold because they can't get anyone to join. We end up relying on retired people, which has the effect of skewing things. If

you're dealing with youth issues, you have more credibility if your own youth is not so remote – some other parish councils are worse than us, they're full of old fogies. The plant and garden society is thriving, but almost everyone in it is retired. Various groups which need volunteers in the village all say they're only just about surviving.

The average age of a councillor in Britain has risen to fifty-seven, and almost 40 per cent are retired; the Improvement and Development Agency for Local Government talks of 'a missing generation of twenty-five- to forty-year-olds'. One man emailed to say that his resignation as a local councillor had been a condition of his being offered a job – the company simply did not believe he could do a good enough job unless he devoted all of his energy and time to it.

Patterns of volunteering have changed, and people are more reluctant to make ongoing commitments, preferring instead to give a limited/one-off amount of time. By far the largest factor preventing people from volunteering is lack of time (in 1997, 58 per cent of people cited it as a cause, an increase of nearly 20 per cent since 1991[39]). Voluntary organisations are acutely aware of the impact of people working harder and working atypical hours, and believe it is one of the reasons for their difficulty in recruiting volunteers. Evening work, weekend shifts and unpredictable working hours make it difficult for people to sign on for regular commitments. Steve Peck of the Scout Association points out the competing pressures: 'People are encouraged to have a work–life balance and spend time with their families, but when people work very long hours, they want to spend the time they have left with their families. Yet government initiatives encourage people to make a contribution to their local communities, through for example being a school governor.'

One man described how when he was growing up in his home town outside Paisley, near Glasgow, dads would be home from work shortly after five, and would eat tea with the family before going out to meetings and activities in the neighbourhood. Now, in his thirties, his contemporaries are lucky to get home much before eight, and by then they're too tired to do more than see their children and eat.

There has been little research to back up such anecdotal evidence of the impact of overwork on social capital in Britain. Nor is it clear what the impact has been of women's shift into the labour market on their patterns of volunteering; the picture has been muddied by the rising levels of education among women, which are usually linked to higher levels of volunteering. So it's hard to tell whether the women who once formed the backbone of the local Women's Institute and the Parents' Association are now too busy running corporations. Historically, work has led to stronger social capital – those in employment are more likely to have lots of friends and to be members of organisations and volunteers – but does there come a point at which time and energy run out?

American sociologist Robert Putnam, in the foreword to his exhaustive survey of social capital in the United States, *Bowling Alone* (2000), cites longer working hours as one of the five key factors contributing to its decline in American society. He has little time for the claim that the social capital of the local community has been replaced by new relationships at work; the social capital of waiting in line for the copying machine rather than over the back fence, as he puts it. Putnam argues that there is no evidence that such workplace socialising has increased to compensate for the decline of outside work, and that studies in the United States show that relationships at work 'tend to be casual and enjoyable, but not intimate and deeply supportive'. He cites research which showed that when people were asked to list their closest friends, fewer than half mentioned even one co-worker, while neighbours were more likely to be listed. He quotes one commentator's conclusion: 'Friendships and connections developed at work are generally assumed to have a more instrumental character; we use people, and they use us, to solicit more business, advance our careers, sell more products, or demonstrate our popularity . . . If so, it follows that even if the decline of civil ties in the neighbourhood is being compensated by new ties formed at work, the instrumental character of the latter cannot be an adequate substitute for the loss of the former.'

As their personal connections to a geographical community shrink, so people look to work to compensate; volunteer schemes organised through the workplace and corporate social responsibility programmes become a substitute. Putnam quotes one commentator's conclusion: 'As more Americans spend more of their time "at work", work gradually becomes less of a one-dimensional activity and assumes more of the concerns and activities of both private (family) and public (social and political) life.'[40]

It is the corporation which hands out advice on toddler potty-training and childcare, offers parenthood classes and sets up a reading support programme in a local school – all of which exist in British corporations – rather than the social networks of family, friends and neighbours. This amounts to a form of corporate neo-paternalism which binds the employee ever tighter into a suffocating embrace, underpinning the kind of invasive management techniques described in Chapter 4.

'Work promises more to our lives than it can deliver,' says Joanne Ciulla in her book on the United States, *The Working Life*. 'We have gone beyond the work ethic which endowed work with moral value and now dangerously depend on our jobs to be the primary source of our identity, the mainspring of individual self-esteem and happiness. Work sometimes substitutes for the fulfilment we used to derive from friends, family, religion, community . . . this substitution is risky because the economy is unpredictable and the employers are sometimes feckless.'

The great US sociologist C. Wright Mills worried in the 1950s that white-collar workers sold not just their time and energy, but also their personalities to their employer; he believed that work took up too much of people's time, and shaped them in such a way as to destroy meaningful life outside work. The overwork culture makes his fears as real as ever. Arthur Miller's character Willy Loman in *Death of a Salesman* (1949) is described as 'a man who by the very virtue of his moderate success in business turns out to be a total failure in life'. These critiques of mid-twentieth-century corporate America were scornful of how the individual, the 'organisation man', entrusted so much of his (it was usually his) life to the company in exchange for security. Fifty-odd years later, the terms of that Faustian bargain, when stripped of the seductive rhetoric of self-development and autonomy, have become much harsher – more is expected, and less is given back in terms of security.

For the twenty-first-century equivalent of Willy Loman, the 'moderate success' exacts even more effort, is always precarious, and when it finally crumbles (for most of us, it's only ever a matter of time) there is little left to fall back on. Only if you are comparatively lucky can you count on good health or strong relationships to survive your work patterns, while the pleasures of the amateur – a 'hinterland', as Denis Healey described it – have been squeezed out of the compass of the successful life. A swelling work ethic has monopolised our understanding of success, to the impoverishment of lives and the betrayal of the great promise of technology, the leisure age.

8

The Care Deficit

Something has been creeping up and creeping up on me which I've been trying to 'reason away' with male doggedness. I work in further education in the south-west, running a good Media/Comms depart-ment, and like everyone else I know, work very long hours. At home I've been saying 'Not now' with growing frequency to my three kids and equally hard-working wife, whilst marking, lecture prep and work-based admin all compete with trying to have some semblance of a social and emotional life with them. It's become almost impossible to keep a balance, and the price is high. My wife, faced with just the same if not worse pressures, says to me, 'Is this what we married and had children for?' And I've started to say, even to her, 'Not now.'

I've never been a whinger, I don't look for affairs or fantasy escapes, I don't believe in magic cures. I don't think there's anything I'm going through which thousands of others aren't too, but I do know that families like mine can't breathe freely, can't live in harmony with the world and each other while this obsessive work-only culture continues to be seen as 'normal'. It's true – for me, anyway – that work brings non-material rewards: self-esteem, satisfaction that students are ques-tioning the world around them, that results are good, etc. But when those become just about the only thing that life revolves around ... then something's going badly wrong. As an alternative, saying 'Get a life' to yourself doesn't crack it, though; it's all there the day after you say 'That's enough!' I live in hope this might change.

This eloquent email was one of those which prompted me to write this book, because it articulated so powerfully how the overwork culture is generating a care deficit, and eroding our responsibilities towards those dependent on us – and how we seem to have become trapped, unable to see a way out. I have looked at one dimension of the care deficit – looking after ourselves – and this chapter looks at another, more familiar part of the equation: the care deficit towards those dependent on us – children, the elderly and each other – and how the overwork culture is exacerbating the contradictions built into the separation of work and family ever since the Industrial Revolution.

The dual-earner family has been called a 'controlled experiment in chaos'.[1] Commentator Charles Leadbeater argues that 'The instability and flux of the modern economy makes it all the more difficult to maintain its social foundations. At the centre of this tension is the modern family . . . [which] is beset by all the pressures, fissures and fractures of the modern labour market.'[2] Work's enormous drain on time and energy is depriving relationships of care and dependence, the investment they urgently need right now. At the same time, it often adds new demands on those relationships as the stress and exhaustion spill over. Overwork erodes intimate relationships, which have never been so brittle and which, in a competitive, individualistic society, have never been so essential in supporting individual well-being, identity and security. Never have we so needed a place to call *home*, a place of refuge from the dictates of the market, from its crude calibration of value and its demands on us to perform. Yet at the very same moment, the time we have at home is shrinking, and the privacy we have there is fast disappearing.

What is in conflict here is a labour-market ethic of individual achievement and effort, versus older ethics of the dignity of dependence and the fulfilment of selflessness. As Penelope Leach put it in her book *Children First* (1994), the social ethos of individualism and competition is 'inhospitable to all personal caring roles because caring always demands a sharing, even subsuming of self'.[3] The overwork culture demands that we belittle and marginalise the ethic of care; it promotes and imposes, as requirements for successful participation, habits of mind which are incompatible with caring. One such habit is the calculation of how much of oneself to give, and what is expected in return; the focus is a short-term contractualism and a chronic provisionality of always being alert to whatever might be a better offer. Richard Sennett asks in *The Corrosion of Character*: 'How can long-term purposes be pursued in a short-term society? How can durable social relations be sustained?'

The American commentator Sylvia Ann Hewlett summed up the clash between the overwork ethic and care in a 1993 UNICEF report: 'The hard-edged personality cultivated by many successful professionals – control, decisiveness, aggressiveness, efficiency – can be directly at odds with the passive, patient, selfless elements in good nurturing . . . Qualities needed for career success also include efficiency, a controlling attitude, an orientation towards the future and an inclination towards perfectionism, while their virtual opposites – tolerance for mess and disorder, an ability to let go, an appreciation of the moment and an acceptance of difference and failure – are what is needed for successful parenting.'[4]

We are aware of the increasing damage our overwork culture inflicts on our relationships: nearly a third of workers now say they have less time for their caring responsibilities than they would like (compared with 21 per cent in 1992).[5] A study of those working over forty-eight hours a week found that 45 per cent said it had contributed to strain and arguments in their relationship or marriage, 20 per cent that it had damaged their relationship with their children, 17 per cent that it had contributed to the break-up of their marriage or relationship, and 12 per cent (19 per cent of women and 10 per cent of men) that they had decided not to have children because of their long working hours.[6]

In another study by *Good Housekeeping* magazine, 61 per cent of women working full-time said it had damaged their family life, and 25 per cent that they had delayed starting a family in the hope that things would get easier when they were further up the career ladder. The disinvestment in relationships of care and nurturing which the overwork culture demands is one we can ill afford. There is a widespread perception that the fabric of too many families' lives is fraying under the increasing strain.

The overwork culture is one of the main contributors to a crisis in human sustainability, because it is depriving us of the time and energy to sustain and nurture lives. What makes its impact quite so damaging is how it is interacting with a complex set of other factors, ranging from the role of the state to the increased complexity of personal relationships, as this chapter will chart. We need more time, not less, to negotiate the high expectations between men and women, and the difficult process of growing up in a highly competitive, individualistic culture. But as we have seen, families are getting less time – nearly eight weeks on average less a year than in 1981 – as British fathers work the longest hours in Europe, and the working hours of women are increasing more rapidly than any other group; between 1998 and 2003 their average hours jumped by 3.5 hours per week.[7] As American sociologist Arlie Russell Hochschild comments of America's overwork culture, 'While the mass media so often points to global competition as the major business story of the age, it is easy to miss the fact that corporate America's fiercest struggle has been with its local rival – the family.'[8] This is an increasingly plausible scenario for the British worker who struggles to protect family life from the demands of the boss.

Sue is the sort of professional career woman who understands the fierceness of that struggle. Both she and her husband work in demanding jobs, and theirs is the kind of predicament which has been most closely associated with the work–life balance agenda (although the number of such dual high-earner families is in fact statistically small). They have always had enough money to pay for childcare and the home, but such are the pressures of her work that she comes home 'not wanting to talk to a soul':

> I come home absolutely wrecked. I don't want to be like that for my family. You bottle up your frustrations in the office – there's a lot of emphasis on no bullying in the office, and you wouldn't dream of shouting at someone. But at home, no one's going to sack you. You forget that at home, your family deserve just as much respect and they're more valuable. My husband is the one who gets the raw deal: work gets most of my energy and the kids get what's left.

Sue was prompted to take several months off because it was 'the last chance to re-engage with my teenage son before he becomes irretrievably independent'. She reflected:

> I've always thought I've managed a reasonable work–life balance – certainly in terms of the hours I work. Over the past five years I've probably averaged sixty hours of active work a week, including travelling. I've tried to compensate in longer summer holidays and being there for the family at weekends. We all have breakfast together. We don't speak much, but it reassures me that we're making the effort, and then we eat weekend lunches and Saturday dinner together.
>
> The children have had to become self-sufficient – they're brilliant about getting on with homework, and it's half done by the time I get back. [My working] has deprived them of emotional support and energy at times. Will that be of lasting damage? Would it have been better if I'd stayed at home? These are questions I've asked myself regularly over the last six or seven years as my job has become more demanding. Before, when I got home I could semi-automatically read a story, and

212

the problem was physical strength. When they were small, I had nannies and au-pairs and I would avoid coming home before they'd had their bath and were in their pyjamas; six o'clock is a grim time with small children.

Now it's trickier. From eight or nine years old it's emotional energy I've needed, and they can really benefit from my being around, but they won't ask me to be around. My teenage boy retreats into himself, and I want to keep the lines of communication open, I need to keep open and emotionally attuned – and that means changing my relationship to my work.

When I get stressed my daughter tells me to calm down. I rely on her to raise the red flag. She's never liked me going out to work – she's made me highly aware of the work–life balance. My daughter says she doesn't want to go out to work herself.

Sue's description reflects the sense of near crisis management which underpins the dual-earner, twenty-first-century family, and the constant apprehension that at any point the delicate construction of work, childcare, family finances and education can buckle, bringing a whole series of undesirable consequences, from cancelled meetings to finding cover for a sick childminder at short notice. Run-of-the-mill events such as school holidays or an overnight work trip become an additional source of stress: there is simply no *elasticity* in the system to accommodate anything other than a standard day. The paradox is that as work has grown more flexible – its demands have become bigger and more unpredictable – the family has become less so, its fragile structures barely able to support one worker and their caring commitments, let alone two.

One mother complained:

I work full-time and have two kids. I dread the summer holidays when the kids are off. Holiday clubs cost a fortune. My partner and I do not take holidays at the same time – we need to cover as much of the holiday period ourselves. I am lucky in that I work in local government and my council allows staff to take up to thirty days' unpaid leave a year. I take ten days – as much as I can afford. We still struggle to cover holidays and days when the kids are off sick. I know I have sent the kids to school when they are ill as neither of us could take the time off. I'm just waiting for my son to start senior school and then that will be just one child to pay after-school care for. I'm lucky that my job is close to home and means I can pick up the kids before 5.30 when the After School Club closes. The Out of School Holiday Club struggles to get kids – most people round here don't need it as they have family around them or they think it's too expensive! We have no choice. Life is just one massive juggling game of arrangements of who can pick up who at what time.

These are the kinds of dilemmas which have become central to the whole 'work–life balance' debate. The word 'balance' aptly captures the precarious instability of the relationship between work and family life, and the phrase also conveys the onerous obligation thrust on us to become tightrope walkers – particularly women, who still carry the primary responsibility for caring. The greater the demands of the overwork culture, the more precarious becomes the tightrope. But what is misleading about the phrase and how it is used are the implications that 'balance' is achievable, and that it is down to the individual's personal skills – or lack of them. Thus, inbuilt contradictions between the organisation of how we work and how our families function are thrown on the shoulders of individual women – and to a lesser extent men. Failure is then perceived as being due not to those contradictions, but to your own personal inadequacies: you aren't well enough organised, you need better time management or you need to boost your energy levels with vitamin supplements and aromatherapy.

Given the care economy's importance to our well-being, it is staggering how we have reduced these issues of human sustainability to simply a matter of personal efficiency – of skill as a tightrope walker. It's an effective way of deflecting attention and trivialising the real problem. It also feminises it, so that 'work–life balance' becomes a women's issue rather than a central issue of our humanity and how, as a society, we order the processes of reproduction and dependency through the entire life-course. The feminisation of the issue opens it up to misogynies such as women 'trying to have their cake and eat it'. Not for the first time, social contradictions are attributed to a problem of female character.

What is at stake here is not women's strength of character, but the impact of a market economy on human sustainability: the reproduction of daily life, the routines of daily life that meet our physical and emotional needs, which are by far the biggest part of personal well-being, and which gives rise to and reinforces the relationships of interdependence within which people flourish. Human sustainability is about all those points of connection, from the shared meal and the cupboard full of freshly washed clothes to the clean sheets and the mown lawn. It is those patterns of dependent living – the emptying of the dustbin, the mending of the washing machine, the paying of household bills – and it is the continuity of relationships, within a community and within an extended family, which provide the context for intimacy. Who has time to call to arrange for a child's friends to come round for tea? Who has time to visit an elderly relative? Who has time to remember a nephew's birthday? Human sustainability lies in the question 'Who found time to care for whom?'

In the past this question was never asked; it was simply assumed that it was women's work, and would continue to be so. We can no longer be so complacent. There is a lag in our thinking as we struggle to adjust to the transfer of a proportion of women's labour from the home to paid employment in the course of just one generation. It is this historic coincidence of a dramatic shift in the employment patterns of women and the acceleration of the overwork culture which is driving the growing care deficit. What makes that deficit acute is the reluctance of the state to take on the kind of radical programme required to make up the deficit, through regulation of the labour market and the provision of childcare.

Women's shift of labour from the home to the workplace is bringing an end to a two-hundred-year-old division of labour between men and women. It was industrialisation which split men and women's productive and reproductive activities into separate spheres. In pre-industrial society the household was the economic unit, and women were often major participants in issues affecting the family business, craftwork or farm. But with the construction of factories, men left the home to work, and increasingly women left employment to look after children and care for the home. It was, as Adam Smith noted, the first, most fundamental division of labour. It heralded a much sharper segregation of men and women, as both sexes developed social networks to support their roles – men in the pub, the trade union and the working men's association, while the family relationships fell to women to maintain. Women were exiled from public life, and men from the intimate relationships of the home.

As the rational economic competition of a market economy gained hold in the male public sphere over the course of the nineteenth century, women were idealised as 'angels of the hearth', a gentler, kinder breed of human being who softened, civilised and offered men and children an emotional refuge from a cruel world; the economic division of labour led to a division of emotional labour. From the outset, this emotional and caring labour operated entirely outside the market economy, economist Shirley Burggraf pointed out in *The Feminine Economy and Economic Man* (1997). It was thus never measured or given any value by the market, but was simply taken as a given, rather as factories assumed they could use the resources of a river or the air. So, from the point of GDP, our grandmothers and great-grandmothers who bore and raised children did nothing; they may have been providing the next generation's labour force, but from the point of view of economists, they were 'economically inactive'. Such a perspective is still deeply rooted in contemporary culture; in June 2003 the government's Women and Equality Unit caused an uproar in the media by implying that the 52 per cent of women with children under two years of age who were not in a job contributed nothing to the economy, and this low employment rate was a problem.[9] In fact, the government's statistics department has been working on a valuation of the total unpaid labour of home-making and care, and has come up with the staggering provisional figure of £929 billion, or 104 per cent of GDP.[10]

A huge chunk of society's wealth-generating capability, the process by which society reproduces its own human capital with the appropriate socialisation and education, has simply been written out of the picture for several hundred years. It amounted to a parallel female economy of caring for human beings in the dependent phases of their lives (childhood, sickness and old age) while providing the essential support that enabled men to participate in the industrial economy. The employer using male labour was basically getting two for one – along with every man came a woman at no extra cost who ensured that his time and energy were fully available for his work, and free from any distractions.

Women began to challenge the rigid separation between public and private during the early part of the twentieth century, culminating in the work of feminist writers such as Betty Friedan, who described the stultifying emptiness of life as a suburban housewife. Over the course of the following decades women have returned to a model closer to the pre-industrial household, mixing some work with their domestic activities and child-rearing. Women's employment rate has risen from 59 per cent in 1984 to 70 per cent in 2002;[11] most dramatic of all is the rise in the number of women of childbearing age in employment, from 40 per cent in the mid-seventies to

70 per cent in 1998.[12] The increase was sharpest in the nineties, when the employment rate for mothers rose from 57 per cent in 1990 to 65 per cent in 2000 (the vast bulk of these women work part-time).[13] The pace of change in the role of women in the late twentieth century has been quite simply astonishing, and is one of the most dramatic changes to have taken place in the structure of the family in Western developed nations. Britain now has one of the highest rates of female employment in Europe.

We still have only a clumsy grasp of what's missing. Never having given full recognition to the female economy, we don't now quite understand what makes life without it so difficult. It's as if we've magicked out of the picture the essential tasks which underpin daily life. The only missing piece of the puzzle we have acknowledged is childcare, and I will turn to that vexed question in a moment. But the rest of the care economy we ignore. We presume it is still possible for someone to do the same job without a traditional wife as with; men and women are expected to devote even more of their time than ever to the single-minded pursuit of the job, free of all domestic responsibilities.

We assume that the tasks of home life can be squeezed into odd moments of time at the beginning and the end of the day, and the rest can be outsourced, or dealt with by technology and take-aways. When this doesn't quite work (the washing machine floods, the bills pile up and a child needs some extra help with homework) we blame ourselves, and then console ourselves with the possibility that the solution lies just around the corner – when a child is older/ the house is sorted out/my mother is out of hospital. But, of course, it's in the nature of family life that no sooner has one challenge eased before another has arrived – rather like buses which arrive in unpredictable convoy. Underpinning the 'it'll get easier' fantasy is what American sociologist Arlie Russell Hochschild describes as 'emotional asceticism',[14] which forces families onto anorexic or bulimic emotional diets: emotional needs are squeezed into the gaps, and stored up for the summer holidays, so that bonding becomes intermittent and intense.

This care deficit is made all the sharper by the fact that greater demands than ever are being placed on the 'care economy'. The emotional labour of family life has become considerably more complex, and what could once be taken for granted is now subject to intense scrutiny and negotiation, whether that be the marriage or the relationship with the difficult teenager. Relationship breakdown adds considerably to the emotional labour of a family; there are particularly delicate relationships to negotiate, such as those in stepfamilies or with former partners, while the strain on single parents can be colossal. The family is also under greater pressure as the primary support mechanism to offset the high anxieties generated by a competitive culture which affects even young children, as well as adults.

The most blatant feature of the care deficit is that the political restrictions on the welfare state in Britain have crippled the provision of childcare; unlike most other European countries, Britain rejected the idea that childcare is an essential part of the modern state's infrastructure. Successive Conservative governments insisted on privatising the raising of children, regarding it as a personal choice in which the state had little role; the Labour government has only just begun to challenge such assumptions. At the same time, an overstretched welfare state has increasingly pushed other, demanding care responsibilities back onto the family, for example to look after the convalescent (now turfed out of hospital with indecent haste) or the growing proportion of the elderly.

Here then are the outlines of a crisis – a disinvestment by women and an underinvestment by men in the care economy, and a state ambivalent about its responsibility to fill the gap. I've picked out five points where the care deficit is particularly evident, but there are others – these are only the most widespread: the care of very small children; the support for school-age children; the elderly; the relationship between partners; and our sense of home. In all five areas, the overwork culture is interacting with other trends to leave individuals scrabbling to pick up the pieces.[15]

1. Who Holds the Baby?

Over the last two decades we've seen a social revolution in the role of motherhood of small children. In the middle of the twentieth century few women worked outside the home when their children were under five; by the end of the century, the majority of their daughters did. Of all the statistics on women's employment, the most dramatic is the leap in the proportion of mothers returning to work within one year of childbirth from 24 per cent in 1981 to 67 per cent in 2001, while the number of mothers of children under five who are in paid work has increased from 28 per cent to 58 per cent.[16] Most of this work is part-time, and represents women reverting to a pre-industrial pattern of combining some work and some caring.

The typical model of a dual-earner family is known as '1.5', with the woman usually in the part-time role. One wouldn't think this was the case, to judge from much of the media coverage, which is polarised around old stereotypes of working mothers trying to 'have it all' and 'having none of it'. In fact, only 16 per cent of mothers with children under three are working full-time,[17] and of these, a disproportionate one-third are middle-class professionals. They are not typical, but their predicament fascinates – witness the success of Allison Pearson's novel *I Don't Know How She Does It* (2002), about a mother struggling to cope with the conflicting demands of a high-powered career, her marriage and her small children. The experiment of the dual full-time-career family in an overwork culture attracts a ghoulish interest from a *Daily Mail* readership, fascinated by the absurdity of baking cakes in the middle of the night for the school fair and seeing a child for only half an hour in the evening. It speaks to the deep internal conflicts of a generation in transition between models of motherhood.

While the number of mothers of small children in full-time work may not be increasing, their plight is worsening; as we saw in Chapter 1, the section of the labour market whose working hours are increasing the most dramatically are women in full-time jobs. Between 1992 and 2002, the number of women working more than forty-eight hours increased by 52 per cent, and the number working more than sixty hours more than doubled, from 6 to 13 per cent.[18] Women's average working week increased by 3.5 hours in just five years, from 1998 to 2003.[19] As the hours demanded by professional careers lengthen, those women struggling to keep up are being stretched, as if on a rack, between the office and the home. While those in work, work longer and longer hours, there has been an increasing recognition of the toll this exacts on women and their families. The long-term rise in the number of women in full-time work halted in the early nineties, just as the overwork culture began to gain its grip, as women seemed to decide that overwork and caring responsibilities were simply not compatible.[20]

Life for the full-time dual-career couple may be excruciatingly painful in terms of the parents' own time and energy (particularly for women), but in terms of childcare things are not necessarily much different from how they were for their grandparents. Sections of the English upper-middle class have always paid others (not very much) to look after their children; where once the mother may have attended cocktail parties and the hairdressers, now she's chairing meetings. Both lead to a care deficit for children, but the contemporary version is more troubling, because of its interaction with other developments which make parenting more demanding than ever; but before we consider this theme, we need to return to the mainstream.

Alongside the dominant model of the mother who combines part-time work and caring is a significant proportion of mothers who do not go out to work: 33 per cent of mothers are at home full-time in the first year of their child's life, and this increases as children grow older, so that of women with children under five, 42 per cent are full-time mothers.[21] More than ten years after the birth of their first baby, fewer mothers are in full-time employment than had been in the first twelve months of the baby's life. The question which dogs all the debate on women's employment and raising children is whether the two options of part-time work and staying at home full-time are what women actually want, or whether they end up doing one or other of them because they don't have any other choice. The balance of the evidence is that most women choose to work part-time because they want to spend time with their families: only 7.5 per cent of mothers said lack of childcare was stopping them working full-time, while 56.3 per cent said they didn't want a full-time job.[22] But they do want to work: according to government research 63 per cent of non-working mothers and 78 per cent of lone non-working mothers say they would work or study if they could find appropriate childcare.[23]

But finding childcare is a lottery determined by the family's level of income and postcode. A quarter of all families said they couldn't find a childcare place when they needed one,[24] and the shortage is particularly acute in poorer neighbourhoods. The deficit of care of small children is caused not simply by the fact that their mothers are working, but that many of the sources of childcare on which they have previously been able to rely are simultaneously shrinking. (The belief that a woman should have sole charge of her children is a curious historical aberration, peculiar only to a few twentieth-century Western industrialised nations.) Leaving aside the crucial issue of how the overwork culture cripples fathers' capacity to care, which is the subject of the next chapter, the second most important form of non-maternal childcare is grandparents. According to a government study, grandparents are more than twice as important as nurseries or friends in providing childcare. But the care which grandparents can offer is shrinking. Increasingly, they no longer live close by, as their children have moved away to find jobs; as the average age of first-time parents rises, grandparents become older and less able to look after small children; and as the retirement age rises and the older stay on at work, they can't offer care. Finally, there's some indication that grandparents have had enough of looking after their grandchildren: 40 per cent of them told one survey they wanted less involvement in the family.[25]

Increasingly, the family is looking beyond its own resources to formal childcare, but a different permutation of the care deficit is evident here. Government plans to expand the provision of childcare are hitting a major constraint: given the low pay and low status of working with children, there simply aren't enough people wanting to do it. One of the most important and most flexible sources of childcare, childminders, has contracted at a particularly alarming rate: their number dropped from 98,500 in 1997 to 68,200 in 2003[26] (the most recent evidence indicates that the figures have now stabilised). It's not exactly clear what is causing this, although it's possible that childminders are finding other, better-paid forms of employment, and it is also due in part to efforts to tidy up registers and to raise standards with better regulation. But the drop is of particular concern to parents working atypical hours – either late in the evening or early in the morning – because childminders are more adaptable than nurseries.

The one area of childcare provision which has been expanding is nurseries, which Labour increased from 193,800 places in 1997 to 383,200 in 2003.[27] There is now almost universal provision of part-time nursery care for three- and four-year-olds. The next stage of government policy is to extend provision for children under three. According to Department of Education figures from 2001, roughly 11 per cent of children under two and 16 per cent of two-year-olds attend a day nursery, which amounts to just over 200,000 children under three. But care of this age group is hugely labour-intensive. A Number 10 review of childcare in 2002 found that half of all nurseries have problems filling positions, and 23 per cent in 2000–01 had unfilled vacancies; yet expansion will require an 8 per cent annual increase in the workforce in the coming years.[28] Because of its low status and low pay, childcare work depends on a ready supply of cheap, usually young and female, labour; it is notorious for high turnover, and in tight labour markets it is having to compete with other types of work which are often better paid. Faced with an expanding range of opportunities, women are no longer entering care employment; if even nursing foresees a future in which demand for recruits will always outstrip supply, then what hope has childcare?

Furthermore, as an ageing population requires more care, and a wealthy economy wants to invest more resources in services such as health and education, where will all the care workers come from? One proposed solution is that technology will ease this care deficit: in Japan, the elderly have health checks at home courtesy of a computer which collects information on blood pressure and sends it to a doctor. A future of computerised robotic care is not fanciful; it is already being devised, as emotions are built into the software for robots.[29] Do we want a robot programmed to show appropriate facial expressions and sing nursery rhymes to be the one holding the baby in 2050? Or will we opt instead to import our care through controlled immigration, an option already evident in the NHS, where nurses are recruited from developing countries.

Underlying the recruitment crisis is the vexed issue of who is paying, because improving recruitment requires higher pay and a better-trained workforce. Childcare is famously expensive, beyond the reach of most families. It is particularly expensive in the first two years, when government standards rightly insist on high staff–child ratios. In much of Europe, childcare is highly subsidised; yet Britain, almost alone, has resisted this responsibility of the modern state. While other countries expect parents to contribute only 30 per cent of childcare costs, the average for British families is 75 per cent. The costs of childcare still deter parents even after Labour's introduction of a Childcare Tax Credit: the maximum allowances of £70 per week for one child and £140 for two don't cover the full cost, particularly in expensive areas such as London and the south-east. No provision is even made for more than two children. Total government spending on all early-years programmes, including Sure Start (integrated childcare, health and education targeted at the most deprived neighbourhoods) and childcare tax, comes to a paltry 0.3 per cent of GDP, compared with the investment Sweden makes in its very young, at 2 per cent of GDP.[30]

However, there is a dangerous tendency to regard childcare as the magic wand which will solve the inherent conflict between the overwork culture and raising small children. Even if there was the collective will to pay for it through increased taxation (which, at present, there is not), we cannot endlessly extend the opening hours of nurseries, or impose on the lives of childminders for the flexibility required for the 24/7 working week,[31] or assume we will easily find other people to provide the care needed for our children. Nor can the government duck its responsibilities to provide adequate support to those caring for very small children and dependent on benefits by continuing to argue that the best route out of poverty for single-parent households is if the parent has a job. Labour was right to embark on a strategy to increase the provision of childcare for three- and four-year-olds, but extending that provision full-time to children under three would be a grave mistake. Playgroups and half-day care can be very beneficial for two-year-olds, but they are complementary to, not a substitute for, parental care. Government policy should be to help parents do what the majority of them want to do – care – rather than to encourage parents prematurely back to work. That means that instead of inducements to get a job, parents are offered support and encouragement for the job they've already got – namely, being parents.

The research evidence on both sides of the Atlantic is increasingly clear that for children under about two and a half years, large quantities of nursery-based care have some damaging effects. Such findings are rarely addressed with the kind of honesty they warrant: the Labour government buries them in the small print, because they run counter to its priority of getting mothers off benefit and into work. It wants benefit bills cut, not distracting debates about the impact of nursery care on the tiniest children. But there are clear signs that while for children above the age of three, nurseries advance cognitive skills and socialisation, before that age they have a damaging effect on emotional development, leading to more anxious and aggressive behaviour. As the biggest British government research project on pre-school education, the Effective Provision of Pre-School Education (EPPE), commented: 'High levels of group care before the age of three (and particularly before the age of two) were associated with higher levels of anti-social behaviour at age three.' EPPE's report concluded that higher-quality group care may reduce the level of 'anti-social/worried behaviour', but probably not eliminate it, and that children's cognitive skills and 'peer sociability' benefited, but their sense of security suffered, showing itself in higher levels of anxiety and aggression.[32]

It is findings like these that concern childcare expert Penelope Leach: 'The cognitive outcomes are the ones which we're better at measuring, while emotional outcomes are more difficult to assess, either you do it through an expensive psychologist's study or you depend on the mother's report.'[33] What worries her is the danger that the research gets skewed to focus disproportionately on cognitive skills, while emotional development is overlooked. 'Children who are put into group-based care too early can't soothe themselves, can't wait for satisfaction, can't calm themselves down, and eventually they become more aggressive. Boys appear to be more vulnerable to this than girls, although girls get sent into day care earlier than boys. The younger the child, the greater the advantage of domestic-scale care – that's why childminders score so highly in the first year to eighteen months. The figures for behaviour disorders such as attention deficit disorder are zooming, and very small children are very anxious. I can't believe they're not connected,' comments Leach.

The EPPE findings are echoed in a major American study by the National Institute of Child Health and Development (NICHD), which has been following a thousand children since their birth in 1991. In 2003 the NICHD concluded that 'The more time children spend in childcare from birth to age four and a half, the more adults tended to rate them . . . as less likely to get along with others, as more assertive, as disobedient and as aggressive.'[34]

Professor Jay Belsky of Birkbeck College, London, has attracted considerable controversy by arguing that 'The more time they spend in childcare in the earliest years of life, irrespective of the quality of that childcare, it has downsides – less harmonious mother–child relations, more problem behaviour and more aggressive disobedience.' His fiercely contested conclusion is that 'There is ever more evidence to raise concerns, especially in the first year of life, especially long hours and especially in centre-based care.'[35]

This is not to say that children become psychopaths after being in a nursery; the impact may be small on each individual child, and there are many variables which can affect the outcome. But the questions Belsky poses are valid: what is the cumulative impact on general behaviour of a classroom where the majority of children have had large amounts of nursery-based childcare? Could there be a link between increased aggression amongst adolescents and childhood experience of insecurity?

Some research has found that boys are worse affected than girls, although it is generally agreed that this is not definitive. One of the most respected studies, by John Ermisch and Marco Francesconi at Essex University, followed 516 pairs of siblings born in the 1970s. It found a link between mothers' full-time employment before the age of five and lower subsequent educational achievement and a higher risk of psychological distress as a young adult. The link was still there, although much weaker, when mothers worked part-time before their children were five, while the effect of fathers' employment was much less important.[36]

The dilemma for parents of new babies is sharpened by recent research on how the care of a child affects not only the development of their emotions but also of their brains. As Dr Peter Hobson of London's Tavistock Clinic comments, 'What happens between an infant and her care-giver is vitally important, not only for the way the infant will come to relate to herself and others, but also for her developing capacity to think.'[37] The first three years of life, we now know, have an enormous impact on the rest of our lives, because this is the period when the brain is growing most rapidly, with thousands of connections being forged between brain cells in what psychologist Oliver James describes as 'the laying down of our mental wiring'.[38] For example, the auditory centres of the brain are stimulated by the repeated sounds that infants hear, and this has been shown to affect later language development and reading ability; social-class differences in language skills have been traced to the quantity and variety of language to which children are exposed as early as six months.[39] The care of small children was once regarded as a matter of wiping both ends; the last few decades of research have revolutionised such attitudes.

This leaves society with a conundrum it insists on ignoring: we now realise just how important the care of small children is, yet we are reluctant to set aside the required resources, either collectively or individually, either of time or money, to meet that challenge. What can one say about a society which has begun to lose its capacity to mobilise the best resources to care for the dependent and to nurture its own future? We have a care deficit in a culture driven by over-work, which neither enables parents to care properly for their own babies nor encourages the provision of alternatives. Parents are left unhappily scrabbling to stitch together the compromises that allow them to work and to care. The price of those compromises is their own exhaustion and the welfare of their tiny children. We have to ask what kind of society a Generation of the Anxious might create. Is this the right kind of care to be providing children who will require a strong sense of security, resourcefulness and adaptability to chart a course through complex social change in the twenty-first century? We are in the process of taking the 'institutionalisation of childhood' into a new realm; but where is the thoughtful debate about what that will mean for small children, and what kind of care do we really want for them?

2. School-Age Children

Parents go to considerable lengths – often at some personal cost as they cut down on sleep or relaxation time – to mitigate the impact of the overwork culture on their school-age children. That is clear from time-use studies which show that mothers are actually spending more, not less time on childcare than they did in the seventies – from less than forty minutes a day in 1974–75 to more than ninety minutes in 1999, despite the increased employment rates.[40] Once children are at school the available time they have to interact with their parents tends to be much the same, regardless of parental employment patterns.[41] Studies show that in the United States employed mothers spend about 86 per cent as much time directly interacting with their children as non-employed mothers. Working mothers spend on average 26.54 hours a week directly interacting with their children – forty-eight minutes more than *non-working* mothers in 1981, but six hours, forty-nine minutes less than their non-working counterparts in 1997.[42] Obviously these averages mask an enormous range, and some working mothers find little time to spend with their children. Some of the gap for working mothers is made up by fathers, who spend on average fifty-four minutes more a week directly interacting with their children if their wife works. Interestingly, children get to spend slightly more time with *both* of their parents now – there's been a rise in the number of families eating a home-cooked dinner together every night from 12 per cent in 1961 to 19 per cent in 2001.[43] For most children in this age group, the care deficit is not primarily one of parental time, but of the quality of attention.

Once children are old enough to go to school, they begin to tell their parents what they think of their working lives. Many parents have had to confront the shrewd, insistent questions of their children: 'Why do you always have to spend so much time working?' But surprisingly, in Britain we only have personal anecdote to guide us on what children think (my daughter at the age of three told me she was never going to work because she didn't want to be tired all the time); there has been no systematic research. It is not an easy issue to analyse, given that children are not always well placed – knowing no different – to assess the impact of their parents' working patterns.

We have to look to the United States for the most comprehensive analysis, in Ellen Galinsky's *Ask the Children* (1999). The American overwork culture is even more entrenched than that of the UK, and Galinsky's findings provide important clues to what a British study might reveal. She argues that it was not work *per se* that children didn't like – on the contrary, they appreciated the income that their parents brought into the family, and when they were asked what they wanted to change about their mothers' work and family lives, money came top, with 23 per cent saying they wanted their mothers to earn more money. Not far behind, though, was 20 per cent of children wanting their mothers to be less stressed by work, and 14 per cent wanting them less tired. Time was not a major issue: only 10 per cent wanted their mothers to spend more time with them. In America it's not that children want more time with their mother, it's that they want more of her attention and energy when she is with them. Two-thirds of the children said they worried about their parents, and one of those worries was that they were tired.

Galinsky argues that it is *work intensification* which affects children most deeply, and points to the American escalation of work intensification in the nineties, which was similar to that experienced in Britain as the proportion of employees experiencing heavy workloads and having to work very fast increased. The result is a spillover of work into family life: Galinsky found that 18 per cent of parents admitted to thinking about their work often or very often while they were with their children, and another 23 per cent sometimes thought about it. The rising incidence of stress is also likely to have detrimental effects on family life: studies of men suffering from stress have shown that they express less warmth and affection, and withdraw emotionally.

What the time-use studies and Galinsky's work suggest is that parents are protecting children from the big time-squeeze better than they are protecting themselves.[44] But if parents are spending more time with their children and more time working, what gets cut? The answer is sleep, time for one's partner and time for oneself. The concern must be that we are raising a generation of children who understand hurrying better than they understand leisure; a generation who are growing up worried about their tired, stressed mothers and fathers; a generation brought up, in a reversal of roles, to do some of the caring for their own parents.

The public debate has focused with particular intensity on the care deficit of very small children, but that doesn't necessarily reflect the point of most emotional pressure on parents. Many parents will agree that things get more difficult as children grow older, not easier. In part this is because they can express (volubly) their views on how they want to be looked after, but it also reflects several other developments. Parents are acutely aware of how brief the window has become when they can have a significant influence on the development of their child; they have much greater expectations of themselves as parents. The more critical the parents are of the surrounding culture, the more anxious they are to buffer their children from it, and instil a different set of values – a tough task to squeeze into a couple of hours at the end of the day. If parents don't provide the close interaction of discussion and observed behaviour which reinforces a set of values, children will be influenced by other models – from television, the internet and their peer group. Schools find themselves with a heavier burden for inculcating basic standards of behaviour. The very independence which children of working parents develop makes the task of passing on values more difficult: the parents find themselves as just one amongst a range of influences.

The second development is increased anxiety about the safety of children. The number of parents happy to let their children play out in the street has dropped considerably. Traffic and highly publicised cases of violence have generated a real fear about children's unsupervised play. The low figures of direct maternal interaction with children recorded in time-use studies in the past indicate how much time children used to spend playing on their own, away from adults. Now 'childcare' is an issue which lasts longer for parents, often until after the child reaches secondary school.

The third development which impacts on parenting, but is harder to quantify, is the greater expectation on children to achieve academically, in order to succeed in a knowledge economy characterised by sharpening inequality. This particularly concerns American sociologist Martin Carnoy, who emphasises in *Sustaining the New Economy* (2000) the importance of the family for nurturing and developing the kinds of cognitive skills required for academic achievement: 'The new workplace requires even more investment in knowledge than in the past, and families are crucial to such knowledge formation, especially for children but also for adults. The new workplace however contributes to greater instability in the child-centred family, degrading the very institution that is vital for future economic development.'[45] Parents feel a greater sense of responsibility for supporting their children's education and development; it's not just work which has intensified, but many aspects of child raising too. One British study found that in affluent two-children families, parents are co-ordinating an average of eight to ten activities a week for their offspring.[46] A time-use study shows an increase in the amount of time parents help with homework from one minute a day in 1961 to fifteen minutes in 2001.[47] Studies suggest that the impact of parental involvement in their children's education accounts for a quarter of potential attainment.[48] Certainly government policy has been to encourage parental involvement; schools expect and ask parents to read daily with their children, for example. The regime of testing places unprecedented pressures on children, who then require educational and emotional support from parents.

What intensifies the debate about the care deficit of our children are highly emotional anxieties about childhood. Previous generations had a much more hard-headed approach towards their children as financial investments, but as sociologist Zygmunt Bauman says, we have turned children into objects of emotional consumption. Arguably, we worry about our children even more than our ancestors did – now we're not so worried about whether they will live or die as about their intellectual and emotional well-being. We have taken on the huge responsibility of their happiness. The only innocence and spontaneity many of us know is our children's; through them, we live some aspects of human experience vicariously. We want for them the authenticity and spontaneity of human interaction which we no longer expect for ourselves in our working lives outside the home. Childhood is the last refuge from the pressures of the market mentality – they, alone, are *price-less*.

Springing from that idealised intensity, there is considerable resistance to the idea of paying other people to care for our children, and even more resistance to the idea of private nurseries making a profit out of it. Nor is state provision of childcare the panacea it is sometimes promised to be. Not only are the increasingly fierce competitive disciplines of the market as common now in the public as in the private sector, but we have lost considerable faith in the ability of the state to provide the quality of service required – if it can't succeed in running good schools, why should it run good nurseries? Those advocating wider availability of childcare often choose to overlook the fact that in Britain there is a strong desire on the part of many parents, particularly mothers, to undertake a large proportion of the care themselves; around half of mothers say they would like to give up work if they could afford to, and stay at home to look after their children.[49] The expansion of certain types of state childcare is a necessary step to ease some aspects of the care deficit, but it can never solve it. This is the hole in current government thinking, with its emphasis on a paid work ethic: the solution to the care deficit must be to encourage people to put back the investment in their own relationships. The role of government should be, above all, to ensure that the obstacles to that investment are removed, and that those who make it are not penalised. The crucial piece of the puzzle is the unfinished revolution at work – the restructuring of jobs and work cultures – which frees parents to be the kind of parents they want to be, and to provide their children with all the care they can.

3. Mind the Gap

In the coming decades, care of elderly parents will become as much of an issue for the overstretched resources of the family as children, as the demographic structure of the population shifts. By 2001, 18.4 per cent of the population was over pensionable age, and this is projected to increase by nearly *a fifth* between 2006 and 2021, from 11.2 million to 13.1 million.[50] Six million people in the UK currently look after a sick or disabled relative, and 300,000 people become carers every year.

This is not only an issue of the elderly, but also of the long-term sick: conditions which might previously have killed someone can now be stabilised. In 1991 there were 6.42 million people in Britain reporting a 'long-standing limited illness'; if the rate of increase remains the same, that could reach 10.2 million by 2037. It's an uncomfortable fact that our increasing longevity is vastly increasing the need for care. People who are kept alive by today's extraordinary medical technology need a high degree of both physical, intimate care and emotional support and companionship. The needs of the elderly and the long-term sick are rising just at the time that their traditional support mechanisms – in families and close communities – are shrinking. We've been far better at discovering how to cure people than how to care for them.

The bulk of this caring burden is still falling on women, who now have a fifty–fifty chance of providing significant amounts of care before their fifty-ninth birthday; it is not until their seventy-fourth birthday that men have the same odds.[51] But the gap between the sexes is much smaller when only childcare is taken into consideration: women broadly do two-thirds of childcare and men a third, while the proportions of those caring for the elderly are 18 per cent of women and 14 per cent of men. One-quarter of all adults in the forty-five-to-sixty-four age group are now carers, according to the National Census of 2001, which defined caring as anything over an hour a week, and many shoulder the burden at a time in their life when their own energies are declining. Caring is increasingly becoming a full-time occupation: the number of carers giving more than twenty hours of care a week has risen sharply from 1.5 million in 1985 to 1.9 million in 2000; those providing over fifty hours of care have risen from 750,000 in 1985 to 1.25 million in 2001.[52]

Eight out of ten carers are of working age, but by the time they reach their mid-fifties a large proportion have given up work because the struggle to balance caring and employment becomes too difficult. One in seven workers combine work and caring responsibilities; 13 per cent of full-time workers and 17 per cent of part-time workers. In one study, a staggering half of carers in employment were providing a hundred hours care a week in addition to their job.[53] Such responsibilities reduced their earnings (either by having to go part-time or cut back on overtime) by an average of £121 a week, or £5,625 a year.

These figures are dramatic enough, but it is the detail which can make the load unmanageable. Often carers also have children of their own to look after, and juggling the two commitments as well as a job can be impossible; a task not made any easier by the fact that the elderly person being cared for may live some distance away. The complaint of organisations such as Help the Aged and Carers UK is that the entire work–life balance agenda and public policy is oriented around childcare, despite the growing proportion of other caring responsibilities. While parents have now won the right to request part-time work, a Joseph Rowntree Foundation study found that employees are far more circumspect about pressing requests on employers for greater flexibility to cope with caring responsibilities.[54] There is no level playing field. This is an issue which is simply not yet on the political agenda, yet carers are a source of labour which effectively contributes a considerable subsidy to the welfare state.

4. Until Death – or the Office – Us do Part

While parents go to great lengths to protect their children from the time-squeeze in the overwork culture, they are much less successful at protecting the relationship with their spouse or partner. One in three partners of people who work more than forty-eight hours in a typical week say the long hours are having an 'entirely negative effect on their personal relationship';[55] 70 per cent of partners say the long-hours worker is sometimes too tired to hold a conversation; for 29 per cent this is true 'quite often' or even 'all the time'. Over half of their partners said their sex life was suffering because the long-hours worker was too tired, and 43 per cent said they were fed up with shouldering most of the domestic burden. The long-hours workers themselves admitted they had the wrong work–life balance, with 56 per cent saying they dedicated too much of their life to work, and 40 per cent admitting that it had led to arguments with their spouse or partner in the last year. The same proportion feel guilty that they are failing to pull their weight on the domestic front. As one teacher commented in an email: 'My wife has got so bored of talking to the wall in the evening that she has decided to go out to work in a call centre for two nights a week so that she can speak to someone who gives more than a grunt in response. I also find the weight of work tremendous. I have thought at certain times recently that I cannot work any harder. Very few times have I felt that in my chequered career.'

Too tired for sex, too tired even for a conversation, arguments and guilt: none of this bodes well for relationships. It would be ludicrous to draw a clear causal link between the rising divorce rate and work intensification or long hours; relationships have become more fragile for a whole range of reasons, but at the same time it's clear that they are a contributing factor, and that long hours deprive couples of time and energy to tackle the demanding task of staying together. This is borne out by research which found that the relationships most likely to break down were in dual-career families. Least likely to break down were those in which the woman worked part-time and the man full-time. The traditional model of full-time mother and working father was sandwiched between the two.[56]

A 1991 study found that the most critical issue for a woman's satisfaction in a marital relationship and her life was the extent to which the father shared in the care of the children.[57] If the father is overworking, and can't therefore contribute to the care of the children, it will affect his partner. The study revealed a particularly disturbing trend: the discontent of women with partners not involved in the care of their children increased with the number of hours they themselves worked. Forty per cent of women working more than thirty-five hours a week reported that they were unhappily married and generally dissatisfied; put simply, the harder women work, the more frustrated they are by the double shift and the more disappointed by their partners. That figure could be even higher now, given the rapid rise in the number of women working more than forty-eight hours since 1991. This is probably a particular problem for high-status, high-earner couples, where agreement on the principles of gender equality breaks down in the face of the overwork culture.

Strains are also visible in low-income households, where the opposite is increasingly occurring: while there might be quite traditional views on gender roles, the couple will arrange their working shifts in atypical hours to care for the children in a relay system. The result may be a much more egalitarian share of the care and employment, but the brunt of that is borne by the couple's relationship: 41 per cent of workers with atypical hours were dissatisfied with the amount of time they spent together as a couple.[58]

Sue, the senior executive quoted at the beginning of this chapter, admitted that such were the demands of her work that her order of priorities was her job, followed by her children, with her husband coming a poor third. This echoes the conclusion of a therapy group for professional career women with children in London: they reported great satisfaction with their roles as mothers and as workers – the problem was their marriages. In dual-career families, what seems to get squeezed out between the demands of work and children is the relationship with the partner.

As men take up a greater role at home, women have to cede their dominance, and as women move into the workplace, men do likewise; for both, new territory is opened up for negotiation (and, unfortunately, conflict). It's a messy process of rapid change in some areas and stubborn conservatism in others, and of a proliferating variety of divisions of labour between different couples. It requires considerable emotional self-awareness and time on the part of the couple to negotiate. There is increasingly no clear convention at all, and such is the fluidity of the situation that it appears the pace of change will continue – we haven't reached a point of stability. It seems likely that more women will work harder in future, and that the rate of childlessness will continue to rise; it is also possible that more men will work part-time to share the caring, and a growing minority will become the primary carers. Where once our grandparents had a clear sense of their respective responsibilities within the family when they embarked on marriage, now it all has to be worked out. Who's going to be the main breadwinner, who the primary carer, and if both are to be shared, how? It takes a remarkable degree of emotional maturity to work out the allocation of roles. It is in the relationship that the conflicts between care and overwork get played out – often with catastrophic results.

The destabilisation is increased by the fact that work has now become the main arena in which men and women meet each other. Shere Hite in her book *Sex and Business* (2000) found that 62 per cent of women and 71 per cent of men have had a 'love affair' with a colleague. Almost half of us find a long-term partner through work. Where once men and women flirted at drinks parties, in the pub or at dinner parties, now they do so in the office; psychoanalyst Professor Andrew Samuels argues that the 'heterosexual site is now at work not home': 'When it was just the man who went to work, he found the social/sexual life at home . . . now all that energy and encounter is at the office not in dinner parties with the neighbours (now we have lunches instead). When a marriage breaks up because of a third person, it is often a work colleague.'

This is exacerbated by the changes in the workplace discussed in Chapters 3 and 4. If we are encouraged to take more of our personality to work, and we build our career on the quality of our personal interactions, how we determine the boundaries of those interactions becomes a fraught territory. Employers have been drawn in to police relations between male and female colleagues with codes of practice, for fear of harassment claims. This is part of the breakdown of the convention of 'the professional' as formal, distant and emotionally self-controlled. It is another sign of how the separations of work and home, the public and the intimate are being eroded; as therapist Susie Orbach points out, more and more of our life is taking place at work, so that 'work–life balance' is a misnomer. In a telling metaphor, the former Head of Brand Communications at Orange quoted in Chapter 4 described her attitude to the brand as a 'love affair'; emotional engagement, energy and time are finite resources – the more they are invested at work, the less there is available for home. One American computer company, recognising the gap between work and intimate relationships, decided to bring the latter into its orbit: employees had to specify at monthly meetings their professional and *personal* targets, and assess how they had matched up to them – the ultimate absorptive corporation which makes it its business to ensure the success of your private life.

In the overwork culture, personal relationships are forced to take on the role of offsetting the stress: love, like leisure, is purloined as an adjunct to keep the worker going. After the worker has spent a gruelling day in the office or the factory, his or her partner can expect little in return. Meanwhile, the emotional engagement in work is reinforced by employers who specifically address the emotional needs of their employees in a way that a working spouse and parent could never hope to emulate. They satisfy the employee's introspection and self-absorption with coaching sessions or mentoring. The focus is skewed from the reciprocity of intimacy to the preoccupations of the self – its promotion, development, growth and career advancement. None of this helps to nurture a resilient basis for the kind of emotional intimacy to which people aspire, let alone for the kind of complicated negotiations required to raise children.

No Place Like Home

The point of primary emotional focus has shifted from home to work, claimed the American sociologist Arlie Russell Hochschild in her controversial book on corporate life *Timebind* in 1997: 'In this new model of family and work life, a tired parent flees a world of unresolved quarrels and unwashed laundry for the reliable orderliness, harmony and managed cheer of work.' She has a point: if Microsoft is offering you free ice creams on a hot summer afternoon beside their delightful lake and nature reserve, why hurry back to your desk so that you can leave in time to get home to fractious teenagers, supper to prepare and a house to tidy up? The intense emotional labour required by relationships with children and partners leads to many finding home a great 'disappointment', comments Susie Orbach. It was a syndrome accurately captured in Allison Pearson's bestselling novel *I Don't Know How She Does It*: 'By the time I reach the haven of my desk, I've regained my composure . . . I love the work: the synapse-snapping satisfaction of being good at it, of being in control when the rest of life seems such an awful mess. I love the fact that the numbers do what I say and never ask why.'

Yet recent surveys in the UK increasingly show up the importance of the family to both men and women. Perhaps Hochschild's perception was an early-nineties phenomenon which has now been offset by the corporate betrayals of the restructurings of that decade. We may be shifting our emotional centre of gravity back to the home, but our use of time and energy does not reflect that. There's a growing sense of resentment and frustration at the mismatch amongst both men and women, between their aspirations and the reality of home life.

The overwork culture inflates the ideal of home as a place of rest and refuge, so that as we work harder, we romanticise even more intensely the ideal of home. This idealisation has roots going back over two hundred years, when industrialisation set the home apart as a sanctuary from the rough and tumble of the competitive market economy. Home was a place of rest and repair for men from which they emerged on Monday mornings, refreshed, to start a new week's work. French writer Alexis de Tocqueville coined the phrase of home as a 'haven in a heartless world' when he visited the United States in the 1830s, and he was echoed by American commentator Christopher Lasch more than a century later when he described the role the family took on after it lost its economic roles in the Industrial Revolution: 'Shorn of its productive functions, the family now specialised in child-rearing and emotional solace, providing a much-needed sanctuary in a world organised around the impersonal principles of the market.'[59]

Indeed, as the world becomes more 'heartless', the pressure to perform more relentless and the competition more intense, we increasingly yearn for somewhere we can take off our armour and rest from the battle. This drives the 'spiritualisation' of the home, lit with fat church candles, perfumed and decorated with statues of Buddhas (David and Victoria Beckham's English sitting room was dominated by a large gilt Buddha). It also drives the 'aestheticisation' of the home evident in the proliferation of television programmes devoted to transforming house and garden, the magazines and the booming DIY sector. We are spending more money than ever – £100 billion at B&Q in just the Easter weekend of 2003 to buy 1.5 million garden chairs and 53.5 million busy lizzies (one for every person in Britain). Home has become a canvas on which to paint the escape fantasies which console us, whether of the past, of rural simplicity, or of the exotic. But home is not simply an aesthetic experience. A sense of home is more than a question of furniture and paint; it is the knitting together of physical and emotional care, the sharing of lives and the expression of interdependence. Our endless fascination with the idea of home fuels a property market, a boom in television series on property, while bookshops groan under the weight of magazines and books. But the vacuum at the heart of our resurgent preoccupation with home is the home-maker: who is putting in the time and energy to *care* for the home?

This is another part of the female economy which has been airbrushed out of the picture. We so trivialise the tasks and skills of the home-maker that we imagine they can be simply squeezed in at the ends of the day; the emotional skills of empathy and warmth to intuit the human need for comfort, and the organisational and managerial skills to ensure the fridge is full, the carpet hoovered, the floor washed and that there are enough clean towels. These are all the tiny details of daily life which make the difference between the smooth running of a home and stressful crisis management, and make a huge contribution to the quality of life and the sense of personal well-being. It is these incessant daily needs of a household which can make a woman feel like the many-limbed Hindu god Vishnu. We simply haven't reckoned honestly with the scale of the task, remaining awed by a superwoman myth and the belief that our failure reflects our personal inadequacy.

This sense of inadequacy is perpetuated by the images of perfect homes in the proliferating television programmes and magazines. But the houses featured have been tidied up, sterilised into stage sets – there are no piles of dirty laundry and kids' toys. The key ingredient missing in these images is the *labour* of home-making. No one wants to be reminded of the daily tidying up, cleaning and repair, because no one is doing it, and the list of chores never gets smaller. Our home becomes a reproach to us. The paradox is that as the overwork culture fuels our yearning for home, so it also deprives us of the time and energy to be home-makers. That, in part, is what people are escaping from when they say they have to go on holiday 'to get away'. Home is no longer a refuge; that's provided by the *gîte* in France, the flat in Majorca or the package deal in Greece, or the second home, that perennial fantasy of the urban middle classes; a study of British second-home owners in France found that their decision to buy a second home had been prompted by the fact that the first was invaded by work or the pace of urban life, or both.[60]

Furthermore, technological development is knocking out the key-stone of the entire edifice of industrialisation's idealisation of the home – the spatial separation of home and work; 'getting away' is a means to reinstitute that separation. Ever since men and women started working in factories in the eighteenth century, and in offices in the nineteenth century, home has moved further and further away from work. Suburbs grew up, serviced by trains, to make the separation of home and work even more distinct. All of that is now being subverted by technology; 'going to work' can now mean going no further than the spare bedroom. Home has become an outpost of the office. BT has over eight thousand homeworkers. Nearly half of those working long hours (47 per cent) do some work from home,[61] while another study found that 52 per cent of managers have a desk where they can work at home, and 25 per cent have their own home office.[62] Magnet, the fitted furniture manufacturer, advertises offices which fit into a spare corner of your bedroom: what more tangible evidence could there be of the place work now has in our lives, and the privacy we have sacrificed for it to be there?

The interweaving of work and rest in the home is not new for women, and their traditional experience is a warning: as the saying goes, 'a woman's work is never done'. Living in the same place as you work makes it much harder to put boundaries around work; this kind of flexibility is a Trojan horse. All the more so if it has become harder than ever to define 'a good day's work': when is enough ever enough? If one of the defining characteristics of contemporary work is its lack of boundaries, how much more worrying that we are bringing this protean monster into our homes to gobble up spare pockets of our time and energy.

'Home is not just an absence of work. It's not merely a moment of relaxation, grabbed wherever and whenever we can ... It's certainly not a matching set of furniture or the largest roof possible over our heads ... it is a refuge for our humanity, a time and place intentionally crafted moment by moment ... without shelter, we lose our best chance for intimacy, quiet and privacy. Without a home, we're hardly human,' writes the American commentator Maggie Jackson in her book *What's Happening to Home? Balancing Work, Life and Refuge in the Information Age* (2002).

For many people, home has become little more than a pit stop for refuelling between laps. Home-making is by definition *time-consuming*: it is the expression of care and time made concrete in a myriad of tiny details. One of the most memorable experiences of childhood is the sense of home, a shared space and time, the interweaving of lives and activities, some together and some separate, the coming and going which provide a child with the deepest experience of security. It is in the home that we first explore the world – its textures, smells and sounds – and as adults, the more unpredictable, demanding and insecure our overworked lives become, the more we need a home and the less time we have to create one.

9

An Unfinished Revolution

By a cruel coincidence, women have entered the labour market in huge numbers over the same time period as the pressures at work have increased. That has hit women in two ways. First, it raises the bar at work. Work has become harder, so they get home tired and stressed from the ward or factory. What would have been considered a good day's work in managerial or professional jobs twenty years ago is now perceived as demonstrating a lack of commitment – many teachers, for example, are struggling with several hours of extra work every night. For those in middle management, a nine-to-five day is not good enough, while at the highest income levels, jobs which might once have required a forty-hour week are now closer to sixty; for instance, the target for billable hours for corporate lawyers has risen well beyond what their predecessors could have imagined twenty or thirty years ago, and the financial markets now open at 7 a.m. instead of 9 a.m., to provide a global twenty-four-hour financial market.

What makes this overwork culture so punishing for women is their second shift. Once home, they then have the housework, cooking and childcare to attend to. While technology and outsourcing has reduced the labour of the domestic shift in some important ways, the division of domestic roles is stubbornly entrenched.

Women do three-quarters of the housework – an average of 18.5 hours a week compared to six hours for men – even if the woman is in paid employment.[1]

Secondly, the overwork culture makes men work harder, restricting their share of the second shift. Depressingly, the working hours of fathers are significantly increasing: one in four fathers works fifty hours a week or more, and one in ten works sixty hours or more.[2] Men are also more likely to work atypical hours: 41 per cent of men work between 6 and 8.30 a.m. or late evenings, 5.30 to 8.30 p.m., several times a week, compared with 21 per cent of mothers. Two in three fathers regularly work in the evenings or at weekends, and one in three at night.[3] Nearly half of all fathers admit that their atypical hours limited the time they could spend reading and playing with their children, and helping them with homework.

The overwork culture is reinforcing gender segregation in the labour market – women cluster in jobs (particularly in the public sector) at the lower to middle levels, which are prepared to accommodate their caring responsibilities. They end up dropping three to four skill levels to find part-time work which will fit around their caring. They are in jobs which are less well-paid, sometimes insecure and usually characterised by the worst pay gap: in part-time work women earn only 41 per cent as much as their male counterparts, compared to full-time work, where the pay gap is less than half that at 18 per cent. The result is that women are being penalised in the labour market for their caring; motherhood, and the compromises it frequently entails, carries a 'penalty' of £140,000 in lifetime earnings.[4] Women's caring will also cost them in old age, when they are far more vulnerable than men because they haven't been able to build up a decent pension: a quarter of single women pensioners live in poverty.[5]

Many women suffer from the double whammy of how the overwork culture is interacting with the increasing instability of long-term relationships. When marriages were more stable, women's caring was effectively subsidised by their husband's earnings; but as the breakdown rate in relationships continues to climb, the position of women becomes precarious. Caring for children full-time becomes a dangerous strategy, because women run the risk of losing the employability which is their best guarantee against poverty in the event of a relationship breakdown. This is how women can be caught in a spiral of downward social mobility, without adequate benefit support to prevent them and their children ending up below the poverty line.[6]

The most powerful and lucrative jobs in the economy remain a largely male preserve, and when women manage to break in, they often do so at the cost of having their own children; a significant percentage of women in senior positions are childless. Fertility is falling, and an increasing proportion of women are resolving the conflict between work and care by delaying having children or choosing not to have them at all. One in four women born in 1972 will be childless at forty-five.[7] Women are still being forced to choose, in a way that our grandmothers would well understand, between family and career. They are under-represented at all the higher levels of the occupational hierarchy. This is all the more striking as women now represent over half of those entering such professions as law and medicine. For example, the proportion of female partners in the hundred top legal firms now stands at 18 per cent, despite women solicitors accounting for 37 per cent of the profession. Only 8 per cent of working women were in higher managerial and professional occupations in 2002, compared with 18 per cent of men, although women outnumber men significantly in lower managerial and professional occupations – 31 per cent of working women are at this level, compared to 25 per cent of men.[8] In terms of career progression, women get well and truly stuck under the glass ceiling.

When challenged on the common 4:1 ratio of men to women at senior levels, companies tend to be defensive. While many claim to be concerned and to be trying to 'address' the problem, if pressed they will argue that basically women choose not to aim for the highest jobs because of the pressure and responsibility they entail: 'Women look at how big the big jobs are and decide they don't want them. Women take that choice, and we're educating people to make those choices. Loads of jobs are very demanding and very challenging. As companies go more global, there's more travel around Europe and the US, and that's really hard to balance with the family. I agree then, there's a problem with a lack of role models,' said Steve Harvey, Director of People and Culture at Microsoft.

Birmingham-based law firm Wragge & Co. is typical of its sector, with nineteen female partners out of 116. The imbalance is a cause of concern, says Pat Evans, the head of human resources, and she acknowledges that the work has got harder in the last fifteen years: 'The understanding of commitment has changed; it means longer hours, information overload. We're absolutely bombarded with emails. We can't change the nature of the work. To a great extent, it's dictated by the demands of the client. When I think about many female associates [lawyers who have not yet made partner] I get the gut feeling that they just look at it and it's just not what they want. Women come to that decision themselves.'

Companies such as Asda make much of employing large numbers of women, but the organisation is a sharply pointed pyramid. Eighty per cent of Asda's workforce is women, but only 10 per cent of its general store managers are. The flexibility and family-friendly shift patterns of the till operators are not matched by those of the store managers, admitted David Smith, head of HR at Asda: 'There is peer pressure amongst the management: "I must pull my weight, I can't let my colleagues down." There's a tendency to workaholism in retail.'

At one company, when I asked about the ratio of men to women at senior levels, the human resources director got irritated – the

4:1 split had nothing whatsoever to do with the long hours put in by the management, he insisted, and then drew the interview to an abrupt halt. Afterwards, his press officer thanked me profusely for raising the issue; she didn't doubt that the long hours deterred women from advancing in the company.

The overwork culture has crippled the equal opportunities revolution for both women and men. It was always going to take generations to shift the old patterns of intimate relationships and of how we are socialised as children into our understanding of the role of caring mother and breadwinner father, but the pace of that change has been hobbled in Britain by a labour market characterised by intensified competition, job insecurity and the overwork they both engender. The conclusion of sociologists Deborah Swiss and Judy Walker in 1991 was that 'for twenty years now, working mothers have done all the accommodating in terms of time, energy and personal sacrifice that is humanly possible, and still they have not reached true integration in the workplace. [They still] find themselves in an intense battle with a society that cannot let go of a narrowly defined work ethic that is supported by a family structure that has not existed for decades.'[9] It is now even worse than Swiss and Walker's eloquent conclusion found: the 'narrowly defined work ethic' is operating in an even harsher labour market, one characterised by intensification and insecurity.

Old gender stereotypes are being revived – so that, for example, the man's career is frequently privileged over his partner's, and macho managers warn that 'If women can't stand the heat, they should get out of the kitchen.' The struggle for equality is not gathering pace in the way it was predicted to do, and it has certainly not reached tipping point. Instead, persistent old myths of how a woman has to choose between career and family remain firmly in place. There is an increasing concentration of women taking those jobs which enable them to manage their double shift of employment and work at home – jobs which, while they may offer flexibility, are often also worse paid, and/or insecure. How did our generation end up with this shabby compromise?

The answer is that the revolution was left unfinished. The feminists of the sixties and seventies challenged the rigid division of labour between men and women; they wanted women to have access to the workplace, and men to rediscover their role at home. The psychotherapist Susie Orbach reflects on the thinking of the seventies: 'We wanted to challenge the whole distribution of work and leisure – we wanted to put at the centre of everything the reproduction of daily life, but feminism got seduced by the work ethic. My generation wanted to change the values of the workplace so that it accepted family life.'

This radical agenda for the reorganisation of work and home was abandoned in Britain. Instead we took on the American model of feminism, influenced by the rise of neo-liberalism and individualism. Feminism acquired shoulderpads and an appetite for power; it celebrated individual achievement rather than working out how to transform the separation between work and family, and the social processes of how we care for dependants and raise children. Trade Secretary Patricia Hewitt remembers a turning point in the debate in the UK when she was at the National Council for Civil Liberties: 'The key moment was when we organised a major conference in the seventies with a lot of American speakers who were terrific feminists. When they arrived we were astonished that they were totally uninterested in an agenda around better maternity leave, etc. They argued that we couldn't claim special treatment in the workplace; women would simply prove they were equals. You couldn't make claims on the workplace. We thought it was appalling.'

Only now are we beginning to realise this was a dead end. We were blinded, says Lynne Segal, Professor of Psychology and Gender Studies at Birkbeck College, University of London, 'to the continuing clash between the demands of the workplace and the lives in which we are able to fulfil desires and obligations to others. It shows the incredibly troubling intractability of the issues that feminism came into being to address . . . one of the main problems they face is a world which prioritises individual success and achievement, and on the other hand likes to pay lip service to women's role in caring and nurturing others.'[10]

The unfinished revolution left unchallenged the 'two for one' model that each employee is freed of domestic responsibilities by a wife at home. It left untouched the idea that commitment is measured by the employee's sacrifice of time, and by the single-minded dedication to work during that time. It is a definition of commitment in which the odds are stacked against women from the start, given their requirement to do the double shift. For the working women of the eighties and nineties, the consequence was exhaustion. They found the time to do the double shift only by 'shedding load' – reducing housework, leisure or sleep, or seeing less of friends and relatives – all of which are the vital determinants of mental health and personal resilience.[11] Women argued that far from 'having it all', they had none of it, either at work or home.

The sight of them struggling with this unfinished revolution has been a powerful deterrent to the next generation of women. Here are the stories of five women at different points in their careers, describing how the overwork culture halted their climb up the career ladder.

Kate is a junior civil servant, and she emailed:

Many of the people I work with, especially in the grades above me, work excessively long hours. I am one of the few people at work who refuses to buy into this culture. This can be difficult. I often feel guilty for leaving at 5.30 or 6 p.m., even though I have done a full and productive day's work, when I know that colleagues will be staying on for another hour or two or three. I do not believe that because someone puts in a marathon day they are 'better' workers. I think long hours can cause you to lose the ability to focus on what really needs to be done and what can wait. Sadly, to progress to a higher grade in my job it is a given that you work the mad hours. I don't think I want to do that and so will probably stay on the middle rung of this civil service ladder. This is a shame as I think I could achieve more and would like to be more challenged, but I am simply not prepared to sacrifice my personal life to do so.

Jane, in her late twenties, has worked in corporate law and is now in banking:

A lot of my female contemporaries in law will get pushed out sooner or later. The women have to show that they are not going to have babies and will put in the time as partners. The role models are awful; there was one partner who was seven months pregnant and did two all-nighters – it's masochism. I saw a partner whose children wouldn't speak to her because she was still on the office phone one evening. I saw her sadness, but she was incapable of changing.

There's a snob value in certain firms, that they offer a 'Rolls-Royce service' of 24/7 service; they expect to be able to get you on the phone until you go to bed and as soon as you get up. They schedule conference calls for the weekend. When you are under so much stress (fourteen hours a day, etc.) it makes it very difficult to have a relationship. A lot of women find it very difficult to switch off, and your partner has to give you a lot of support – not many men are prepared to do that.

I see three routes to choose: first, not to have children at all; secondly, do a Nicola Horlick and do all-nighters and have the baby, which is not successful for either the children or the woman; thirdly, never become a partner but take legal-related work where the pressure is less.

Women either give up or drop out because the caring responsibilities of women is a problem; they don't try and change the system because there's not yet a sufficiently critical mass – one partner did try a four-day week but she left because she couldn't cope with the stress.

The company want a level of attrition, it is a pyramid structure; out of every seventy trainees, four get to partner level, and hard work is a way of whittling them down; there's an element of thinking that dedication is more important than talent. It's even worse now in banking – there are no role models for women at all, so you end up with the 'impostor complex' which undermines women's confidence and adds to the stress. You need to be seen after 7 p.m. in the office.

Already, Jane had rejected the childless option, and she was horrified by the Horlick-type scenarios she'd witnessed, which left her with effectively just one option when she wanted to start a family: she would scale down her work. She admitted that despite her MBA and her substantial income, consideration of the whole issue was prompting her to question her understanding of success and to wonder if, after all, her mother, a primary school teacher, hadn't in fact been very successful.

Liz works in another male-dominated sector, the oil industry, in Aberdeen. She had her first baby a year ago, and after struggling to continue working, she has decided to hand in her notice:

I'm really panicking. It's difficult to give up a career after fifteen years. I'm scared I'm not going to be able to cope with my baby day in, day out with no stimulus. I earned £35,000 last year and my salary covered all the basics, so we are worried about that. I know I'm a hard worker and I have a lot of skills for any organisation. But I'm not prepared to go into any organisation that expects me to be 120 per cent work and nothing else. In the UK, you're not allowed another life – UK companies want everything.

It's made me really angry. I don't want the constant guilt, I don't want to work less hours or work part-time, because it would make it even more difficult – I would never be taken seriously; that's been enough of a struggle already. In a male-dominated business you have to be the same as the men, and when you have children, you can't do that. A lot of it comes from me; I used to work ridiculous hours and take a lot of work home and I went to a lot of social events: that's how I was successful.

In a way, us women have ourselves to blame. Men don't help – they're not expected to pick up the sick kids – and my husband is away on work a lot. I just can't be everything to everyone. Internally, it's just too much of a battle. I want to be in an environment where I'm respected; what motivates me is being recognised as doing a good job, and if that's not the case, what's the point?

Jackie, a middle-ranking civil servant in Yorkshire, says the only way she has found to cut her job down to size to fit in with family commitments is to go part-time officially, but still work a full week:

I get paid for thirty-three hours, but – my husband goes nuts about this – I do about forty-five hours a week on average. I'm not always getting paid for all of it, but if I went full-time, I'd have to work about fifty-five hours a week. I've kept a nominal record of my flexitime and I'm owed about ninety hours – that's just the bit I've recorded. I didn't use to feel resentful because I had a good job and liked the people I worked with, but it's become expected to work ridiculous hours. Now they're extending the retirement age, and I don't think I'll last until then. I'm forty-seven and I didn't use to look it but I do now.

Tracey has reached board level of a major UK company. A single mother of two school-age children, she has decided to step down to go part-time:

As the company grows, I would have to gear up to another level of energy, and I haven't got that capacity right now. I don't want to step out of this level of responsibility so it will be a sideways move to a three-day week, but what I'm trading in is the 'How much further can I go?'

I was a Thatcher babe, and we thought we had to have lots of male qualities to succeed. The things that were valued weren't family but earning lots of money. The way to find your place in society was to have a lovely home and get to the top. I came from Dagenham, Essex, and my father was a lorry driver; we were working class. My parents are so proud of me; all through my career I couldn't believe how successful I was, and that was a pressure not to give up. But I now feel so unfulfilled as a mother. I thought after the toddler stage it would all be plain sailing, but the last few years have been a big shock. Now the children need help with homework and friendships. I feel this decision was hugely liberating. When I go part-time, I'm redefining success and I'm free of the Thatcherite definition of success. I won't have as much money, but I'm not materialistic.

The company hadn't 'cut her any slack', she said, despite her domestic responsibilities, but she had no criticism of it for that. Both she and the company had decided that the long hours and a lot of travelling were essential for the job, and it couldn't be done on a part-time basis.

What was noticeable about these women was their lack of radicalism to challenge the definitions of commitment and hard work. It was not that they hadn't noticed how increasingly oppressive these had become; it was that they had no sense of how they could be changed either by company policy or government legislation. Many women criticised how their colleagues wasted time in the office, how long hours often included gossip, surfing the net to book holidays, and a pernicious presenteeism, but none of them had sought to challenge the habits of working. Some, no doubt, felt they were too junior to question the status quo, and felt trapped by a system of which they were often contemptuous. But even those in more senior positions were reluctant to rock the boat, and often they made the arguments one might expect the boss to make: 'The client expects it,' 'The company has no choice – it would lose to competitors,' 'There's no other way to do the job.' Women find private solutions on their own, such as opting out, rather than challenging the organisation of work.

This fragmentation of experience is the most striking contrast with the seventies, comments Susie Orbach. Thirty years ago, women shared their experiences and tried to develop a common understanding of their situation and what constrained their choices. Now they struggle on their own, isolated by a prevailing rhetoric that their circumstances are of their own choosing. They fumble after an understanding of success which reflects the true value and worth of caring, but which has no resonance or affirmation in a market-driven society and the overwork culture it breeds. The story of contemporary feminism is of millions of women struggling to accommodate the clashing priorities of the overwork culture and their intuitive understanding of another kind of success, and of how in the end, like Tracey, they are often forced into a choice between them.

At least these women quoted have a degree of material security which underpins their decisions. For less skilled women, the double shift can trap them in low-paid work. Maggie, the single mother working at Asda in York, was full of praise for the company despite the low pay, because it enabled her to fit work in around her children: 'Every time I've had a problem I go to them – and sometimes I've had problems with childcare, and I can swap my shifts. It's never been a problem, even when things were difficult when I split up with my partner.'

She was now working three shifts which dovetailed exactly with the times she could arrange childcare – either from her mother or boyfriend. Asda's flexibility – as few or as many hours as Maggie could manage around her children – and adaptability as her needs changed had ensured a loyal employee. No wonder the company has pursued flexible, family-friendly policies at the lowest level of its workforce – it has found that women's traditional double shift effectively subsidises its wage bill.

Catherine, another single mother, is caught between the demands of the overwork culture and the domestic shift. Her job may give her the flexibility to care for her two daughters, but it is demanding, badly paid and insecure. Such circumstances can coalesce even in jobs once regarded as safely professional. She's been working as a lecturer at the same Liverpool college of further education for six years, but she's on short-term contracts, so is never sure from one term to the next whether she'll have a job or what course she will be teaching. One of the most complex tasks she continually has to juggle is ensuring that she is doing enough work to qualify for Working (Families) Tax Credit (minimum of sixteen hours a week), but not too much to prevent her doing the school run. She also has to estimate how much preparation each course will require, and how she can be sure she will be able to sign on for income support over the worst period of all, the summer, when she has no money coming in. If things get really bad, she relies on a friend who brings carrier bags full of food round.

Catherine is paid £13.94 an hour by an agency (in the seven years she's worked for the agency, the hourly rate has *fallen* by 1p). When she includes all the time she spends in preparation and marking, it probably works out at less than £5 an hour. She'd be paid more if she went back to college to qualify as a schoolteacher, but that would mean she wouldn't be able to take the children to and from school. It's the flexibility of the part-time employment offered by further education which keeps her, and many other single mothers she knows, working there.

Catherine's computer, desk and files fill half the sitting room, and she often has work to do in the evenings after the children are in bed. She has to supplement her income with private tutoring for 'A' levels, because her work at the college is so uncertain. For her, the care deficit is not an abstract idea, but a concrete problem every week:

After seven years of it, I'm really tired. The kids are always saying, 'Why can't you be a sandwich-maker so you don't bring your work home with you?' The problem is finding someone to look after the kids. I feel terrible – this isn't good – but I leave them. On Mondays it's only for one hour and twenty minutes; on Saturdays it's a bit longer. They don't go near the stove and usually they have a couple of videos. I was left when my mum went out to work as a cleaner – she left me in charge of my three brothers, and the neighbours would watch out for us. But I haven't got that kind of support network, because I'm working. I can't ask people to babysit. The family is two buses and one and a half hours away.

Catherine doesn't get any sick pay, so she can't afford to miss work for anything other than an emergency. 'When one of the kids is ill, I'm not supposed to take them in but I do. I can't take them in if they're on the point of throwing up, but if they've got a fever then they have to come to college and they sit in the staff room.'

The children are a great support:

I have a bad back and my oldest child massages it for me. I'll try and sit with them for an hour and play in the evening, but I'm so tired. You make more of an effort with the kids because you're aware they might be being short-changed. I try to do the work after they've gone to bed and sometimes it's hard to think straight – I was up sorting out registers last night until 11.30 p.m., and there were still the school uniforms and dishes to do. The kids see you struggling and they try to help out. My daughter says I'm always tired. Something has to change. I can't do this, I feel robotic. I wake up in the night and I'm making lists – I've a pad by the bed. I never wanted to be in the rat race. You don't have the energy to reflect – you're just coping.

What About Daddy?

If men took on more of the domestic shift, it would enable women to make more of a commitment to work, and it would also mean that they would no longer have to meet unrealistic expectations in the workplace. This was another part of the unfinished revolution: men's and women's lives are so interconnected that the radicalism of the seventies' feminism always understood that men's roles as well as women's would be transformed. This is the point in the debate where many men begin to look edgy; they may subscribe to the idea of gender equality in principle, but as they reach their thirties and have children, many revert to traditional gender stereo-types under the pressure of the overwork culture. Demanding, insecure work is hard to combine with being an involved father.

Women can see that as clearly as their partners. The chatroom on the website mumsnet gives a fascinating glimpse of how individual couples fall into the pattern. One new mother reflected: 'Re comments on husbands not helping, he can't help it, he works very long hours, sometimes weekends, his salary pays our mortgage and everything else, and in his line of work, you have to do what you have to do, and there's no excuses (apart from really serious emergencies), and you may think you can do it, but you would be first on the list for the next round of redundancies!!!!'[12]

The biggest determinant of how men and women divide up the employment and caring roles is not traditional assumptions about gender roles, but money: the job of whichever partner earns most usually comes first; and the harder that job is, the more adjustments the other partner has to make in his or her own work. The result is that the pay gap becomes self-reinforcing, and much harder to break: women earn less than their male counterparts within a few years of joining the labour market, and by the time they have children the gap is significant. It becomes a rational decision for the secondary earner to scale down his or her work so as to support the primary earner. The most powerful predictor of the pace of change in men and women's domestic roles is the income of the woman: the more women earn, the more men take up the caring responsibilities at home.

This was confirmed by the Equal Opportunities Commission report in early 2003 which found that in dual-earner families the father's share of childcare has risen from a fifth in 1974–75 to a third in 1999.[13] Within a generation, the role of the father has been transformed in a large number of families. In one study of thirty-three-year-old mothers, the father was the primary carer in a third of households.[14] On average, the time fathers spend on childcare has increased from ten minutes to fifty minutes a day, with much of the increase since 1985.[15] There has been a particular increase for fathers with children under five, from twenty minutes a day in 1974–75 to about 120 in 1999.[16] This is perhaps the most striking demonstration of the sea-change in attitudes to fathering: once, small children were the preserve of women, with fathers appearing only briefly and intermittently in their lives. Now 87 per cent of fathers say it is best for a father to be 'very involved in bringing up a child from an early age'.[17]

Men are also doing more in the house – albeit starting from a low point: over the last forty years the amount of time they spend on cooking and housework has tripled.[18] Another study found that men's involvement in routine tasks was increasing, and significantly more so in households where the wife works long hours and earns more than her husband. The most egalitarian sharing of tasks was in households where both partners were working full-time.[19]

But the big brake on this transformation of fatherhood is the overwork culture. British fathers work forty-seven hours a week – the longest average working week in Europe – and longer than

British men who do not have children, as their new responsibilities add to their sense of insecurity. Once the father begins to work more than fifty hours a week – only slightly over the average – his involvement in the home begins to decline, the research found. Men have taken on new responsibilities at home while at the same time being expected to work as hard as, and often harder than, their fathers. They have protected their employers from the new demands of their lives at home. Trying to meet expectations both at home and at work exacts a toll, and many men now find themselves in a similar position to women – with a sense of overstretch, and of personal inadequacy either on the work front or at home, or both.

Commentator Richard Reeves points out that work–life balance issues were once seen as women's problem, but no longer: there was a marked increase between 1992 and 2002 of men complaining that their work intruded into family time.[20] In response there has been a rapid increase of men looking for working hours that would accommodate their family responsibilities: nearly half of men in full-time employment want flexitime, while four out of ten would like compressed hours.[21] Men in demanding jobs now routinely express guilt at not being able to do more with their children; for example, Niall Fitzgerald, Chairman of Unilever, told an interviewer from the *Financial Times* that he has breakfast with his two-year-old daughter, and added, 'I try to get home to see her before evening engagements and work more from home. I still don't do anything like enough; but I do it and I make it known I'm doing it.'[22] It's inconceivable that a man in his position would have mentioned such issues ten years ago.

Similarly, a decade ago it would have been hard to imagine the situation of Daniel. A civil servant in the Treasury who works a four-day week, he's quite sure that, as a man, he wouldn't have been able to get that arrangement in the highly competitive engineering company for which his wife works; there is no level playing

field. He's acutely aware of how men and women's roles inter-
connect.

I need to play an important role in the home for my wife to stay in her job, because it's very demanding. As long as I can remember I've had a gut feeling about egalitarian relations between men and women. But apart from that, I just sort of blundered into it, and I had the example of a part-time father in the Treasury – there's about 10 per cent of us at my level – and my wife was going back to work four days a week. When I took a secondment in the City, I insisted at the interview that I wanted a work–life balance, and the manager was fine about that.

Fathers of my generation are tremendously more involved, but they're a long way from that sense of ultimate responsibility that mothers have. But the impact of my being around on the children is unbelievable; my child is just as likely to run to me as to Harriet when she falls over. Because we've both spent the same amount of time with her, we've both got a similar level of expertise. Being with children is often about multi-tasking, and on that I do conform to the stereotype [of women being better than men], but the quality of the intimate relationship is just as good.

In my professional career, there are things I could have done if I'd been willing to work longer hours – but I've always hated long hours anyway. Work has its place, but I don't draw all my self-esteem from work. I feel quite missionary about my life choices – why aren't there more men like me? Then I realise so many factors have to be in place in London for it to be possible. Money is such a help, and we can manage on part-time salaries because we have a small mortgage, but some people aspire to a certain kind of lifestyle which is difficult to achieve without high-pressure jobs. The route to where we are has so many elephant traps that few couples last the course.

Men like Daniel are still regarded as pioneers in Britain, yet his story would not be uncommon in other European countries such as Denmark or Sweden. Why is it that we have a society which makes it quite so difficult for the kind of shared responsibility which Daniel wants? The odds are stacked against many fathers willing to take a greater role in the home.

First, they are still having to combat the weight of a history in which industrialisation exiled men from the home and the family, argues sociologist Michael Kimmel in *The Gendered Society* (2000). Industrialisation's curtailment of fatherhood was so effective that the absent father became a great source of concern. Kimmel quotes the Revd John S.C. Abbott, writing in *Parents Magazine* in 1842: 'Paternal neglect at the present time is one of the most abundant sources of domestic sorrow.' The father 'eager in the pursuit of business, toils early and late, and finds no time to fulfil . . . duties to his children', wrote Theodore Dwight as he tried to persuade men to resume their responsibilities at home in *The Father's Book* (1834), one of the first advice books for British men.[23]

A new generation has rediscovered fatherhood, but there is a real gap between these aspirations and how they are being accommodated in the workplace. Richard Reeves points out: 'Fatherhood is being renegotiated at home [while] the debate at work has barely begun.' He goes on to argue that any chance of gender equity now depends on men as the critical agents of change: only if they press for reform, so that they can fulfil their family responsibilities, can women make headway in the workplace.

Secondly, it requires an unusual strength of character and self-confidence for a new father to reject the overwork culture's dominant male pattern of long hours, competitiveness and insecurity. Women are expected at some point in their career to have caring responsibilities; men are still regarded as unusual if they point out that they also increasingly have them too. Nor have fathers had much help from government policy: paternity leave has been painfully slow in arriving, and pitiful in quantity – in April 2003 fathers finally won the right to two weeks' paid leave. At the same time, women won the right to up to a year off, with six months paid and six months unpaid, which tipped the scales even further against any couple wanting the father to be the primary carer in the baby's first year.

The government claims that it wants to extend choice on how families divide work and care, but the choices for men are still limited. The lobby group Fathers Direct argues that Britain now has leave policies which entrench traditional gender stereotypes more forcefully than those in any other European country. In Sweden and Denmark, parents can use parental leave to share equally the care of their children. The most useful lever of change for British fathers is the introduction in April 2003 of a right to request flexible working, which applies to both parents of children under the age of six; but the right is hedged round with qualifications, and for the pioneer fathers seeking to break the mould, it's not easy.

Tony is a computer programmer in Manchester, and because his is an industry which employs few women, his requests for part-time working were considered very strange. But he managed to arrange a three-day-a-week contract, and his wife also worked three days: 'When the oldest child was born, I was working full-time, but when she was three months I went down to two days a week until she was two and a half. So for just over two years I looked after the kids two or three days a week, and spent a day windsurfing. We shared all the responsibilities and the routine decision-making processes over the care of the children. I was competent and in charge instead of just "standing in for someone else".'

Then Tony lost his part-time contract, and because the IT market was very slow at that time, he didn't feel he had much choice about the next job he took; they couldn't live on just his wife's part-time income.

I raised the issue of going part-time when I took the job, but the agent who fixed the job didn't push it. The employer's reaction was positive, but they're not doing anything about it, and I'm reluctant to 'throw the book' at them. I know there's legislation now, but my concern is not to antagonise them. My best chance is to play it cool, and then I'll get it. When I started last year I realised how hard I worked – I did in hours what took them days. When I started working part-time in my previous job I got into the habit of working very hard, with high levels of concentration and focus, but I can't keep that up. I'm burning out. My health is suffering. Either I slow down and make coffee, browse the internet – and that's not the point – or I go down to three days.

Examples such as David Beckham's conspicuous fathering, and the decision of Alan Milburn to resign as Health Secretary in June 2003 in order to spend more time with his family, may help shift the tone of the national debate on the role of the father. The danger is that the overwork culture will slow down the pace of change, making our rediscovered fatherhood more rhetoric than substance. In concluding *The Gendered Society*, Michael Kimmel throws down the gauntlet:

The second half of the transformation of gender is just beginning, and it will be, I suspect, far more difficult to accomplish than the first. That's because there was an intuitively obvious ethical imperative attached to enlarging the opportunities for and eliminating the discrimination against women. But the transformation of the twenty-first century involves the transformation of men's lives.

Men are just beginning to realise that the 'traditional' definition of masculinity leaves them unfulfilled and dissatisfied. While women have left the home, in which they were 'imprisoned' by the ideology of separate spheres, and now seek to balance work and family lives, men continue to search for a way back into the family, from which they were exiled by the same ideology.[24]

Kimmel recognises the ethical imperative, but he overlooks the economic one driving women's move into the labour market. Employers over the last twenty years haven't done women a favour by employing them: they wanted their labour for many reasons, ranging from the fact that it was cheap, to the fact that many of the emotional skills women have honed for generations are in demand in running organisations. The danger is that there is no such economic imperative to drive men's redefinition of masculinity; indeed, there is a considerable danger that it will be crippled at the higher end of the labour market by the overwork culture.

The problem of how men and women divide care and work will not go away. On the contrary, it is likely to become even more pronounced as women form an increasingly large part of the labour force: 82 per cent of the jobs created between 1998 and 2011 will be taken by women.[25] Finishing off the revolution is no longer solely a feminist cause. It has been recast in the language of 'work–life balance', and round that standard men and women can find common cause. The battle lines are not drawn along gender lines so much as between different definitions of success and fulfilment, and the nature of our responsibilities to those who depend upon us for care.

Part Five

What Can be Done?

10

In Our Own Time

I started this book by describing the predicament of several people who felt trapped by the demands of their job, and many more of them cropped up in the course of my research. Some were determined to find a way off the treadmill, and I went back to them after nine months to see if they had succeeded.

Pete, the engineer working for a big multinational, has finally found a way out:

I've needed to help more at home because my partner has been ill so I've had to get more organised. I've also realised that it's not necessary to run around and be at everyone's beck and call to get your work done. I treat work as a means to an end much more now, which means that I've got a tighter grip on what's acceptable to me – that's partly been forced on me by home circumstances.

I've made the decision to leave the company and set up on my own. We're in a very specialised area and we could stand on our own and we'd make more money: why don't we reap the rewards of our efforts instead of lining other people's pockets? I'm in talks with two or three of my colleagues. I think I could work two or three days a week and earn more money and undercut the prices my company charges clients now.

What Can be Done?

I look at my company and I ask, 'What's in it for me?' They've cut a lot of the benefits such as company cars. The hierarchical management has been flattened [so there's no promotion]. All I get is a regular income. There's less of the long-hours culture in the office. Other people have realised that the company doesn't have any respect for its employees. Even those who used to work late are now leaving on time. The diligent are in a minority, and they know that. There's one colleague who's very diligent, and some would say it's out of all proportion, but he has a sense of loyalty and duty. I often ask him why he's working so hard; he's working blindly for a company which doesn't respect him, and he knows all this but can't change.

My boss used to work very hard, but he's changed his attitude – he was really upset about the new company-car policy. Plus there's a freeze on recruitment, so we're still run ragged trying to service the market with too few people, and it wears you down. There's a lot of disillusionment. I speak to a lot of people in other companies, and it's the same everywhere. Because of the flattened hierarchy, the middle and senior management are so far removed from what we do that if my boss left, there'd be no one to interview candidates to replace us, because our work is so specialised. They don't know what we do, and they don't know that we're not replaceable. If we all leave, the company will lose the business and a turnover of £2.5 million. Perhaps that doesn't matter much to them. The company has brought all of this upon itself.

It's been a long process working out what to do next; you question your own sense of diligence, and you have to do a risk-assessment on going alone. It's a very large decision, but when you put on one side of the scales all the risks of leaving and on the other all the risks of staying where you are, it becomes clear.

It takes a long time to gain the impetus and confidence to do something about your job and to get up and do it. But I'm hopeful now that I've made the decision. It could open doors to a brighter future. I'm very lucky. I have skills which I can use, and opportunities.

Now the presence of hope in my day-to-day life gives me more energy and determination to see it through.

Sarah, the civil servant in Yorkshire, went ahead with her plan to downshift.

We moved to Lancashire a month ago and my husband started his new job three weeks ago. I'm not working, so I've gone from absolutely no time at all to having all the time. It feels very strange. I've been trying to treat it as an extended holiday, so I've been reading a lot, doing housework, decorating and doing the garden. I'm getting back to my patchwork. I feel better, I've got more energy and I'm more relaxed. I'm getting more sleep. I feel a weight's been removed from my shoulders.

I was the main breadwinner, and dropping my wage has been a bit frightening. But I went back to where we used to live, and popped into work. They looked so grey, drawn and tired. They all looked so down in the dumps. Everyone said I looked fabulous, and that really decided it for me that I'd definitely done the right thing. We've reduced the mortgage by about half, and we have about the same disposable income because my husband's travelling costs are much lower.

My husband now gets up much later for work – instead of 5.30 a.m. he gets up at 7.30 a.m., and he has time to sit down for breakfast with me for a cup of tea because his commute is only seven and a half miles instead of thirty-eight. He works a normal day, has a decent lunch and he's often home before 5 p.m. We've got a huge park at the end of our road, and we're in there every evening either before or after tea.

On Saturdays I used to have to do all the housework, but now it's the beach. I'm going to train in reflexology, and when I'm qualified I'll be my own boss. I'll be in control. I want to spend some time helping other people who haven't got the opportunity or the means to do something as radical as I've done.

What Can be Done?

Sarah has achieved what millions dream of – downshifting and trading in property equity to end up with roughly the same standard of living and disposable income. She, like Pete, dreams one day of the autonomy of being self-employed and having complete control over the hours she works. Significantly, she looks to complementary health to express her desire to care for others, rather than to the traditional caring professions such as nursing and teaching, now tyrannised by a cult of efficiency. It's an indictment of Britain's overwork culture that Sarah has decided, at the age of twenty-seven, to have no further part it. She has lost all hope of finding work which would enable her to keep healthy and to find fulfilment. Her decision is echoed in surveys of young adults who have no wish to follow in their parents' footsteps.

One email, signed 'Disappointed of Brighton', poignantly summed it up:

> I am relatively new to the world of full-time work, having graduated three years ago. I have spent my working life in two busy offices surrounded by the type of work ethic you describe. As a result I find that I am at a complete loss as to what to do next, although I have become very sure about what I do not want to channel my efforts into. This is a shame, as I feel that I have a lot to offer and was keen to offer it, but not on the terms that the modern world of work dictates. What is wrong with me? Do I lack drive and ambition? I never have before, but nothing about the work ethic of today excites or motivates me.

Another of my interviewees was Maev, the cleaner in a London hospital; when I went back to see her, I barely recognised her. She was a different woman, smiling, laughing and meeting my eyes. After attending several training courses run by her union, Unison, she was one of a team of four who negotiated a new employment contract with the private contractor ISS. She gave me a poem she had written for a public meeting campaigning for a living wage:

People think I was born a cleaner,
But wher I was young, I never planned to be a cleaner.
When I put on my uniform, I'm a cleaner.
When I take it off, I was born a leader, I was born a singer.
On my days off when I put on nice clothes, people call me a lady,
*   not a cleaner.*

Under the terms of the new deal, Maev got an immediate increase of 57p an hour, bringing her basic hourly pay to £5, which amounts to a significant increase of almost £25 for a forty-hour week, or 13 per cent. In April 2004 it increased by another 35p an hour, or 8 per cent. But the real coup was an agreement to harmonise the pay and conditions (excluding pensions) of the old NHS staff and the ISS staff: the much-prized end to the 'two-tier workforce' in the hospital is due by 2006. More hefty increases in pay, of between 8 and 12 per cent per year, are in the pipeline to bring ISS staff up to the NHS pay level (which is itself being increased with the introduction of the national Agenda for Change agreement for NHS staff). By April 2006, the basic hourly rate will be at least £6.40.

When the harmonisation is implemented in 2006, ISS staff will get benefits such as better sick-leave entitlement, and their holidays will *double*, from twenty days a year to forty. Prior to the agreement, ISS had exploited a grey area in the Working Time Regulations, which don't make clear whether the twenty days' holiday they specified were on top of, or included, bank holidays. The company interpreted it as the latter, and gave their staff no bank holidays off until 2003, when it agreed bank holidays were additional.

What's more, the harmonisation of NHS and private-contractor pay is binding on all new contractors. If ISS loses the contract, the union won't have to start negotiating all over again. The shop steward who led the talks with the company admitted, 'If you'd asked me at the beginning of the negotiations if we'd get so much, I'd have been very sceptical.'

But while the pay deal and the union had done a huge amount for Maev's sense of pride, they had done nothing to reduce her hours. She was still working double shifts, and a fifty-hour week including overtime: 'My sister has been diagnosed with AIDS and I am paying about £120–150 a month for her drugs. I would love to go home to Africa, but at the end of the day people need me. I plan to work hard, and I can go home when I've saved up enough money. So many people need things. I want to go home and set up a primary school, but I can't save much because I have to spend money on looking after so many people.'

We counted up how many people are dependent on Maev's wages as a domestic auxiliary. In addition to her sister's AIDS drugs, she sends money back to her husband and three children in Africa, she has adopted ten orphans there whose parents have died of AIDS, she is supporting an orphaned niece through university, and her sister's five children. It came to a total of twenty-one. What keeps Maev going are her strong Christian faith and her dreams; she is a teacher by training, and her head is full of plans for the projects she will set up to help women and children when she finally returns home. Until then, she can see no way out of the overwork culture.

Sue, the senior media executive quoted in Chapters 3 and 8, returned to work after three months off.

For much of my leave I had no energy. I was fundamentally exhausted, and it was only three weeks before I was due back that I began to feel like my old self of several years before. I felt more creative and energetic. People say I look fantastic, and that's got to be good for energising my team. It drags everyone down if you come in looking tired.

I didn't want to get sucked back into the workaholism when I got back. I was offered a big job to run a new project. The easiest thing was to work hard; it needs a lot of self-discipline to resist that. I decided I had to regain my weekends, and to do that I would work at home on Fridays. I do a lot of thinking and there's no additional stimulation, so I can draw a line under work on Friday evening. I also try to organise Monday mornings so they're not full of important meetings which I have to start preparing for on Sunday afternoon.

I used to feel working at home was skiving – that work ethic is hard to overcome. Overwork is 75 per cent about the individual at my level. Of course, there are lots of demands on senior management, and you can't come in at 10 a.m. and go home by 4 p.m., but you can decide to put clear boundaries around different parts of your life. You need inner strength to put them there and to hold to them.

A lot of individuals get sucked into the workaholism. I think they're deeply fearful that if they're not on the case seventy hours a week, they'll fall behind. It's very human; it's about security. It's in about 50 per cent of them. They're in a hard-won position in a very competitive environment, and they think that if they take their eye off the ball, they might lose their position.

But on the issue which most concerned Sue in our first interview – thinking about work at home – it was more difficult to put down boundaries:

Any job which involves a lot of interaction with people is almost impossible to leave at work. What I love about work is interaction with people – it gets into my soul. Sometimes you go home with lots of negative stuff, and you need to switch off from that. The obvious way is meditation, but it is totally impractical: I can't carve out fifteen minutes at the end of the day, because I want to be with the kids. It used to be a glass of wine, but I've managed to cut down on the alcohol. I go to the gym a couple of times a week now – the busier I am, the more important it is. I've taken up singing lessons. I'm not very good, but I've always wanted to learn and now I do fifteen minutes' practice every morning, and it's a fantastic way to clear the head and switch off. It uses different bits of your brain.

What Can be Done?

In the evenings you do need to digest the day, I woke at 4 a.m. the other day and I was thinking about work because I hadn't given my brain an opportunity to wind down and get things in order. TV is a brilliant way of unwinding, but it's not very sociable.

I'm better at getting out of the office on time and not staying on to finish off things which would take me half the time the next morning. Obviously when something big gets thrown your way you have to get stuck in, and when there's a crisis you have to put in long hours, but the challenge is to regain the good habits after the crisis.

One of my colleagues who overworks said to me, 'Help me get my work–life balance back.' She needs permission from me. What people need to hear is that the organisation doesn't want you in the office at 7.30 p.m., it wants you balanced and healthy. You have to experience the way out of workaholism to know how it's possible.

These four individuals were a random sample, and three of them were on the point of finding a way out of the overwork culture. This is possible for many workers – though, tragically, not for those in the kind of desperate predicament described by Maev – but it requires a lot of thought, determination and courage. One can wonder whether Pete's dream of a two-day week will ever be realised – the self-employed tend to work longer hours than the employed, often driven by a greater degree of insecurity. But going self-employed would ease his bitter sense of resentment at the company's cavalier attitude towards its workforce. Dig a bit deeper beneath Pete's complaints about loss of control over his time, and one of the things that most irked him was the lack of respect it symbolised; time gets caught up in issues of respect and power. Once he's self-employed he may end up working as many hours as before, but his sense of self-respect and dignity will be restored.

Tony and Lee, the car-plant workers whose stories are described in Chapters 1 and 7, have both reached a decision. Tony has joined a union, Amicus: 'I've been very reticent about trade unions. I was in the pit strike at the age of eighteen. I went back to work after the union shitted on everyone. I went back with seven or eight of my friends, and two days later my car was petrol-bombed. I refused to go to work in the armoured buses they provided, and I walked through the lines. I was threatened in the pub, they tried running me over. After that, I was wary of unions. But the long hours at the car plant are so bad, I had to join a union. Someone had to do something. We're trying to get the hours cut back, and I'm in there for the long run. It's going to be difficult, because the union only covers about 40 per cent of the workforce.'

Lee is trying to purchase a shop. 'I'll leave before Christmas. I'm planning to set up two businesses: one will be a computer build and repair shop, and the other is with my wife and will be a beautician's. I could work seven days a week for myself. I don't mind that, because it's for me. Besides, at least I'll spend a lot of time with my wife this way.'

Jane, the Gloucester teacher interviewed in Chapter 7, is trading in equity to move to Worcestershire. This is the dream of many Londoners: that one day they will cash in their overpriced homes as tickets to a life of rural simplicity in France or Devon. The dream is beyond the reach of many who don't own their homes or don't have enough equity, and beyond the courage of most. It takes considerable resolve to leave behind all one's connections and friendships, and start afresh. Downshifting is only ever going to be a possibility for a minority who are wealthy enough and who have few responsibilities, as one contributor, Jim, who emailed the 'Working Lives' website pointed out:

I didn't decide to change – the decision was made for me. I had a typically meaningless media/marketing-type job. PR agencies don't need creative directors. It took them four years to make the same observation. Since then I've done bits of freelancing. I go out with a friend as his gardener's labourer sometimes – for buttons. I moved to a smaller house and dumped my two largish mortgages on my house and my buy-to-let flat, which means that instead of my buy-to-let being my pension, it keeps me afloat right now. I am now shopping at Primark, but I sleep like a baby.

Another correspondent emailed describing how he and his partner had built into their life-circumstances decisions and choices which enable time-wealth:

We have two children (fourteen and almost eleven) and live in London. My wife works three days a week as a health visitor and I work the same, part-time teaching and some research. We have a modest, comfortable income.

The main benefits: have time to fully engage in the life of our kids – both school governors, ferrying to Scouts, Guides, drama groups, etc., inviting their friends and other parents in after school, etc.; have time for each other – we have nearly every Friday in term time together, chores get done in the weekdays so weekends are less stressful.

Disadvantages: accept limitations of where we might get in our careers.

Key decisions to enable this balance of income, work and leisure: rule out any consideration of private schooling but give our time and support to our local state school; live a car-free lifestyle, which means you get to know people locally, and give your local area your commitment. In practical terms, we have helped bring about a traffic-calming scheme and got a tree preservation order on a row of chestnut trees.

Many who emailed felt that it was impossible to find a solution in Britain, as the overwork culture and the values it breeds are so pervasive that the only way out is to move abroad – as one emailer argued:

My husband and I were both self-employed with three children and had to work very long hours to maintain our reasonably modest standard of living. Only problem was that we rarely had time together as a family and were permanently exhausted. Our solution? We took a year out to live in Turkey, my husband's country of origin, where I continue to work as a freelance writer for my British clients. Life is cheaper here so my husband doesn't have to work. We now have the support of an extended family. We keep a horse, goats, and now my perspective on the UK way of life is so different – I think we all get caught up in a kind of madness. Once on the moving stairway, it's hard to jump off or go back. For those of us lucky enough to be able to work at home – why should home be in the UK? If quality of life is better elsewhere, then more people like us will just pack their bags and find it.

Another correspondent emailed:

I am writing this whilst sitting under a vine-buried pergola watching two iridescent hummingbirds feed on the purple flowers and listening to a family of ring-necked parrots squabbling in the mango trees at the edge of the garden.

Until December 2001 my wife and I lived and worked on the Isle of Wight with our son. As a head teacher my wife was accustomed to sixty-plus hours a week, seventy hours during periods of crisis such as school inspections or the end of term when the paper mountain had to be shifted prior to the arrival of the next term's lorryload of paper. I had a busy clinic as an acupuncturist working mainly for the NHS.

Both of us were working so hard that we drifted into a compensatory lifestyle where a foreign holiday was not a luxury but a necessity in order to stay sane, a good bottle of red an essential . . . Between us we were earning well, but at the end of each month there was nothing left to compensate for the mind-numbing exhaustion our jobs induced. It costs you money to work. We were living in order to work, as opposed to what the smart people do – work in order to live. In the public sector this is difficult to break out of. In December 2001 we flew to Trinidad, and I have set up a clinic here; my wife flies back to the UK to do various bits of consultancy work.

People work hard here, Trinidad is not your typical Caribbean Island. There are no tourists, but there is industry, oil, gas and a thriving business community that could teach the UK a thing or two about where to draw the line. The major difference between here and the UK is that most people here know when to stop. If they have to work late they will do so, but they won't do it habitually. It is understood that such work habits destroy efficiency and the quality of one's life, which, after all, should be important.

I am not knocking Britain – I love it. What I'm knocking is the doctrine that unless you work yourself into an early grave you are somehow not committed to the profession, company, clinic or whatever. This is so counterproductive and expensive in terms of ill-health, lost ideas, damaged relationships and creativity, which drowns in an ocean of tiredness.

Few of the people who emailed or whom I interviewed talked of collective solutions to the overwork culture. There was a distinct gap between their analysis of the problem and their suggestions of how to resolve it. While they realised that overwork was an endemic problem of the British economy and society, apart from Tony's decision to join a union to campaign against long hours, they could see only personal means of liberation – everyone thought it was up to them individually to find a way out. The personal solution was pursued in the face of cultural norms which reinforce the overwork culture. It's not that it's impossible to find a way out, but it is often difficult, and it is easy to lose sight of what is at stake; the overwork culture feeds off collective inertia and failure of imagination.

Pete and Sarah both opted for self-employment; they couldn't find a way to change the organisational culture. Their decision reflects a common pattern, and the result is that the impetus for reform is privatised, and the status quo perpetuates itself. Only those who will put in the hours rise to the top, and once they are there, they see little need for change. Furthermore, in Pete and Sarah's kind of white-collar work, long hours are seen as a problem of organisational culture, on which legislation and government regulation would have little bearing. It's a perception which the Labour government has been happy to reinforce, in order to let itself off the hook. In the hundreds of emails sent to the site, no one mentioned the need to remove Britain's opt-out from the Working Time Regulations. The majority accepted it as self-evident that, for all but the poorest, overwork 'is your choice'. And yet there was a widespread acceptance that this purported power to choose was often exceptionally hard to exercise – one of the many riddles that characterise our working lives. Richard Sennett describes this powerlessness in his book *The Corrosion of Character*:

> *Confronted by something conflicted, a person's attention can become riveted on its immediate circumstances rather than on the long view . . . When a person lacks belief that anything can be done to solve the problem, long-term thinking can be suspended as useless. However, focal attention may remain active. In this state, people will turn over and over again the immediate circumstances in which they are caught, aware that something needs to be done even though they do nothing. Suspended focal attention is a traumatic reaction found in all higher animals: the rabbit's eyes dwell on the fox's paws.*[1]

This kind of paralysis is common: those endless conversations with friends, colleagues and partners which go round and round, searching for some accommodation or some way out of a situation which seems unbearable and inescapable; the job change which never quite comes off; the postponed dreams of a different life. All are blamed on a lack of courage or of opportunity; the failure to act and bring about change breeds a special kind of humiliation, because it brings together two contemporary phenomena: it combines the taboo of failure with the fetishising of change. We live in a culture intoxicated with dramatic new beginnings, starting over again and transformation – whether of our faces, our partners, our homes, our gardens or our lives. We want those transformations to be rapid and compelling – a contemporary form of magic. The stories which fascinate are the bank manager who becomes the olive-tree farmer, the nurse who ends up running a hotel in Spain – but they will be lived out only by the most reckless and the most courageous. For the majority, they serve merely as a tantalising distraction from the kind of incremental change needed to dismantle the overwork culture. They sap the energy and determination which could be channelled into a campaign or 'a time movement' in which we search for collective as well as personal solutions.

Agents for Change: The Unions?

Historically, trade unions have been the collective vehicle for achieving change in the workplace. Work–life balance is a reconfiguration of one of their longest-running struggles. In the 1870s the Nine Hours League attracted trade unionists and non-trade unionists alike to its campaign for a shorter working day; the first meeting of the International Labour Organisation in 1919 called for a forty-eight-hour working week – which nearly a century later has still not been implemented. The 'drive for thirty-five' – as the engineering unions described their 1989–90 campaign – is a battle which is still to be fought; and the strike fund of £15 million raised then is still available for those wishing to fight it.

Work–life balance is a term closely associated with women. During the early nineties the trade unions were preoccupied with redundancies and the decline of manufacturing, and the issue languished close to the bottom of the in-tray. Beleaguered after nearly two decades of Tory restrictions of union rights, the movement struggled to develop the new thinking and the confidence to respond to the way technology, the 24/7 society and the influx of women were changing the labour market. It was cut off from the kind of meaningful social partnership which made unions powerful and innovative in Germany and the Netherlands.

The wildcat strikes at British Airways in the summer of 2003 marked a new phase in the trade union movement's fight over working time. That dispute took both the unions and management aback, because desk staff walked out not over pay, but over their shift system. What they objected to was a new swipe-card which they feared would lead to annualised hours (where staff are expected to alter their hours in line with demand over the course of a year). Seventy-four per cent of BA desk staff are women; the jobs are not particularly well paid – a starting salary of £10,000 – but they could be fitted around caring responsibilities, a fact which BA had promoted in its recruitment literature. The perceived threat to the delicate arrangements of work, childcare, school hours and partners' shift patterns was enough to prompt a costly dispute. It was eventually settled that the swipe-cards would not be used to change shift patterns, but the incident sent a clear message to the union movement, that to some sections of the workforce working hours rather than pay have become the single most important issue. The conclusion of Kevin Curran, General Secretary of the GMB union, was: 'It was a twenty-first-century dispute where the low-paid, mainly women, workers stood up and demanded dignity, respect and consultation from their employer. I believe that this dispute proves that time is the new money, and work–life balance and the quality of people's lives will become a major part of the collective bargaining agenda.'[2]

At a conference in Nottingham organised by the trade union Amicus in November 2003 as part of a programme of shop stewards' meetings around the country, this change of gear in the debate on working time was strikingly evident. It was standing-room only. Three-quarters of those present were men, and the intensity of the debate made a nonsense of the idea that the work–life balance agenda is mainly an issue for women; all the issues of stress, health, time for the family and relationships were self-evident to this audience. The majority of them worked in manufacturing, in sectors ranging from the car industry to textiles. Over the last two decades they have experienced job intensification as well as the reorganisation of shift patterns to cover nights and weekends.

Many of their stories had much in common. The basic working week may be as low as thirty-five hours, but companies have overtime policies which can increase it to sixty hours or more a week. Some companies make the overtime compulsory, others stipulate a 'reasonable amount of overtime' in employees' contracts – and sometimes bring very unreasonable amounts of pressure to bear to get it. The room went particularly quiet as one speaker detailed the impact of stress and long hours on health, with graphic images of the damage they could cause to heart vessels. These are not abstract warnings: one man said a colleague had a heart attack at forty-two, after working sixty hours a week, another had two friends who died of heart attacks after overwork. These workers know the high price exacted by the overwork culture, and that is the reason they had travelled to Nottingham to spend a day talking about it.

What they disagree about, however, is whether anything can be done about it. The debate kicked off immediately the official speakers finished. There were none of the usual diffident pauses one expects at a public meeting. One man argued that he was of the 'fixed generation' that has become attached to a certain standard of living, and that can't forgo the income from paid overtime. The only hope, he concluded, is to educate our children to avoid the 'pitfalls', and to adopt a 'contentment lifestyle'. On the contrary, responded another, we're the 'changeover generation', and the only way to educate children is by showing them the way. Only if there is a cut in working time will members focus on getting a better deal in their basic pay, rather than relying on paid overtime, said one unionist. People get into debt, said another, and have no choice but to keep up the overtime. They want their consumer goods; how can they be educated to want less and appreciate a better quality of life? How can they be persuaded to take a small pay cut for the sake of better health and a better family life?

'What's the point of the fancy car sitting outside in the car park for twelve hours a day and the DVD machine when you're working so hard you can't use them?' said one member of the audience, but another disagreed, arguing, 'If I went back to my members and said we were campaigning for the government to drop the opt-out on the Working Time Regulations, they would slit my throat. Yet every one of our engineers has left the company on grounds of ill-health in recent years, four from breakdowns.' He was backed by another speaker, who said, 'My company reorganised the shifts to do away with overtime and increased pay, but the employees were like babies throwing all the toys out of the pram – they wanted the overtime back.'

This is the sharp end of the working-time debate. About 1.6 million of the four million employees who work more than forty-eight hours a week are paid for their overtime. Dropping the opt-out on the Working Time Regulations would amount to a pay cut for many of them. In Nottingham the divisions in their own minds, as well as between them, were evident. What was clear was the link between consumption and overwork; they were grappling with an understanding of what constituted the good life – consumer goods, or their health and the harmony of their home lives?

Gary regularly worked a sixty-hour week at his engineering company; it wasn't compulsory, but workers came under a lot of pressure from management to do it. He made a point of not doing any overtime shifts in August, when his five-year-old daughter was off school, and he knew the difference that made: 'I felt a lot better. I was more placid and I didn't get wound up. I could do things with the family and do things on the house which I don't usually have time for. We could manage without my overtime; we'd have to cut out luxuries such as going out to a restaurant sometimes and going on holiday every year. I'd adapt if the opt-out was dropped.' But he reckons about 25 per cent of his colleagues wouldn't agree with him, and concludes that 'education' of union members would be an essential part of any campaign to reduce working hours, because some loss of pay would be almost unavoidable. Another shop steward, from the textile industry, where pay levels are lower, put the proportion of his members who would want to keep overtime even higher – perhaps as many as 50 per cent.

What made the debate so fascinating was how finely balanced it was. The appetite for the fight was there, but so also was a deep sense of pessimism that the consumer culture had too many people too tightly in its grip. Despite that, a majority in the room seemed to be in favour of shorter hours, even if it meant a pay cut.

Trade union members hope that shorter working hours without loss of pay can often be achieved as part of a reorganisation of shift patterns. The increasing demands of covering a 24/7 service culture open up new areas for negotiation; the GMB negotiated a deal with the gas maintenance company Transco which reduced a fifty-five-hour week to forty-seven in exchange for covering a new 24/7 shift system. Where social partnership between trade unions and employers has been strong in Europe, for example in the Netherlands, Scandinavia and Germany, they have developed projects on a 'dual agenda' of integrating measures to increase productivity and innovation, and at the same time improving the quality of workers' lives. This is what the trade unions are now trying to spearhead in Britain, and they are involved in some of the most interesting and innovative projects on work–life balance. Jo Morris, a senior policy officer at the TUC, has pioneered two projects with PCS (Public and Commercial Services), the civil service union, at the Inland

Revenue in Sussex and in Bristol City Council; both employers wanted to extend opening hours to improve service to the public, while employees wanted more flexibility. The projects were slow, hard work which involved lengthy discussions between employees and employers to establish how both sides could win. Employees outlined what kind of hours they wanted to work, and provided the workforce was big enough, almost all the requests could be accommodated, and at the same time the hours of service were extended. Both projects have been copied in other parts of the public sector.

Morris admits the process is 'front-loaded', requiring a lot of time and effort to produce any dividends, but what inspired her was how the work–life balance opened up other issues in the workplace: in Bristol, employees opted for 'self-managed shifts' – they worked out among themselves how to staff the service. The process of discussion and consultation changed people's relationships and how the organisation worked. What was vital, argued Morris, was the involvement of the union, which gave employees confidence that they weren't going to be taken advantage of. She comments: 'The part-time, job-share agenda is old hat, we should have done all that by now. The interesting work now is addressing productivity and work–life balance at the same time.'

Morris also recognises that increased flexibility in Britain's labour market has bred a more innovative approach than in some other European countries: 'The need is greater because we have to find ways to reconcile work and the rest of our lives. We work harder in the UK and for longer hours, and we have a higher participation rate of women in the labour market. That leads to greater pressure. We have to be creative about finding new ways of working.'

The problem is that the kind of projects Morris has pioneered cover a tiny fraction of the British workforce. Many companies still haven't even got to the point which she regards as 'old hat'. The weakness of British trade unions has left employees of many small- and medium-sized companies with no representation. This cripples the advance of the dual agenda, which is only possible where there is a strong, constructive basis of social partnership – where unions and employers work together. That kind of partnership has only taken root piecemeal in Britain, the legacy of the bitter industrial conflict of the sixties and seventies.

The trade union movement may have been slow to see the significance of work–life balance as a campaigning issue in the nineties, but it's got there now. In 2002 the TUC published its analysis of 'long-hours Britain' in a pamphlet, 'About Time', and launched it with a big conference; John Monks, the former General Secretary of the TUC, and his successor Brendan Barber have both championed the issue, and there's now a TUC website dedicated to it, 'Changing Times'. The unions have raised their standard on the politics of time, but they are still struggling to rally the troops, as large sections of the workforce remain reluctant to express their grievances through a trade union. Less than 30 per cent of British workers are members of a trade union. The result is a vacuum in the body politic: employers need to be challenged on how they use – and steal and waste – the time and effort of their employees. For over a generation, trade unions have been too beleaguered and embattled to develop new battlegrounds which would resonate with British workers, and the result is that employers have got away with an unproductive overwork culture. The pressure needs to be stepped up on those who cream off the benefits of burnout Britain.

Agents for Change: The Boss?

Work–life balance needs effective working-time legislation, but it is also an issue which can be embedded in the culture of an organisation, and that is often beyond the reach of government. Even after the implementation of the Working Time Regulations in 1998, many white-collar workers are working just as hard as before – some even harder. Their problem lies partly in a culture which rewards long hours, and puts employees under intense pressure to perform. When long-hours workers say they do so out of choice, many are simply responding to that organisational pressure, and don't want to let their colleagues or teams down. To reverse that, it often takes an enlightened employer to push through dramatic change, and to give permission to employees to manage other responsibilities in addition to their work. Most workers want their line manager's approval and respect; there's a world of difference between a boss who grumpily allows someone to leave early to attend an evening class or pick up a child, and one who is encouraging. You can't pass laws about the kind of cultural change which is necessary; there is also the danger that the poisonous legacy of Britain's history of industrial relations, the suspicion with which employers regard workers, could seriously inhibit the change that's needed. So who does manage to make the changes, and why? And the million-dollar question: does it pay off?

Gerry Farrelly prides himself on being a pioneer; his small company, Farrelly Facilities & Engineering Ltd, in the West Midlands, makes the bold claim of having solved the conundrum of being competitive *and* ensuring its workforce have reasonable working hours. By the time I reach its doors on a back street in Sutton Coldfield, Farrelly is used to explaining what he likes to call the 'Tao Farrelly Facilities & Engineering Ltd's Way'. What makes his company – which installs air ventilation and heating equipment – such an interesting case is that its success challenges two common assumptions: firstly, it is in the construction industry, which is notorious for long hours; and secondly, it works for clients who expect almost constant availability, and who often make enormous demands on their contractors. In the debate about what can be done to reduce working hours, companies often claim that nothing can be done in client-driven businesses where there are high expectations of availability and tight deadlines, and that in a competitive market you have to meet them. Gerry Farrelly disagrees:

> *I noticed in 1998–99 we were working long hours seven days a week. We had fifty full-time staff and we were all working sixty- to seventy-hour weeks. Everyone thought they were indispensable. It was chaotic. The first thing we said was no overtime, no working on Saturdays and Sundays, and we would finish work at 5.30 p.m., with a thirty-seven-hour week. Now it's down to 5 p.m., and 4 p.m. on Fridays. We all leave together in the evening, and if anyone needs a hand to meet a deadline then we all help.*
>
> *Occasionally we have to work over that to meet a deadline. We'll ask for more time, but the customer sometimes insists. We have deadlines all the time, but we tell our customers that we allow the right amount of time, and that way we will deliver on time, sensibly priced, and things don't go wrong. We try to educate clients, because when client work is rushed, there are mistakes. So far, it's never cost us good work.*
>
> *It's cut-throat competition in our industry, so the client has to know you're going to give 110 per cent; but he doesn't buy because you're in the office until midnight. We offer a twenty-four-hour service, and calls after 5 p.m. go to managers who are on a weekly on-call rota, but it's very rare to get calls, because customers' complaints have dropped. In a lot of big companies they say, we need to be there all hours, but if you allow the customer to bully you, they will, and will carry on. But if you explain and you're good, they want to keep you. Why take people on and then burn them out? The construction industry can be very adversarial – it's as if you're going to war every day. What's the point if you end up going home and worrying about work, and you have a file of paperwork beside you on the settee, and the wife and kids are thinking, 'I know Dad is at home, but he's not at home.' I don't want to be responsible for marriages breaking down.*
>
> *I could relate to this, because that's how I was – taking work home,*

taking calls on the mobile. I thought, if it was happening to me, then it was happening with everyone else too.

Farrelly set the business up with his brother and his wife Cathy, who remembers how her husband used to set off to work by 6.15 a.m., and was often not back until 9 p.m.: 'The business needed to change, our family was growing up and our children never saw their father. We outlawed work at the weekends. He's more understanding of the children now, he sees them in the evenings whereas before he'd be back after they'd gone to bed.'

Along with the reduction in hours, Farrelly changed the way people worked. Individual managers became entirely responsible for the projects they took on; they knew exactly what profit was made on each one, and were subject only to periodic reviews of what they were doing. He gave his staff full responsibility for hiring new recruits – after all, he reasons, they're the ones who have to work with them. He wanted them to take full responsibility for their work and declares, 'Trust is given, not earned.' Some people had made expensive mistakes, he admitted, but that was no reason to change. 'I had [management consultants] KPMG come round, and they were amazed at the lack of scrutiny and checking we did of our employees' work. They said we'd done the impossible – work less hours and achieve more.'

James is a manager who has been at Farrelly's for four years and in the industry for fifteen: 'No other company in construction has the kind of ethics of this company – it's a bullying, bang-on-the-table type of industry. Wherever I've worked, you never leave before the boss, but here I leave at 5.30, and I've started playing football again and I get to see my wife.'

In the course of my research I bumped into others like Farrelly; they had the same evangelical fervour that it was possible to make radical changes to how people worked. What's crucial is that those people are either at the top of their organisations, or have the full backing of those at the top. Chief executives have a huge impact; they can shift the entire culture. The difficulty, as has been noted, is that it is the most driven people who succeed at the highest levels, and they are often the least likely to acknowledge the cost of overwork.

The government has couched its push on work–life balance in terms of the business case. Backed up by research, it argues that allowing employees flexibility improves staff recruitment and retention, and reduces absenteeism. The Department of Trade and Industry argues that this is a win–win scenario, in which companies benefit as well as employees. Big companies such as BT, Sainsburys, Lloyds TSB and Asda agree, and have very publicly associated themselves with the work–life balance agenda, offering their thousands of employees different forms of flexible and part-time work. There are deals for term-time working only, school-hours working, compressed hours (working longer hours on fewer days). Companies which need to accommodate longer opening hours (such as in the retail sector) or fast turnaround times on orders, have an interest in greater flexibility than the old standard working hours. One study claims that as many as 78 per cent of workplaces now have some form of flexible working.

One of the most progressive pioneering schemes anywhere is that of Lloyds TSB; their Work Options programme, offering a range of six choices including term-time working, teleworking and part-time working, or any combination of them, was introduced in 1999 and is open to all employees, not just those with children; 86 per cent of all requests are accepted. The results are impressive: there has been a 40 per cent increase in the number of women going into management, and 80 per cent of applicants felt their performance had improved (90 per cent of their managers agreed). But there were some disappointments: only 16 per cent of applications to the scheme were from men, and only 18 per cent from managers.

Such pioneering schemes often founder at the middle and senior management levels. It is the unchallenged work intensification which ensures that the work–life balance agenda seldom makes it to the top. The result is a two-tier culture: the bulk of an organisation's workforce may have the option of part-time work, but above a point in middle management, the overwork culture remains intact.

Caroline Waters, head of human resources at BT, is widely respected for her advocacy of the work–life balance agenda, and proud that the company now has over 8,000 homeworkers, 750 job shares and 6,000 part-time jobs out of a workforce of 103,000. Much of that take-up has been by men, and more than half the workforce are on a non-standard working week. But she insists that individuals at the highest levels of an organisation must make a choice about the commitment required of them: there are no part-timers among employees at senior levels of BT, of whom only 15 per cent are women (the low figure is partly a legacy of BT's engineering, male-dominated past). She herself works fifty hours a week, which she says is not 'ludicrously long'.

It is at the pole ends of the labour market, the top and the bottom, that the work–life balance is the most difficult to resolve. Jayne Buxton, author and work–life balance consultant at Price Waterhouse Cooper, regretfully acknowledges that.

I thought any job is do-able part-time but I don't think that now. Above a certain level, when you're managing thousands of people, it's hard to check out two or three days a week. In competitive industries, managers are responsible for the success of the business, and they must put their heart and soul into it. Perhaps the solution is not always part-time. Rather careers must have scope to be full-time and then part-time; there are ebbs and flows in careers, otherwise the risk is of burnout.

In the last five years the level of understanding has advanced enormously, but progress in organisations has been slower than the debate has suggested. There are some sticking points. The first lies in the capacity of managers to manage differently, and a new set of skills is required: instead of measuring inputs – everyone is in the office all the time – you have to measure outputs and what's expected of each employee, and that requires a lot of forethought and a lot of managerial time. The very success of work–life policies at below managerial level may make it more difficult at managerial level.

What often happens at the senior levels of organisations is that in return for long hours, employees have a degree of flexibility; for example, the chance to take a couple of hours off in the afternoon to catch a school sports day. Will Hutton, Chief Executive of the Work Foundation, suggested in a column for the *Observer* that 'time sovereignty' is the key. People didn't mind working long hours, he said, as long as they were in control of those hours: 'What we all hate – from supermarket till operator to Cabinet Minister – is the loss of control. It is this "time sovereignty" that makes my life bearable . . . When lack of control encroaches on your evenings and weekends, with no compensating gap in your time elsewhere, however much you may love your work, you feel like a rat in a trap.'[3]

Certainly people are much happier (and tend to have lower levels of stress) if they have control over their hours of work. Hutton argues, rightly, that time sovereignty can be extended into jobs such as agency nursing or working in supermarkets, so that staff choose what shifts to work, and can swap them if they wish. But 'time sovereignty' is meaningless without any consideration of workload. A frequent comment of senior managers is 'I don't care where or how you do the work, just that it gets done.' If the workload is onerous, this is a spurious form of sovereignty; all the indications are that workload is the biggest driver of long hours, and that it is getting worse, not better.

One problem with the government's 'business case' is that some companies take the view that it is more profitable to take five or ten years of hard work from an employee, and then shed those who burn out. The most difficult workplaces of all are those where there is a predominantly male workforce. Changing the macho culture of an oil refinery in Aberdeen or a bank in the City is very hard, and requires a rare consistency of effort and drive from the top levels of the organisation. As for diversity; companies may pay it lip service, but only in some sectors does having women at the top affect their profit margins: for example, a tobacco company wanting to market cigarettes to women found a significant improvement in its bottom line after it put women in senior positions in its marketing department, but that wouldn't necessarily be the same for a corporate law firm. Progress is not just slow in certain sectors, it sometimes goes into reverse: the proportion of women in information technology has significantly declined in recent years.

There are three factors which may help change the macho institutional overwork culture: the first is that as the emotional labour required in managing an organisation intensifies, it may find women's emotional skills increasingly valuable, and be less willing to see large numbers of women fall away on the narrowing pyramid. It may find it needs women at the top of the organisation as well as the bottom. Secondly, consultants McKinsey's attracted much publicity for its concept of the 'war for talent', in which companies compete to attract the brightest employees. Developing the same theme, a recent article in the *Harvard Business Review* argued that the battle lines were now drawn not between labour and capital but between talent and capital, and increasingly it was the former which could dictate terms. The ludicrous salaries of the elite are a result of this, but they could also use their talent as leverage for time rather than money. In response, far-sighted companies will have to shift to assessing employees not merely on the basis of the amount of time they spend at their job, but on their effectiveness while they're there. This could lead to an inequality of time distribution, with leisure reverting to being high-status. Thirdly, diversity has become an issue of corporate social responsibility. The public reputation of a company which has no senior women and does nothing about it suffers: it has less legitimacy as an institution.

Jayne Buxton admits she's been very disheartened at various points in the last few years, despite the high profile of the whole work–life balance agenda. There is now a Work–Life Balance Week in September, with events all over the country; the government's Work–Life Balance campaign, launched in 2000 by the Prime Minister, produces material and offers companies consultancy services to implement flexible working through the Challenge Fund; Employers for Work–Life Balance, an organisation dedicated to promoting flexible working, tries to spread models of good practice. Buxton remembers how at one event a group of consultants in this area asked themselves, 'Why are we still saying the same things, and the same barriers still exist?'

One reason is that the business case doesn't always work. Buxton explains: 'The reality is that those numbers on absenteeism and retention [caused by inflexible working conditions] don't show up on the balance sheet in that form, so people can ignore them. Shareholders can't point to those losses. The losses occur in lots of different cost centres, so they are easy to hide. The average company does just enough to keep the workforce happy to avoid major unrest. It will be immensely slow progress.'

There's another hole in the business case, she adds, which is that the much-prized 'dual agenda' of raising productivity and cutting down hours by reorganising work 'demands a huge amount from management. It is very time-consuming, and sometimes the force of events can take it over.' The sheer pace of work makes it extremely difficult to undertake the unpicking and rethinking of how work is organised: the problem itself militates against a solution.

Perhaps it was a mistake of government rhetoric to couch work–

life balance in terms of the 'business case'. It would have been more honest – and in the long run perhaps more effective – to tag it onto the corporate social responsibility agenda. Just as companies now audit for their impact on environmental sustainability, so they should audit for social sustainability: have employees enough time and energy for their caring responsibilities, to exercise or to pursue other interests? An audit would identify where pressure in an organisation is tipping over into stress.

Much has been made recently in the media of the risk of a backlash from employees, who can become resentful of colleagues whose shorter hours mean their own burden is increased. One woman emailed the website:

> At my husband's work, the [flexible work] packages are offered – unofficially of course – only to mothers, and the accommodation made for them is sometimes ridiculous. The result is that the childless women and men (most of whom are fathers) have to work longer hours to cover the phone calls from clients. It's very nice the women get to see more of their families, but everyone else in the department gets to see less of theirs.

The way to kill off the danger of a backlash is to make flexibility an option for everyone, not just parents, as Lloyds TSB has done. The backlash may continue to exist in some places, but I've become suspicious of the way it is used by employers to resist further changes.

Ultimately, the biggest pressure point on employers doesn't seem to be the carrot of the 'business case', but the fear of litigation over stress from employees. In the next decade it seems far more likely that this will propel change than a business case for 'family-friendly' policies; already it is forcing employers (many of them reluctantly) to consider far more fundamental issues about the organisation of work than just time; they are having to examine aspects such as workload, work relationships and the pace of work. The Health and Safety Executive's decision to issue an enforcement notice on West Dorset Hospitals NHS Trust which grabbed newspaper front pages in August 2003 (see Chapter 7) sent shockwaves through the public sector. Already the HSE is piloting schemes to audit for stress, and has set targets for stress levels; after years of research there is beginning to be enough evidence for government to intervene effectively. As this issue becomes increasingly important, it generates a pressing task of public education about mental illness. We need a much more sophisticated public understanding of the difference between pressure, which can be fulfilling and can motivate employees, and stress, with its symptoms of panic attacks, depression and damage to health. Low levels of stress should be a crucial ingredient of being a good employer. Given that the highest levels of stress are in the public sector, the government has an enormous amount to do to put at the heart of its reform agenda the well-being of the employees who are essential to its delivery.

There are clear limits to what employers will do to reverse the overwork culture. Some will be pioneers; many others will rely heavily on the argument that competition leaves them no choice, and that that's the way things have always been, so why change now? Employers have rarely led the way in humanising the workplace, and there's no reason why now, in a period of intensely competitive neo-liberal globalisation, they are likely to do so. The challenge lies above all with government to develop a politics of well-being.

11

The Politics of Well-Being

Britain has a choice. It is caught between two models of post-industrial capitalism: the American route of low regulation and high employment exerts a powerful hold over the political establishment of both left and right. But across the Channel is an alternative of effective social democracy which does not shrink from intervening in the economy to achieve a common benefit. Which way will Britain go? One gloomy prognostication is that wherever America goes, Britain follows five or ten years later. If that is true of our working culture, the future looks dire indeed.

American working hours have increased even more rapidly than in Britain, and Americans are now among the hardest workers in the world, and take the shortest holidays.[1] The United States may be the wealthiest country in the world, with an unequalled standard of living, but Americans have singularly failed to translate their wealth into increased leisure. Average weekly hours for full-time workers increased by 3.5 hours, to 47.1, between 1977 and 1997. Eighty per cent of men and 62 per cent of women work more than forty hours a week;[2] these figures represent the reverse of a trend over several decades of declining hours. Working hours are now longer than those of Americans in the 1920s. One in three employees takes work home once or more a week. American workers also take a meagre allocation of holiday: an average of ten days a year, compared to Germany's thirty and Britain's twenty-five; 26 per cent of Americans take no holiday at all. Thirteen per cent of US companies (the figure has more than doubled in the last five years) offer no paid leave at all. Americans work up to twelve weeks more a year in total hours than do Europeans. A series of bestsellers such as Juliet Schor's *The Overworked American* (1991) and Arlie Russell Hochschild's *Timebind* (1997) have struck a powerful chord in the public imagination; 63 per cent of workers say they would like to work fewer hours.[3] America is one of only five countries – the others include Swaziland and Lesotho – that have no statutory paid maternity leave.

The overwork culture has also become entrenched in Australia and New Zealand as a consequence of the deregulation of the labour market. Australia has the second-longest average working hours for full-time employees in the OECD, and the largest proportion of any OECD country working very long hours. The number of male employees working more than eleven hours a day jumped from one in eighteen to one in eight between 1974 and 1997.[4] The Australian Council of Trade Unions has been running a 'Reasonable Hours' campaign in response to members who put long hours and work intensification as their primary concerns. Similarly, New Zealand's Council of Trade Unions has a 'Get A Life!' campaign.

Increasingly, parts of overworked America represent a future where you buy care rather than provide it yourself: you pay people to look after your children and your elderly parents, you pay therapists to provide emotional support and empathy, you pay someone to arrange your children's birthday parties and to help them with their homework. Companies spring up to provide the services to the overworked which were once carried out by the social networks of family and neighbourhood outside the economy. In parts of California's Silicon Valley many of the family's roles have been 'outsourced', comments Hochschild in her latest book, *The Com-*

mercialisation of Intimate Life (2003). The private world is commercialised, contracted out, and thus the logic of capitalism is extended into the personal realms of intimacy and love. Reciprocity and interdependence are the bases of many relationships, and friendships are eroded; love becomes simply a feeling, de-linked from a daily routine of care. Meeting the physical needs of those who require care is split from its emotional and moral content, and the labour to carry it out is bought in cheaply from developing countries and poor ethnic minority communities. Care is commodified.

This is the nightmare scenario, and Britain doesn't have to follow suit. It can fence in the market and its logic of efficiency; it can put up a big 'KEEP OUT' sign and hold true to a vision of humanity which gives proper place to the privacy and authenticity of relationships of care. It can reject the form of economy which feeds parasitically off inequality and creates a servant class to provide care; it is a crucial part of a democratic, egalitarian culture that we each provide the bulk of our care of those dependent on us. Britain could look to Europe for inspiration on how the state can intervene to protect workers and ease the conflict between work and caring: shorter working hours, universal childcare and generous parental leave provisions. All are the product of political cultures which set great importance on the social fabric – the welfare of children, the quality of life and the cohesion of communities and families.

The Working Time Regulations, which place a ceiling of forty-eight hours on the working week, have been implemented across Europe, the culmination of a long tradition of state legislation of working hours – as early as 1936 France passed a law on a forty-hour working week. Only Britain has an opt-out from the regulations which allows individuals to sign a waiver; many countries have legislated to bring hours even lower: Austria, Finland, Spain and Sweden have limits of thirty-nine or forty hours a week. In Germany, Volkswagen has a 28.8-hour week for its 103,000 workers; the Netherlands has a thirty-two-hour week for public sector workers. In 2001 France conducted a bold experiment under the socialist government of Lionel Jospin, introducing a thirty-five-hour week. It became the government's flagship issue; it was controversial among small businesses, but French productivity continued to climb, and it won considerable popularity (particularly amongst women) before it was partially reversed after Jospin's defeat in the presidential election of April 2002.[5] In many European countries working long hours is regarded as a sign of inefficiency or incompetence, rather than of commitment as it is in overwork cultures.

On childcare, the gap is even wider between Britain and the Continent: countries such as France, Denmark and Sweden have publicly funded universal childcare, which enables very high rates of female employment. Provision of parental leave is much more generous both in length – three years in France, Finland and Germany – and in the proportion which is paid. There have been many strategies to encourage men to take such leave; for example, Norway makes some of its parental leave available only to fathers, and as a result the take-up rate has leapt from 2 per cent in 1990 to 85 per cent in 2000. Germany and the Netherlands have given parents the right to request family-friendly working patterns, while in Italy, Spain and Belgium parents can spread out parental leave over a number of years to reduce weekly hours.

Several factors will step up the pressure on the British government to reverse our overwork culture and take more decisive action than the incoherent zig-zag between the American and the Continental European approaches which the Labour government has pursued since 1997. Firstly, the age structure of the population is changing: by 2021 there will be 1.5 million fewer workers aged twenty-five to thirty-five, and three million more workers aged over thirty-five. The competition for young employees will intensify, and the most talented will be in a strong position to dictate their terms. The increase in the thirty-five-plus age group will swell demand for work–life balance policies, because it includes those who are at the peak of their family commitments, and consistently complain of difficulties in balancing work and care. The proportion of people over sixty who remain in the workforce will also rise, helped by the removal of a compulsory retirement age. This is the age group whose job satisfaction has already fallen sharply because of work intensification over the last decade. A growing proportion of older workers will add to the pressure for reform. Meanwhile, those at the beginning of their working lives will increasingly have to consider how they can maintain the intensity of work over the long haul; retirement no longer beckons at sixty, but at seventy or even beyond.

Secondly, declining fertility all over Europe is going to propel the issues of time and care up the political agenda. Encouraging women to have children will be a major political imperative in countries where birth rates have fallen well below the levels required to maintain the population. In Britain the birth rate has now fallen to its lowest level since statistics were first recorded in 1924, while Spain, Greece and Italy all have even lower birth rates,[6] and face a halving of their populations by 2050; that will have an impact on the rest of Europe through EU legislation. It is well established that certain policies encourage couples to have children, such as the provision of childcare and well-paid part-time work.

Finally, the government will face a growing demand for change; in January 2003 a third of workers said they would rather have the option of working flexibly than a pay increase of £1,000.[7] Levels of dissatisfaction with 'work–life balance' are increasing; fathers want more time with their children, women say they are tired of being torn between family and work, and either decide not to have children or wish they could afford to give up working. Those without family commitments angrily demand to know why it is that the only concessions government has made are for parents, and complain that they then have to carry the slack for colleagues.

We are in the middle of a period of extraordinarily fast-paced change. Ten years ago there were fewer women in the labour market, and flexitime was the privilege of a minority; twenty years ago, no one would have understood the term 'work–life balance', and few would have predicted that one in five women would be their family's major breadwinner, or that fathers in dual-earner households would be doing a third of the childcare. The pace of change will continue: in another decade, women could make up more than half the workforce. Ten years ago, there was still a debate about whether women should be working; young women now regard the idea that they should stay at home as simply absurd. Some debates have been settled, but that only increases the stakes of those questions which remain.

A new and dangerous frontier has been opened up: if women have moved into the workplace only for their traditional caring labour to be abandoned, outsourced or squeezed to the edges, we will all suffer for it. The mission of feminism to achieve equality will have been hijacked by a capitalism eager for cheap, flexible labour and emotional skills on its terms. What we will reap is exhausted men and women, neglected children, loneliness, relationship breakdown and everyone short-changed of the well-being which is a product of the bonds of care. This threatens a commodification of the emotional life; in parallel developments, emotional skills play an ever bigger part in the labour market while private emotional relationships are starved of the time and energy which they need to flourish, and are then outsourced. This would be the final triumph of market capitalism, whereby the separate sphere which once belonged to women, and from which the market was excluded – of the private life, of home and family – is opened up for commercialisation. The pressure bearing down on the reciprocity and commitment of these private relationships is colossal; it's a tribute to the strength of many individuals that they struggle to hold true to their intuitive understanding of relationship. It would be a tragic betrayal of the grand vision of twentieth-century feminism if it had inadvertently contributed to the market's conquering of this final frontier, the private realm.

The government has a crucial role to intervene and mitigate the impact of the global market, technology and the 24/7 society. What measures will government take to protect and strengthen the social fabric? This will be at the heart of a new political agenda in the next decade: a politics of well-being which revolves around the interconnected issues of time and care. Its manifesto would include the following:

1. *An average thirty-five-hour working week.*
2. *Everyone has a right to flexible working, which can only be refused on a strong business case. A large proportion of the workforce will be in some form of part-time work. Many parents will be both working part-time on three- or four-day weeks. Many in their fifties and sixties are doing the same.*
3. *Universal childcare for all three- and four-year-olds.*
4. *A care allowance for parents caring full-time for children under three.*
5. *Eighteen months' paid parental leave, available to either parent, which can either be taken in a block at the beginning of the child's life or spread out.*
6. *Six months carers' leave, which can be taken in a block or spread out.*
7. *A universal state pension which compensates for breaks in employment to provide care.*

On Time

The government needs to launch the country on a path towards eradicating the overwork culture, and the most pressing issue to tackle is working time. It could start with a small but essential first step in 2004, when the European Commission reviews Britain's opt-out from the Working Time Regulations. The CBI, the TUC and the government are limbering up for a fight: business argues that cancelling the opt-out would reduce competitiveness, while the trade unions say the opt-out has to go, and that long working hours are part of Britain's 'low road', with low skills, little regulation and low-value products. Already it is suspected that the government will flinch from giving up the opt-out, and will try to sweeten the pill with increased holidays. It's nervous of the impact of dropping the opt-out on 1.6 million long-hours workers who rely on overtime to supplement their pay. Senior government figures argue that the British 'low road' of long hours and low productivity has to be tackled incrementally, or implementing the Working Time Regulations could trigger an increase in unemployment. At present Britain's productivity is too low, the argument continues, to support the shorter working hours and longer holidays found in Europe. This kind of reasoning makes one ask why the British economy should need extra-careful handling. Why can't it stomach the regulation dealt out to weaker economies such as those of Portugal, Belgium and Spain?

It's the old chicken-and-egg question of which will come first. Companies will only invest in reorganising work to use people's time and energy more effectively if there is a pressing business imperative to do so. Trade unions have shown how negotiations to cut working hours can be linked to increasing productivity, job growth[8] and more effective shift patterns, but as long as the 'low-road' option exists, it will be used. A realistic compromise would be to follow Ireland's example between 1997 and 1999, and phase in the Working Time Regulations over several years, to give business time to adjust. Without some commitment to end the opt-out, Tony Blair's launch in 2000 of the government's Work–Life Balance campaign is a nonsense, as is the Trade Secretary Patricia Hewitt's pledge to end long hours by 2007.

The Labour government's timidity is all the more depressing given how many loopholes are built into the Regulations anyway. It hasn't lived up to its promise, succeeding only in halting the increase in average full-time hours rather than reversing the increases of the nineties: one in five of British workers say their hours have actually *increased* since the regulations were brought in.[9] As we have seen, nearly a fifth of the British workforce have signed the opt-out; European Commission-sponsored research has found evidence of employees being put under pressure to sign the waiver, and of companies ignoring the Regulations.[10] Requirements for organisations and companies to keep records were dropped in 1999 after lobbying from business, making enforcement extremely difficult. From the start, there was also an exemption for workers who could claim 'genuine autonomy' over their working time – this effectively ruled out the self-employed and many in senior managerial/professional positions.

But the Regulations did score two significant victories. They increased the annual holiday entitlement to twenty days, with the result that two million workers received paid holidays for the first time, and four million benefited from an increase in holidays – a total of six million workers, predominantly in the part-time and low-paid end of the labour market. Unfortunately they didn't clarify whether the twenty-day entitlement included bank holidays or not, so for many employees their entitlement came to only twelve days plus bank holidays. The second achievement was that the Regulations established an important principle in British law of the state intervening to regulate working hours, rather than leaving them to the process of collective bargaining. This has altered the political and cultural landscape, giving a significant boost to employees' sense of entitlement. The principle of regulation over working time provides government with a powerful lever in the labour market – one of its most powerful in the battle against the overwork culture. While it is difficult to see how the state can intervene effectively to combat work intensification or emotional labour, it can use a strategy of reducing working hours to relieve the pressures in the workplace.

If technology and increased competition drive work intensification, the most effective response is to reduce the time we spend at work. Why not return to the working patterns of some craftsmen in the early Industrial Revolution, as described by E.P. Thompson: hard work for three or four days, and leave the rest of the week to balance caring responsibilities, pursue other interests or rest? The industrial bureaucracies of the twentieth century required conformity, not the intense innovation and emotional labour of the twenty-first century. In parts of the most creative knowledge economy, the length of time spent at work is irrelevant to performance. A shorter working week might be as productive, a point made by Tony, the computer programmer in Chapter 9. Besides, a shorter working week would enable employees to update their skill levels in the type of lifelong learning strategy required in a modern economy. For all these reasons, economic and personal, government has to take the bold step of introducing a right for all employees to work part-time. That would take much further Labour's tentative measure in April 2003 of the right for parents of children under six to request part-time work, which the employer can refuse. The right needs to be extended to everyone, to head off a backlash against those with small children; employers should only be able to refuse if they can prove it will damage their business. It's vital that there is a level playing field in the labour market between those with children and those without, or the former will find themselves disadvantaged.

If more people are to work part-time, much needs to be done to reform the current second-class status of part-time workers. Labour's implementation of the EU part-time directive was a start. In Britain part-time work is less well paid, has fewer promotion prospects, fewer benefits, is usually less interesting and less skilled, and the pay gap between men and women is more than twice that of full-time work (41 per cent compared to 18 per cent). The cause of part-time workers – which is almost synonymous with that of women, who make up most of the part-time workforce – has become a matter of interest to the Treasury, which is concerned that the country is losing out on the productivity of women, who drop as many as four skill levels to find part-time work they can fit around their caring responsibilities. That represents lost revenue to the exchequer and lost skills to the economy, not to mention lost earnings to the woman. It doesn't have to be this way. The Netherlands has a high proportion of part-time workers, who tend to work slightly longer hours on average than those in the UK, and twice the number of men work part-time as in Britain. Dutch part-time workers are better paid (the pay gap between men and women in part-time work is less than 10 per cent), and their jobs straddle all sections of the labour market. The country's strong tradition of social partnership between employers and trade unions has enabled the Netherlands to mesh the contemporary need for flexibility with the needs of employees, so that instead of a full-time/ part-time twin-track labour market, it has developed a spectrum of work schedules.

There are some in the Labour government who understand the politics of time: the Trade Secretary, Patricia Hewitt, wrote a book, *About Time*, in 1993 which called for radical changes to labour and benefit regulations. But now, in office, she cannot provide the required radicalism for fear of losing the support of business, and the approach is softly-softly, persuasion rather than coercion. At its worst, the government comes close to abdicating responsibility altogether, and urging business to do its job for it. It puts itself on the sidelines, simply cheering on those who pioneer new ways of working and encouraging good practice. But it's the role of government to trigger change, lead and shape it, not simply to applaud those companies which see that it is in their interests to introduce some forms of flexible working. It is up to government to champion

an old cause, one especially close to the heart of the Labour movement – the humanisation of the workplace.

Care

Just for once, as a wealthy, progressive country with a keen interest
in our future, let's imagine we can put children's welfare first.
Drawing on the latest research into child development, why not
shift society's priorities and develop a system of parental leave and
care allowances which enables parents to provide as much of the
care of their children in the first two years as they can? Using
child welfare as the prism through which to assess policy, why not
transform the childcare system in this country to one which is not
a means of helping parents to work, but which has child development at its heart? Childcare shouldn't be an adjunct of the labour
market.

Why is it that we pay lip service to the importance of raising
and nurturing the next generation, yet are not prepared to devote
more of our GDP to ensuring it is done to the best of our wealthy
country's capabilities? How can we ignore the findings of increased
levels of anxiety and insecure behaviour among the most vulnerable
members of society? A conspiracy of silence has buried this research
in the small print, because it challenges the direction of government
policy and revives old myths such as the golden age of the stay-at-
home mother. But the time for an honest debate is already overdue.
To put it at its crudest, what is the point of a government policy
which persuades parents to pay other people badly to look after
their children badly? Even without indulging the most alarmist
predictions of a 'timebomb' of emotionally disturbed youngsters,
we have enough evidence to show us the dangers of the country
setting a course towards longer hours, more stress and more childcare to fit around the 24/7 society. This is driven by the priority
of economic growth, not human need, and we will rue the cost.

The answer is not the dangerous dead-end of forcing women, out of a sense of guilt, into staying at home, where they run a greater risk of poverty (for themselves and their children), but easing the conflicts between work and care for both parents.

What is required is a significant shift in Labour's thinking. The rhetoric and the policies need to change, so that those who set aside time to care are given public endorsement and support, instead of being seen as a drain on public resources. Labour needs to fundamentally rethink its exaltation of the paid work ethic, and to re-orientate policies to encourage parents to invest time in their children. It could start by providing a total of eighteen months of paid parental leave, available to either parent. Unless it is paid, parental leave becomes simply a luxury for those who can afford it. We need policies which redistribute time – giving it back to those who are the most time-poor, such as young parents. With the money would come a recognition of the vital unpaid caring work that effectively subsidises the economy. It would be a dramatic shift of direction for a government which has elevated the paid work ethic to unprecedented heights, and thereby reinforced the low value and worth attached to parenting. Only in connection with issues of law and order – vandalism, youth crime, truanting – does the government ever talk about the importance of hands-on parenting. It demands a lot of parents and gives them little in return; because of the colossal pressure bearing down on families, government has no choice but to intervene to give more support – or face a mounting bill for the fraying social fabric.

The mismatch between rhetoric and policy is most apparent in the treatment of fathers, who received a pitiful two weeks of paid paternity leave in 2003 for the first time, but who are discriminated against by extended maternity leave. This eighteen months of parental leave would open up choice for couples as they try to divide and share the responsibilities of work and care. A portion of the leave could be allocated to fathers and be non-transferable, to encourage their engagement with their children. There may always be a preponderance of women who choose to take on the care of children, but there are men who would like to share more of it, and at the moment the odds are stacked against them. Until fathers have more opportunities to do more of the care, women will be disadvantaged in the labour market by the second shift. This is not social engineering, as some critics would claim, but about government policy needing to keep ahead of the rapidly changing roles of men and women, rather than holding them back.

For all its good intentions, Labour's extension of maternity leave in April 2003 (mothers now have a total of a year's leave, of which twenty-four weeks are paid) still lags woefully behind the provision in other European countries. While parents are entitled to thirteen months' leave at 80 per cent of their earnings in Sweden, and forty-two weeks at 100 per cent in Norway, British mothers get only six weeks at 90 per cent of pay, and another twenty weeks at £102.80 per week. Fathers get only two weeks of paid paternity leave at the £102.80 flat rate.[11] Only one in five British mothers gets a better maternity leave package from her employer. Furthermore, Labour's extension of maternity leave has served to entrench the gender division of caring more deeply than in any other European country. In Britain, maternity leave (intended to allow a period of time for the recovery from labour and for breastfeeding) has been conflated with parental leave (for the care of children), whereas many European countries draw a clear distinction between them, and give couples flexibility to decide which partner will take the parental leave. In the UK, if the mother is the main breadwinner and wishes to return to work, her husband does not have the advantage of job protection she would have while on leave, nor does he have the same allocation of paid leave. In fact, there is a real risk that current policy on maternity leave contravenes equal opportunities legislation. As one government figure put it, 'We agonised over whether to extend maternity leave or give fathers more parental leave, but we didn't want to double the burden on business. We don't want to give the Conservatives the business community.'

The kind of scenario which would serve the interests of children best – and which is rare in Britain, though not in countries such as Norway, Denmark and the Netherlands – would be if parents could stagger their working hours so that children spent only a few hours in childcare during the day (the father could drop the child at 10 a.m., before going into work, the mother pick the child up at 2 p.m., after her work) or only a couple of days in childcare (both parents working a three- or four-day week). Once the children are at school, parents could stagger their hours around the school timetable. This would be the best option for children, providing them with both the emotional security of close parental involvement and the stimulation and interest of a nursery or childminder.

Even if all these time policies were implemented, there would still be a need for paid childcare; an emphasis on the importance of parental care *reduces* the need for childcare, it doesn't remove it. Universal, affordable childcare is part of the infrastructure of a modern state, much like transport; just as the country could not operate without a decent railway system, so family life cannot now function without decent childcare. At its best, and at the appropriate age and for the right amount of time, childcare benefits children enormously. All the research shows that the money spent on pre-school education for three- and four-year-olds reaps remarkable dividends in increased educational achievement and social skills, and is one of the most effective forms of public expenditure. Yet it has been an astonishing failure of the collective will that Britain has been so slow to grasp this. In the late nineteenth century, British governments saw the importance of universal free education, and the need for the state to provide it; the comparable challenge at the end of the twentieth century was the provision of childcare, and Britain flunked it. While other European countries pioneered

315

respected traditions of pedagogy and early child development, Britain lagged miserably behind. We failed to make the necessary public investment, and it was parents (usually mothers) who were left to pick up the pieces, patching together the precarious arrangements with carers, friends and relatives which make their lives so complicated and stressful.

Those who suffer most from the lack of affordable childcare are women in lower-paid work, whose wages will never cover the cost of childcare, particularly single parents trying to raise children on one wage. Childcare is expensive, and it hits parents at the point in their lives when they are least able to pay – as they stretch their income to cover a family; it will always require generous state subsidy. Labour's attempts to subsidise childcare through the child-care allowances, nurseries in the poorest neighbourhoods, Out of School Clubs and Early Excellence Centres are all admirable, but they fall far short of the kind of universal, affordable provision for three-year-olds upwards which would ease millions of lives. Sure Start, the government programme to provide a range of services including childcare and parental support in the most deprived neighbourhoods, is pitifully small, covering only one out of every eleven children in the twenty poorest wards in the country. After-school care is still patchy. Labour's National Childcare Strategy has made some headway, increasing the number of after-school places from 115,000 in 1997 to 240,000 in 2002, with a target of 400,000 by 2003–04,[12] but this is estimated to be only 60 per cent of the total needed. Deprived neighbourhoods have a particular difficulty in keeping after-school clubs financially viable even with subsidies. Nor can after-school clubs help with atypical working hours in the early morning and evening, or with weekend working, while school training days and holidays often give parents problems. Labour has adopted a piecemeal approach, inching forward cautiously; child-care is subject to yet another review in late 2003, this time of the Treasury. Margaret Hodge, the Minister in charge of early years and one of a handful of senior Labour women most closely associated with the childcare agenda since the party came to power, has pledged to establish a children's centre in every neighbourhood: not just childcare for the poor, but childcare for all. To do that she needs the Treasury to back her, and they're still biting their fingernails at the size of the bill attached.

What has dogged the campaign for childcare in Britain in recent years is that it is fighting on several fronts. Not only is it campaigning for more widespread provision, but for an improvement in standards *and* significant increases in pay, status and training for the workforce if the massive expansion required is to be properly staffed. These kinds of policies are expensive: income tax would have to be increased to cover them. But the alternative is no less expensive, in escalating levels of stress and depression, strain on families and a weakened social fabric. The task for government is to articulate clearly to the country that the choice is of which bill to pay: for the prevention, or the treatment, of the symptoms?

Here then is a new agenda for the government: a politics of well-being around time and care which asserts human need rather than letting corporate interest and an inhuman pursuit of efficiency set the agenda. There is a growing understanding in the Labour government that its dream of progress cannot be understood simply in terms of economic performance and increased wealth. The politics of well-being is rising up the political agenda as policy-makers grapple with the fact that increased affluence has brought in its train increased stress at work and at home. They are being influenced by a new critique of the market emerging on both sides of the Atlantic from the so-called 'happiness economists', who argue that the market does not deliver increased happiness, and in fact generates conditions which make people less happy. This dislocation can be expressed through the ballot box, as voters lose interest in a politics that does not articulate the sense of struggle in their lives. The American economist Robert Lane points out in *The Loss of Happiness in*

What Can be Done?

Market Democracies that rising GDP does not translate into greater happiness beyond a certain level of wealth; the United States reached that point sometime in the late fifties, and ever since, the proportion of people saying they are happy has been in decline: 'The reason markets in advanced economies fail to do much to promote, let alone maximise, well-being is that the things that contribute most to well-being, especially companionship and family life, are market externalities,' argues Lane, who claims that Western industrialised nations are going through a step-change in personal relations, with steep declines measured in family and community socialising. The result is a 'famine of warm interpersonal relations, easy-to-reach neighbours, of encircling inclusive memberships and of family life'.

What worries Lane is the rising incidence of dysphoria – the loss of what gives security and meaning to our lives. He points out that the best predictor of subjective well-being is the number of friends we have; yet, as we saw in Chapter 7, friendship has taken the worst hit of all personal relationships in the big time-squeeze. Many of us are not choosing what will make us happy, and are instead misled by a culture of overwork and consumption which forces out the time-consuming relationships which bring lasting happiness.

Another happiness economist, Richard Layard of the London School of Economics, argued in a series of public lectures in 2003 that the state should step in; too much paid work is inimical to happiness, he said, and results in a 'distortion of our life towards work and away from other pursuits'. He argues that we should use taxation 'to discourage excessive self-defeating work', and while he acknowledges that this would lead to a drop in GDP, that wouldn't matter, because GDP is 'a faulty measure of well-being'.[13]

Assumptions about the priorities of government could be radically challenged. Do we judge political success by the crude measure of rising GDP, or might the political agenda of 2015 be focused more on life satisfaction than simply on the growth of disposable income? By then, will we be watching indices of mental illness such as depression and stress as closely as we now watch indices of economic performance? Will quality of life weigh heavier at the ballot box than levels of taxation? The politics of well-being offers a set of ideas which might lift the Labour government beyond the managerialism of public service reform and help it to connect to the lives of the electorate; but this would mean squaring up to business and levelling with voters, because it will be expensive. Bold policies on time and care are a form of social investment as vital to a vibrant, cohesive society at ease with itself as good-quality education and health services. Is Labour up to it? Is the taxpayer up to it?

A Rallying Cry

Rolling back the overwork culture will not be the task of governments alone. The changes required must be triggered through the spread of ideas, a growing awareness that shifts the *zeitgeist*; the exchange of personal experiences can help shape a better understanding of the addictive nature of overwork, the care deficit and the politics of well-being. The traditional channels of trade unions and political parties will play their part in identifying the choices we face and the policies we need. But one of the most pressing tasks is to imagine a new future. If what we imagine is sufficiently compelling, and resonates with people's own private dreams and aspirations, then it will succeed in mobilising the will for effective action.

So here's a first draft of what might characterise a new future, and what it requires of us.

As women come to represent a bigger proportion of Britain's workforce, they will revolutionise the work ethic. Out goes the nineteenth- and twentieth-century version of work as the driving focus, the dominating discipline in life and the primary source of identity. In comes a work ethic which is interwoven with a care ethic; it is demanding, but it is also fulfilling, and they have the potential to enrich each other. This new work ethic redefines commitment to the job, which can no longer be measured only in time and availability, but also in ingenuity and creativity. It makes the management of workers harder, as they are less dependent on work as a source of identity and emotional fulfilment because there's plenty of that in the rest of their lives. But it opens up the possibility of a humanisation of work: organisations where people can *become* themselves and develop their talents, where the driving principle is not competition but collaboration, and where the workplace is not crippled by dysfunctional emotions but enriched by the life experiences its employees build up outside it. It requires raising our expectations of the workplace and no longer putting up with the routine disorganisation, dishonesty and lack of respect. This new work ethic demands a lot of workers – that they have the self-assertion and 'inner strength' to which Sue referred in Chapter 10, and that they have the faith that change is possible. Individual workers have to determine their own boundaries about what they can and what they cannot give their employer, and then fight for them alongside colleagues. This alternative work ethic doesn't rule out hard work; it recognises the exhilaration and the need for deadlines, but it also recognises when the deadline has passed and the need is for rest. It recognises workaholism, and knows how to deal with its symptoms.

Already, this alternative work ethic is emerging: for example, a DTI survey in January 2003 found that 30 per cent of respondents said they would prefer a day off to a pay rise. It may mean keeping weekends and evenings clear, it may mean refusing an intranet connection at home and turning off the mobile. People help each other – by not phoning colleagues at home, by recognising each other's privacy; as one corporate PR explained to me, she and a friend agreed to phone each other at 5.45 every evening to remind each other to go home. The alternative work ethic recognises and rejects the insecurity which drives the overwork culture. It puts work in its place; the job may be rewarding, it may be enjoyable, but it is not one's whole life, it is only ever a part. Finally, it is not apologetic; it insists that humanisation of the workplace is not a luxury, but an essential of a wealthy, progressive nation.

In the nineteenth century much was made of the self-discipline and sense of responsibility involved in the work ethic, and the same is true of the twenty-first century. Only this time, the self-discipline and responsibility required is that you owe it to yourself to leave work on time; to complain to the boss if the workload is too heavy and to campaign with colleagues to get impossible jobs redesigned. Don't short-change yourself – allow yourself moments to slow down, to be lazy, to potter, to change speed and to pursue other interests – give yourself a Sunday. Don't short-change yourself on your health, and work yourself into an early grave; you deserve better. Enshrined in the new work ethic is that work can never be at the cost of those for whom you care: no matter how you justify the delegation of that care to others – to those you pay, or to your partner – there are elements which are non-negotiable, and the buck stops with you.

This is the other side of the equation. Alongside the new work ethic we need to assert a care ethic; at this time, it seems the more urgent and neglected. We have to reinterpret our understanding of success and achievement to include this overlooked and under-valued ethic of care. We know we need it; the driven work ethic of the eighties yuppies crumbled quickly, and by the following decade we were already fumbling after a more human formulation of fulfilment. 'Care' and 'caring' became ubiquitous words in the 'caring, sharing nineties'; we told each other to 'take care', and 'caring' popped up in corporate mission statements and slogans. But the word was bankrupted of meaning, reduced to nothing more than a vague, passive intention, and degraded by its association with the shame of dependence, that taboo of individualistic, competitive culture. We need to reassert what we instinctively know, which is that we are all interdependent, and it is in that web of dependence that we find our deepest contentment.

Integral to that is an ethic of care, and far from being passive, this is the most deeply engaged experience of our lives, because it draws so much from us. It is first and foremost about *paying attention* to another's needs and well-being. It is also about responsibility, because it is where we exercise profound moral decisions about our impact on other human beings. It is also about competence. Uniquely, it requires many different qualities from us simultaneously, from the most sensitive empathy to the most mundane of practical skills, such as preparing a meal, polishing shoes or ironing a shirt. Its defining characteristic is that while care begins with looking after ourselves, it goes beyond the self and draws attention out of ourselves towards another human being. It provides the most profound and the most fulfilling engagement – moral and emotional – of our lives, enlarging our imaginations beyond the narrow egotism and narcissism of the self to connect with others. It is quintessentially beyond the reach of the market, it cannot be incentivised or commercialised without compromise. It is rooted in a culture's deepest understanding of what it is to be human.

The great achievement of feminism in the second half of the twentieth century was to dismantle the boundaries which made care the exclusive preserve of women, and men increasingly perceive its rich emotional rewards. Individuals need the time and the support (financial and educational) to care – and government has a responsibility to ensure that these are in place, because it is the strength of those caring relationships which is the basis for a politics of well-being.

An ethic of care will prevent the emotional desiccation threatened by abdicating care to the market. Rather than pay others to care for those we love, we can find and develop in ourselves new skills to raise children, care for friends and develop the relationships which make for a strong social fabric. An ethic of care is an integral part of a democratic, egalitarian culture; care should be DIY, not something to contract out to the cheapest supplier. The provision of care should not feed off the import of low-cost labour generated by inequality which is increasingly evident in the globalisation of care. Developing countries export not just raw commodities, but their female labour to offer care – thus denying it to their own families and communities – to the highest bidder from the Gulf States or western Europe. DIY care is not a proposal for millions to leave the labour market, but a recognition that our fulfilment lies in more than one direction, that the future must be an integration of different responsibilities rather than the painful jostling for pre-eminence imposed by our work culture. Our greatest potential for personal growth comes from integration, rather than the obsessive development of one aspect of ourselves.

But the politics of well-being struggles to be heard over a cacophony of market-driven logic which insists that there is no other way, that Britain cannot afford investment in time and care, and that disorientated, isolated individuals struggling to piece together meaning and purpose in their lives are the unavoidable collateral damage of successful economic performance. With the decline of religion and political ideology, we have lost the inspirational bearings which once provided a compass towards the achievement of social progress. In its place we only have what purports to be realism, with its false promises and shabby compromises. We have narrowed our focus as a culture to one underpinned by an ethos of market efficiency, at a terrible cost to our understanding of the relationship and responsibilities of one human being to another, and of the dignity of individuals in their work.

Marx believed that the circumstances of work are the principal sources of ill- and well-being. Our jobs are making us ill, as the rising levels of stress and work-related depression reveal. And that dis-ease of humiliation and powerlessness is evident at every level of the labour market, in workplaces which emotionally groom dependence. It may manifest itself in the poor pay of a cleaner or in the brutal bullying that is part of the performance management of a City trader. Nor is it enough to argue that the plight of the latter is his or her own choice. In no other circumstances do we blame the bully's victim quite so quickly and thoughtlessly. This is not to belittle material disadvantage, which can be crippling, or growing inequality, but to argue that the psychology of exploitation is devious and pervasive in our culture, and that it insinuates its tentacles into the circumstances of even the most privileged. To understand that, we need to see more clearly what mesmerises us, and to recognise how vulnerable we are to forms of overwork which are addictive, promising the recognition, identity and chimera of control which a chaotic world rarely provides.

We need to be much more wary of organisations which have developed a fine rhetoric of sloughing off their own responsibilities while at the same time increasing those of their employees. We need to tell employers who offer meaning and purpose that we are old enough to find our own, and that all we need from them is the time to do it. We need to be much more wary of the dependency which can grow towards employers, and to develop in its place the 'inner strength' to combat their encroachments, whether through trade unions or individually. We need to challenge a rhetoric of choice which is now being used to prop up the glass ceiling. The choices we're offered amount to 'put up or shut up'. Human creativity can devise organisations which offer a better choice than that.

We're getting there; it just needs a big kick in the right direction, and in a decade we'll look back at the overwork culture as we now look back at the power-hunger, flashy wealth and shoulderpads of the eighties generation, as an emotional dead-end.

What needs to override our work ethic is a *wisdom ethic* – a deep understanding of what constitutes lasting human happiness, and the part our labour plays in it. We need to identify true freedom among the many fake versions available, and keep a shrewd eye on the fancy dress which can disguise the true power relations of the twenty-first-century labour market. These are not all things which can be taught: they are often learnt by example and by experience. Zygmunt Bauman has written of how human beings balance their need for freedom against their need for security: until the middle of the last century it was the latter which predominated, now it's the former. We love our freedom, but the challenge for the twenty-first century, says Bauman, is whether we can now *take responsibility for the responsibilities* which freedom brings. This demands much emotional wisdom and insight. It lies with us to fashion the kind of society in which people will find contentment, security and fulfilment. It lies with us to effect the political and personal change to tame technology and the global economy to meet human needs, rather than exploit human vulnerabilities.

Notes

Introduction

1 M. Jahoda, cited by John Haworth in paper for ESRC seminar on 'Work, Leisure and Wellbeing', www.haworthjt.com/well-being-esrc
2 E.F. Schumacher, cited in John Knell and Richard Reeves, 'Transforming Work', unpublished paper
3 See Global Working Families Project, Harvard University School of Public Health, www.globalworkingfamilies.org

Chapter 1: Working All Hours

1 'Working Time Regulations: Have They Made a Difference?', Chartered Institute of Personnel and Development (CIPD), January 2001
2 Robert Taylor, 'Britain's World of Work: Myths and Realities', ESRC, Swindon, 2002
3 Labour Force Survey (LFS), Office of National Statistics, 2002
4 Eurostat figures, cited in 'About Time: A New Agenda for Shaping Working Hours', TUC, London, 2002
5 Peter Robinson and Nick Burkitt, 'The Challenge of Full Employment', in N. Burkitt (ed.), *A Life's Work*, IPPR, 2001
6 'Living to Work', Chartered Institute of Personnel and Development, September 2003

Notes

7 DTI Work–Life Balance Campaign, *Management Today*, August 2002

8 'About Time', op. cit.

9 Ibid.

10 DTI Work–Life Balance Campaign, www.dti.gov.uk/work-life balance

11 'Living to Work', op. cit.

12 Reed.co.uk July 2002; also 'Living to Work', op. cit.

13 Royal and Sun Alliance survey, BBC, June 2003

14 'Real Time', ICM/*Observer* 'Precious Time' poll; similar findings in 'Living to Work', op. cit.

15 Taylor, 'Britain's World of Work', op. cit.

16 'Living to Work', op. cit.

17 Figures calculated from LFS by Paul Kent of the West Midlands Employment and Low Pay Unit, 2003

18 James Arrowsmith, 'The Struggle Over Working Time in Nineteenth- and Twentieth-Century Britain', in *Historical Studies in Industrial Relations*, no. 13, spring 2002

19 Ivana La Valle, 'Happy Families? Atypical Working Hours and its Influence on Family Life', Joseph Rowntree Foundation, 2002

20 Author's calculations, based on LFS data

21 Transport 2000, National Travel Survey

22 Study by Centre for Economics and Business Research, April 2002

23 Ibid.

24 Author's calculation, based on OECD figures

25 Karl Marx, *Selected Writings*, p.497, quoted in Arrowsmith, 'The Struggle Over Working Time in Nineteenth- and Twentieth-Century Britain', op. cit.

26 'Working Time Regulations: Have They Made a Difference?', op. cit.

27 E.P. Thompson, 'Time and Work Discipline and Industrial Capitalism', in *Customs in Common*, 1991

28 Julia Brannen, 'Lives and Time: A Sociological Journey', Thomas Coram Research Unit, Institute of Education, 2002

Notes

29 'I Want to be my Own Time Lord', *Observer*, 15 June 2003
30 Barbara Adam, *Timewatch: The Social Analysis of Time*, Polity Press, 1995
31 Theodore Zeldin, *An Intimate History of Humanity*, Sinclair-Stevenson, 1994
32 Brannen, 'Lives and Time', op. cit.

Chapter 2: All in a Day's Work

1 Alex Jones, 'About Time for Change', Work Foundation, 2003
2 Taylor, 'Britain's World of Work', op. cit.; 83 per cent of those who work long hours cited deadlines and workload as the cause
3 TUC press release, February 2003
4 Francis Green, 'It's Been a Hard Day's Night', *British Journal of Industrial Relations*, 39 (1), March 2001, pp.53–80. Green states that he checked that the answers to these questions were meaningful by comparing responses from employees with those of their line managers, and found a high correlation
5 He lists them as the Labour Force Surveys: 'Social Change and Economic Life Initiative', 1986; Workplace Industrial Relations Survey, 1990; European Surveys on Working Conditions, 1991 and 1996; 'Employment in Britain', 1992
6 Brendan Burchall, 'The Prevalence and Distribution of Job Insecurity and Work Intensification', in Burchall et al. (eds), *Job Insecurity and Work Intensification*, Routledge, 2002
7 European Working Conditions Survey, 2000
8 Cited in Burchall, 'The Prevalence and Distribution of Job Insecurity and Work Intensification', op. cit.
9 Huw Beynon et al., *Managing Employment Change: The New Realities of Work*, Oxford University Press, 2000
10 Andrew Scott, *Willing Slaves? British Workers Under Human Resource Management*, Cambridge University Press, 1994
11 Les Worrall and Cary L. Cooper, 'The Long Working Hours Culture', EBF, issue 6, summer 2001

Notes

12 Green, 'It's Been a Hard Day's Night', op. cit.

13 Max Nathan et al., 'Getting By, Not Getting On: Technology in UK Workplaces', Work Foundation, 2003

14 David Lewis, *Information Overload*, Penguin, 1999

15 Frazee, cited in Anthony Burgess et al., 'The Message Defects and Tolerance Levels of Email', working paper of Computer Science Department of Loughborough University

16 Ibid.

17 David Ladipo and Frank Wilkinson, 'More Pressure, Less Protection', in Burchall, *Job Insecurity and Work Intensification*, op. cit.

18 Cited in ibid.

19 Les Worrall and Cary L. Cooper, 'The Quality of Working Life', Institute of Management, 2001

20 Francis Green, 'The Rise and Decline of Job Insecurity', paper presented at the ESRC seminar 'Work–Life and Time in the New Economy', February 2003

21 International Survey Research, OECD, 2001

22 Taylor, 'Britain's World of Work', op. cit., p.13

23 Right Management Consultants, 'The Career–Confidence Index', www.rightcoutts.co.uk, November 2003

24 Mark Cully et al., *Britain at Work: As Depicted by the 1998 Workplace Employee Relations Survey*, Routledge, 1999

25 Green, 'The Rise and Decline of Job Insecurity', op. cit.

26 Cully, *Britain at Work*, op. cit.

27 Worrall and Cooper, 'The Long Working Hours Culture', op. cit.

28 Cited in ibid.

29 Yiannis Gabriel, *Organisations in Depth: The Psychoanalysis of Organisations*, Sage, 1999

30 Office of National Statistics

31 Learndirect Office Hours Report, March 2003

32 Ewart Keep and Jonathan Payne, 'What Can the UK Learn from the Norwegian and Finnish Experience of Attempts at Work Reorganisation?', SKOPE research paper no. 41, spring 2002

Notes

33 Cully, *Britain at Work*, op. cit.

34 'A Perfect Union: What Workers Want from Unions', TUC, July 2003; 'Living to Work', op. cit.

35 Ibid.

Chapter 3: Putting Your Heart and Soul Into it

 1 Arlie Russell Hochschild, *The Managed Heart*, University of California Press, 1983

 2 André Gorz, *Reclaiming Work*, Polity Press, 1999

 3 *Financial Times*, 5 December 2002

 4 Gorz, *Reclaiming Work*, op. cit.

 5 Marek Korczynski, *Human Resource Management in Service Work*, Palgrave/Macmillan, 2002

 6 Ibid.

 7 S.C. Eaton, cited in Irena Grugulis, 'Emotions and Aesthetics for Work and Labour', *Business & Management*, 2002/02

 8 Ibid.

 9 Cited by Ann-Marie Stagg, chair of the Call Centre Managers' Association, www.ccma.org.uk

10 Hochschild, *The Managed Heart*, op. cit., p.198

11 M. Noon and P. Blyton, cited in Grugulis, 'Emotions and Aesthetics for Work and Labour', op. cit.

12 Ibid.

13 Glen Owen, *The Times*, 28 July 2003

14 I. Menzies, 'The Functioning of Social Systems as a Defence Against Anxiety: A Report of a Study of the Nursing Service of a General Hospital', *Human Relations*, 13, 1959, pp.95–121

15 Worrall and Cooper, 'The Long Working Hours Culture', op. cit.

16 Worrall and Cooper, 'The Quality of Working Life', op. cit.

17 Michael Moynagh and Richard Worsley, 'Tomorrow's Workplace: Fulfilment or Stress?', www.tomorrowproject.net, 2001

Notes

Chapter 4: Missionary Management

1 Abraham Maslow, *Maslow on Management*, John Wiley & Sons, 1998
2 Ibid., p.8
3 Ibid., pp.20–42
4 Karen Moloney, *People Management*, 5 May 2003
5 Cited in Jayne Buxton, *Ending the Mother War, Starting the Workplace Revolution*, 1998
6 Korczynski, *Human Resource Management in Service Work*, op. cit.
7 Helen Murlis and Peggy Schubert, 'Engage Employees and Boost Performance', Hay Group working paper, www.haygroup.com, 2002
8 Gorz, *Reclaiming Work*, op. cit.
9 *New Statesman*, 5 November 2001
10 Joanne Ciulla, *The Working Life: The Promise and Betrayal of Modern Work*, Random House, 2000

Chapter 5: Government, the Hard Taskmaster

1 Anatole Kaletsky and Robin Marris, 22 May 2001, cited in Nick Timmins and Barry Cox, 'A Public Realm', *Prospect*, July 2001
2 Belinda Finlayson, 'Counting the Smiles: Morale and Motivation in the NHS', King's Fund, 2002
3 John Carvel, *Guardian*, 9 May 2003
4 'Recruitment and Retention: A Public Service Workforce for the Twenty-First Century', Audit Commission, 2002
5 'The Common Good', *Guardian*, March 2002
6 Ibid.
7 'On Target? Government by Measurement', House of Commons Public Administration Select Committee, HC 62-I, www.parliament.co.uk, July 2003
8 Minutes of evidence to the Public Administration Select Committee, 10 December 2002
9 Liberal Democrat analysis of government figures

Notes

10 *Guardian*, 20 December 2002

11 *Guardian*, 10 May 2002

12 *Observer*, 11 May 2003

13 *British Medical Association News*, March 2003

14 Liberal Democrat press release, February 2003

15 BMA briefing, 29 November 2002

16 Mary Riddell, *Observer*, 9 June 2002

17 *Guardian*, 28 February 2003

18 Paul Skidmore, 'Beyond Measure: Why Educational Assessment is Failing the Test', Demos, 2003

19 'Recruitment and Retention', op. cit.

20 'The Common Good', *Guardian*, March 2002

21 Department of Health and Office of National Statistics

22 'On Target? Government by Measurement', op. cit.

23 'Recruitment and Retention', op. cit.

24 Ibid.

25 Ibid.

26 Cited in Timmins and Cox, 'A Public Realm', op. cit.

27 'Recruitment and Retention', op. cit.

28 Cited in Timmins and Cox, 'A Public Realm', op. cit.

29 David Osborne and Ted A. Gaebler, *Reinventing Government: How the Entrepreneurial Spirit is Transforming the Public Sector*, Perseus, 1992, pp.14–15

30 P. Day and R. Klein, cited in Michael Power, *The Audit Society: Rituals of Verification*, Oxford University Press, 1997

31 'The Common Good', *Guardian*, March 2001

32 *Financial Times*, 7 June 2003

33 'Recruitment and Retention', op. cit.

34 Power, *The Audit Society*, op. cit., p.140

35 Ibid., p.135

36 John Clarke and Janet Newman, *The Managerial State: Power, Politics and Ideology in the Remaking of Social Welfare*, Sage, 1997, pp.123–4

Notes

37 Onora O'Neill, *A Question of Trust: The BBC Reith Lectures 2002*, Cambridge University Press, 2003

38 'The Common Good', *Guardian*, March 2002

39 British Medical Association survey, 15 October 2003

40 Prime Minister's speech on public sector reform, 25 January 2002

41 'The Common Good', *Guardian*, March 2002

42 Ibid.

43 Patrick Wintour, *Guardian*, 15 January 2003

Chapter 6: You're on Your Own

1 Alex Bryson and Stephen McKay, 'What About the Workers?', pp.23–48, in fourteenth report of British Social Attitudes Survey, 1997, cited in Jane Wills, *Union Futures*, Fabian Society, 2002

2 Michael White and Stephen Hill, cited in Robert Taylor, 'The Future of Work–Life Balance', ESRC, 2002

3 Ibid.

4 'The National Minimum Wage', Fourth Report of the Low Pay Commission, March 2003

5 TUC

6 Cully, *Britain at Work*, op. cit.; see also Office of National Statistics and TUC opinion poll, cited in Alex Jones, 'About Time for Change', Work Foundation, 2003

7 Stephen Aldridge, 'Social Mobility: A Discussion Paper', in *The New Economy*, IPPR, 2003

8 *Guardian*, 31 July 2003

9 'The National Minimum Wage', op. cit.

10 'Households Below Average Income 2001/2', Department of Work and Pensions, 2003, p.6; see also Low Pay Unit, www.lowpayunit.org.uk

11 New Earnings Survey, Office of National Statistics

12 Linda A. Bell and Richard B. Freeman, study for the National Bureau of Economic Research, 2001

13 Robert Reich, *The Future of Success*, Alfred A. Knopf, 2001

Notes

14 S. Harkness et al., 'Examining the Pin Money Hypothesis', *Journal of Population Economics*, 10, pp.137–58

15 Ibid.

16 Cited in Will Hutton, 'Working Capital', Work Foundation, 2002

17 'A Woman's Place', Chartered Management Institute, 2001

18 Council of Mortgage Lenders, www.cml.org.uk

19 Aldridge, 'Social Mobility', op. cit.

20 'Debt: Behind the Headlines', The Credit Card Research Group, March 2002

21 Datamonitor

22 'Debt: Behind the Headlines', op. cit.

23 'In Too Deep: CAB Clients' Experience of Debt', Citizens Advice Bureau, May 2003

24 Zygmunt Bauman, *Freedom*, Oxford University Press, 1988

25 Roland Marchand, *Creating the Corporate Soul: The Rise of Public Relations and Corporate Imagery in American Big Business*, cited in Sharon Beder, *Selling the Work Ethic*, Zed Books, 2000

26 Cully, *Britain at Work*, op. cit.

27 Ibid.

28 Tony Blair, *Financial Times*, July 1994

29 Desmond King and Mark Wickham-Jones, 'Bridging the Atlantic: The Democratic (Party) Origins of Welfare to Work', in Martin Powell (ed.), *New Labour, New Welfare State? The 'Third Way' in British Social Policy*, Policy Press, 1999

30 Tony Blair, *The Times*, 15 January 1998

31 Adrian Little, 'Rethinking Civil Society: Radical Politics and the Legitimisation of Unpaid Activities', *Contemporary Politics*, vol. 8, no. 2, 2002

32 *Daily Telegraph*, 16 October 2003

33 Michael White and Stephen Hill, cited in Taylor, 'The Future of Work–Life Balance', op. cit.

34 Dora L. Costa, National Economic Research paper, cited in Ciulla, *The Working Life*, op. cit.

Notes

35 Ronald Inglehart, *Culture Shift in Advanced Industrial Society*, Princeton, 1989

36 *Fast Company*, June 2003

37 David Brooks, *Bobos in Paradise: The New Upper Class and How They Got There*, Simon & Schuster, 2000

38 Zygmunt Bauman, *Work, Consumerism and the New Poor*, Open University Press, 1998, p.34

39 Cited in Ciulla, *The Working Life*, op. cit.

40 Cited in Beder, *Selling the Work Ethic*, op. cit.

41 Peter Berger (ed.), *The Human Shape of Work*, cited by Paul Heelas, 'Work Ethics, Soft Capitalism and the "Turn to Life" ', in Paul du Gay and Michael Pryke (eds), *Cultural Economy*, Sage, 2002

42 Ibid.

43 Michelle Harrison, 'Wellbeing 2002', Henley Centre, 2002

44 Yiannis Gabriel, 'Glass Palaces and Glass Cages: Organisations in Times of Flexible Work, Fragmented Consumption and Fragile Selves', *Ephemera*, 2003

45 Cited in Linda Holbeche, 'The Politics of Work', *People Management*, 26 March 2003

46 Judi James, 'You've Got the Look', *People Management*, 3 April 2003

Chapter 7: Keeping Body and Soul Together

1 I use the term 'care deficit' in a much broader sense than that used by academics to denote the growing shortages of recruits to employment in care services

2 Health and Safety Executive (HSE), 3 July 2002 and 11 October 2002

3 Surveys of Self-Reported Work-Related Ill-Health, HSE, SW101/02, www.hse.gov.uk

4 Ruth Wheatley, 'Taking the Strain', Institute of Management, 2000

5 Michael Rose, 'Future Tense: Are Growing Occupations More

Stressed-Out and Depressive?', ESRC Future of Work working paper no. 5, 1999

6 A.P. Smith et al., 'The Scale of Occupational Stress: A Further Analysis of the Impact of Demographic Factors and Type of Job', The Bristol Stress and Health at Work Study, HSE, London, 2000

7 Rose, 'Future Tense', op. cit.

8 Smith, 'The Scale of Occupational Stress', op. cit.

9 International Stress Management Association, November 2002

10 Smith, 'The Scale of Occupational Stress', op. cit.

11 Rose, 'Future Tense', op. cit.

12 Smith, 'The Scale of Occupational Stress', op. cit.

13 S. Stansfeld, J. Head and M. Marmot, 'Work-Related Factors and Ill-Health: The Whitehall II Study', HSE, 2000, www.hse.gov.uk/pubns/stress4.htm

14 Worrall and Cooper, 'The Quality of Working Life', op. cit.

15 Cary L. Cooper, 'Destructive Interpersonal Conflict and Bullying at Work', unpublished research for the TUC, February 2000

16 Stansfeld et al., 'The Whitehall II Study', op. cit.

17 'Trade Union Trends: Focus on Services for Injury Victims', TUC, February 2002, p.4

18 Ibid., pp.4–5

19 Ibid.

20 Cited in J. Rick et al., 'Stress: Big Issue, but What are the Problems?', Institute of Employment Studies, 1997

21 Ibid.

22 International Stress Management Association, November 2002

23 Wheatley, 'Taking the Strain', op. cit.

24 Sutherland and Cooper, cited in Jennie Grimshaw, *Employment and Health: Psychosocial Stress in the Workplace*, British Library, 1999, pp.202–4

25 Paul Landsbergis, cited in *Hazards*, TUC, July–September 2003

26 Occupational and Environmental Health 2002, cited in 'The Time of Our Lives', Amicus, 2003

Notes

27 M. Bosma et al., 'Low Job Control and Risk of Coronary Heart Disease in Whitehall II (Prospective Cohort) Study', *British Medical Journal*, vol. 314, February 1997, pp.558–65

28 Mika Kivimäki et al., 'Work Stress and Risk of Cardiovascular Mortality: Prospective Cohort Study of Industrial Employees', *British Medical Journal*, vol. 325, October 2002, p.857

29 Smith, 'The Scale of Occupational Stress', op. cit.

30 'Living to Work', op. cit.

31 Schleifer and Ley, University of Maryland, cited on the American Psychological Association website, www.apa.org/pi/wpo/niosh/abstract13.html

32 Lundberg of Stockholm University, Sweden, cited on ibid.

33 Cited in *Management Today*, October 2002

34 'Whose Life is it Anyway?', The Mental Health Foundation, April 2003

35 Office of National Statistics, *Social Trends: British Social Attitudes Survey 30*, HMSO, 2000

36 Wheatley, 'Taking the Strain', op. cit.

37 Institute of Social and Economic Research (ISER), Essex, cited by the Future Foundation

38 Stephen Jenkins and Lars Osberg, 'Nobody to Play With? The Implications of Leisure Coordination', Institute of Social and Economic Research, University of Essex, 2003, available at www.iza.org

39 J.D. Smith, *National Survey of Volunteering 1997*, Institute of Volunteering Research

40 Robert Putnam, *Bowling Alone*, Touchstone, 2000, pp.87–91

Chapter 8: The Care Deficit

1 Al Gini, *My Job, My Self*, Routledge, 2000

2 Charles Leadbeater, *Up the Down Escalator*, Viking, 2002, p.191

3 Penelope Leach, *Children First*, Penguin, 1994, p.3

Notes

4 S.A. Hewlett, 'Child Neglect in Rich Nations', UNICEF, 1993, cited in Oliver James, *They F*** You Up*, Bloomsbury, 2002

5 Michael White and Stephen Hill, cited in Taylor, 'The Future of Work–Life Balance', op. cit.

6 'Living to Work', op. cit.

7 Ibid.

8 Arlie Russell Hochschild, *Timebind: When Work Becomes Home and Home Becomes Work*, Henry Holt, 1997

9 'Delivering on Gender Equality', DTI, June 2003

10 Sandra Short, 'Time Use Data in the Household Satellite Account', Office of National Statistics, October 2000

11 'Trends in Female Employment 2002', Labour Market Trends, Office of National Statistics, November 2002, p.612

12 T. Desai et al., 'Gender and the Labour Market', in P. Gregg and J. Wadsworth (eds), *The State of Working Britain*, Manchester University Press, 1999

13 'Balancing Work and Family Life', HM Treasury and DTI, January 2003, p.8, point 2.11

14 Arlie Russell Hochschild, *The Second Shift*, Viking Penguin, 1989

15 Christine Skinner, 'Running Around in Circles: Co-ordinating Childcare, Education and Work', Joseph Rowntree Foundation/ Policy Press, 2003

16 Susan McCrae, cited in 'Raising Expectations', Daycare Trust, May 2002

17 Catherine Hakim, *Work and Lifestyle Preferences in the Twenty-First Century*, Oxford, 2000

18 DTI Work–Life Balance Campaign, *Management Today*, August 2002

19 'Living to Work', op. cit.

20 The number of women working full-time increased from 33 to 38 per cent between 1984 and 1991, but that increase has now tailed off, climbing by only 1 per cent between 1991 and 2001. 'Women in the Labour Market: Results from the Spring 2001 Labour Force Survey', *Labour Market Trends*, March 2002, pp.109–17

Notes

21 'Raising Expectations', op. cit.; see also Hakim, *Work and Lifestyle Preferences in the Twenty-First Century*, op. cit.

22 Cited in Margaret O'Brien and Ian Shemilt, 'Working Fathers: Earning and Caring', Equal Opportunities Commission, 2003, p.22

23 Department of Education and Skills research

24 'Childcare for Working Parents', House of Commons Work and Pensions Committee Report, July 2003

25 Cited in Helen Wilkinson, 'Creche Barriers', Demos, 2002

26 Ann Mooney et al., 'Childminding in the 1990s', Joseph Rowntree Foundation, 2001

27 Registered Childcare Places, Ofsted, September 2003

28 'Delivering for Children and Families', Strategy Unit Review of Childcare, 2002, www.number-10.gov.uk/su/childcare

29 Judy Wajcman, *Technofeminism*, Polity Press, 2004

30 Peter Moss, 'Beyond Caring: The Case for Reforming the Childcare and Early Years Workforce', Daycare Trust policy paper, April 2003

31 June Statham and Ann Mooney, 'Around the Clock: Childcare Services at Atypical Times', Joseph Rowntree Foundation/Policy Press, 2003

32 'Measuring the Impact of Pre-School on Children's Social/ Behavioural Development Over the Pre-School Period', Technical Paper 8b, Effective Provision of Pre-School Education Project (EPPE), Institute of Education/Department of Education and Skills, March 2003

33 Interview with the author, 2003

34 Study of Early Child Care and Youth Development, National Institute of Child Health and Development, July 2003, www.nichd.nih.gov

35 Interview with the author

36 John Ermisch and Marco Francesconi, 'The Effect of Parents' Employment on Children's Lives', Joseph Rowntree Foundation/ Family Policy Studies Centre, 2001

37 Interviewed by Rebecca Abrams, *Daily Telegraph*, 7 June 2003

38 James, *They F*** You Up*, op. cit.

39 Liz Kendall and Lisa Harker, 'An Equal Start', IPPR, 2003

40 Fisher, McCulloch and Gershuny, 1999, cited in O'Brien and Shemilt, 'Working Fathers', op. cit., p.22

41 Bianchi, cited in ibid.

42 Sandberg and Hofferth, cited in ibid.

43 Future Foundation, www.futurefoundation.net/release_families.doc

44 Shirley Dex, 'Families and Work in the Twenty-First Century', Joseph Rowntree Foundation/Policy Press, 2003

45 Martin Carnoy, *Sustaining the New Economy: Work, Family and Community in the Information Age*, Russell Sage, 2000, p.110

46 Cited by Lorna McKee, School of Management, University of Aberdeen, at Tedworth Seminar, October 2003

47 Future Foundation, www.futurefoundation.net/release_families.doc

48 The Campaign for Learning, research commissioned by the Department of Education and Skills, 2003

49 A. Bell and I. La Valle, cited in Dex, 'Families and Work in the Twenty-First Century', op. cit.

50 Census 2001, Office of National Statistics; see also Age Concern, www.ace.org.uk/AgeConcern/information

51 'Without Us?', Carers UK, 2002

52 Figures compiled by Carers UK from General Household Survey and J. Maher and H. Green, 'Carers 2000', Office of National Statistics, 2000

53 'Caring Costs', Carers' National Association, 1996

54 Judith Phillips, Miriam Bernard and Minda Chittenden, 'Juggling Work and Care: The Experiences of Working Carers of Older Adults', Joseph Rowntree Foundation/Policy Press, 2002

55 'Married to the Job', Chartered Institute of Personnel and Development, July 2001

56 Susan McCrae, 'Careers and Motherhood Still Don't Mix', cited by One Plus One, January 2002, www.oneplusone.org

Notes

57 Elsa Ferri and Kate Smith, 'Parenting in the 1990s', Family Policy Studies Centre/Joseph Rowntree Foundation, 1996

58 La Valle, 'Happy Families', op. cit.

59 Cited in Michael Kimmel, *The Gendered Society*, Oxford University Press, 2000, p.115

60 Davina Chaplin, cited in Maggie Jackson, *What's Happening to Home? Balancing Work, Life and Refuge in the Information Age*, Sorin Books, 2002

61 'Living to Work', op. cit.

62 Wheatley, 'Taking the Strain', op. cit.

Chapter 9: An Unfinished Revolution

1 Man-yee Kan, 'Gender Asymmetry in the Division of Domestic Labour', cited in 'Who Does the Housework?', Institute of Social and Economic Research, July 2001

2 Ferri and Smith, 'Parenting in the 1990s', op. cit.

3 La Valle, 'Happy Families', op. cit.

4 'Women's Income Over the Lifetime', ONS Women's Unit, Cabinet Office, 2000

5 Fawcett Society

6 Jonathan Gershuny, presentation to the Cabinet Office, 2003

7 *Britain 2000: The Official Yearbook of the United Kingdom*, ONS, 2000

8 Labour Force Survey, autumn 2002

9 Cited in Buxton, *Ending the Mother War*, op. cit.

10 *Guardian*, 2 July 2003

11 Bianchi, 2000, cited in O'Brien and Shemilt, 'Working Fathers', op. cit.

12 www.mumsnet.com

13 Fisher, McCulloch and Gershuny, cited in O'Brien and Shemilt, 'Working Fathers', op. cit.

14 Ibid.

15 Ibid.

Notes

16 Ibid.

17 Anthony Burgess, *Fatherhood Reclaimed: The Making of the Modern Father*, Random House, 1997

18 Richard Reeves, 'Dad's Army', Industrial Society, 2000

19 Ferri and Smith, cited in O'Brien and Shemilt, 'Working Fathers', op. cit.; see also La Valle, 'Happy Families', op. cit.

20 Reeves, 'Dad's Army', op. cit.

21 Patricia Hewitt, 'About Time', speech to TUC conference, 2002

22 Alison Maitland, *Financial Times*, 17 June 2003

23 Kimmel, *The Gendered Society*, op. cit., pp.114–15

24 Ibid., p.267

25 'Balancing Work and Family Life', DTI/HM Treasury, 2003

Chapter 10: In Our Own Time

1 Richard Sennett, *The Corrosion of Character: Personal Consequences of Work in the New Capitalism*, Norton, 1998, p.91

2 *Guardian* magazine, 13 September 2003

3 Will Hutton, *Observer*, 16 June 2003

Chapter 11: The Politics of Well-Being

1 Families and Work Institute, 'Feeling Overworked: When Work Becomes Too Much', New York, 2001. www.familiesandwork.org

2 Ibid.

3 Ibid.

4 Australian government figures, available at http://www.eowa.gov

5 Susan Milner, 'An Ambiguous Reform: The Jospin Government and the Thirty-Five-Hour-Week Laws', *Modern and Contemporary France*, vol. 10, no. 3, 2002, pp.339–51

6 Cited in M. Taylor and L. Taylor, *What are Children For?*, Short Books, 2003

7 DTI survey with Reed.co.uk, January 2003

8 After the Netherlands cut the working week to thirty-nine hours, the country experienced strong job growth

Notes

9 'Working Time Regulations: Have They Made a Difference?',
   Chartered Institute of Personnel and Development, January 2001
10 Catherine Barnard et al., 'The Use and Necessity of Article 18.1
   (b)(i) of the Working Time Directive in the United Kingdom',
   unpublished EU-commissioned research, December 2002
11 Peter Moss and Fred Deven, 'Parental Leave: Progress or Pitfall?',
   CBGS, Brussels, 1999
12 House of Commons report on childcare, July 2003
13 Richard Layard, 'What is Happiness? Are we Getting Happier?', LSE
   lecture, 2003

Bibliography

Ackers, P., Smith C. and Smith P. (eds). *The New Workplace and Trade Unionism*. Thomson Learning, 1995

Adam, B. *Timewatch: The Social Analysis of Time*. Polity Press, 1995

Anderson, P. and Mann, N. *Safety First: The Making of New Labour*. Granta, 1997

Andresky Fraser, J. *White-Collar Sweatshop*. Norton, 2001

Arrowsmith, J. 'The Struggle Over Working Time in Nineteenth- and Twentieth Century Britain'. *Historical Studies in Industrial Relations* 13, spring 2002

Audit Commission. 'Recruitment and Retention'. 2002

Ball, C. *The Time of Our Lives*. Amicus, 2003

Bauman, Z. *Freedom*. Oxford University Press, 1988

Bauman, Z. *Globalisation: The Human Consequences*. Polity Press, 1998

Bauman, Z. *Work, Consumerism and the New Poor*. Open University Press, 1998

Bauman, Z. *Liquid Love: On the Frailty of Human Bonds*. Polity Press, 2003

Beck, U. *The Brave New World of Work*. Polity Press, 2000

Beder, S. *Selling the Work Ethic*. Zed Books, 2000

Beynon, H. et al. *Managing Employment Change: The New Realities of Work*. Oxford University Press, 2000

Bolman, L. and Deal, T. *Leading with Soul*. Jossey Bass Wiley, 2001

Bibliography

Bosma, H., Marmot, M., Hemingway, H., Nicholson, A., Brunner, E. and Stansfeld, S. 'Low Job Control and Risk of Coronary Heart Disease in Whitehall II (Prospective Cohort) Study'. *British Medical Journal*, vol. 314, February 1997, pp.558–65

Boyle, D. *Authenticity: Brands, Fakes, Spin and the Lust for Real Life.* Flamingo, 2003

Brannen, J. *Lives and Time: A Sociological Journey.* Institute of Education, 2002

Brannen, J., Lewis, S., Nilsen, A. and Smithson, J. *Young Europeans, Work and Family: Futures in Transition.* Routledge, 2002

Burchall, B. et al. (eds). *Job Insecurity and Work Intensification: Flexibility and the Changing Boundaries of Work.* Joseph Rowntree Foundation/York Publishing, 1999

Burchall, B., Ladipo, D. and Wilkinson, F. (eds). *Job Insecurity and Work Intensification.* Routledge, 2002

Burgess, A. *Fatherhood Reclaimed: The Making of the Modern Father.* Random House, 1997

Burgess, A. et al. 'The Message Defects and Tolerance Levels of Email'. Working paper of the Computer Science Department, Loughborough University

Burggraf, S. *The Feminine Economy and Economic Man.* Perseus, 1997

Burkitt, N. (ed.). *A Life's Work.* IPPR, 2001

Buxton, J. *Ending the Mother War, Starting the Workplace Revolution.* Macmillan, 1998

Cameron, D. *Good to Talk?.* Sage, 2000

Cameron, D. 'The Tyranny of Nicespeak'. *New Statesman*, 5 November 2001

Carers UK: 'Without Us?'. 2002

Carnoy, M. *Sustaining the New Economy: Work, Family and Community in the Information Age.* Russell Sage, 2000

Chartered Institute of Personnel and Development. 'Working Time Regulations. Have They Made a Difference?'. January 2001

Chartered Institute of Personnel and Development. 'Married to the Job'. July 2001

Bibliography

Chartered Institute of Personnel and Development. 'Living to Work'. September 2003

Ciulla, J. *The Working Life: The Promise and Betrayal of Modern Work.* Random House, 2000

Clarke, J. and Newman, J. *The Managerial State: Power, Politics and Ideology in the Remaking of Social Welfare.* Sage, 1997

Cooper, C. et al. *Organisational Stress.* Sage, 2001

Coupland, D. *Microserfs.* HarperCollins, 1996

Coyle, D. *Getting the Measure of the New Economy.* iSociety, 2002

Crompton, R. 'Class, Gender and Work–Life Balance'. ESRC seminar series, 2003. http://www.lse.ac.uk/collections/worklife/

Cully, M. et al. *Britain at Work: As Depicted by the 1998 Workplace Employee Relations Survey.* Routledge, 1999

Daly, M. and Rake, K. *Gender and the Welfare State.* Polity Press, 2003

Daycare Trust. 'Raising Expectations'. 2002

Department of Trade and Industry's Work–Life Balance Campaign and *Management Today* Survey. DTI, 2002. Available at http://164.36.164.20/work-lifebalance/press300802.html

Dex, S. 'Families and Work in the Twenty-First Century'. Joseph Rowntree Foundation/Policy Press, 2003

Donkin, R. *Blood, Sweat and Tears.* Texere, 2001

Doyle, J. 'New Community or New Slavery?'. Work Foundation, 2001

Earls, J. 'From Adversarial to Aspirational: A New Agenda for Trade Unions?'. www.unions21.org.uk

Ehrenreich, B. *Nickel and Dimed.* Granta, 2002

Ermisch, J. and Francesconi, M. 'The Effect of Parents' Employment on Children's Lives'. Joseph Rowntree Foundation/Family Policy Studies Centre, 2001

Ferri, E. and Smith, K. 'Parenting in the 1990s'. Joseph Rowntree Foundation/Family Policy Studies Centre, 1996

Finlayson, B. 'Counting the Smiles: Morale and Motivation in the NHS'. King's Fund, 2002

Frank, T. *One Market Under God.* Secker & Warburg, 2001

Bibliography

Franks, S. *Having None of it: Women, Men and the Future of Work*. Granta, 1999

Gabriel, Y. and Lang, T. *The Unmanageable Consumer*. Sage, 1995

Gabriel, Y. *Organisations in Depth: The Psychoanalysis of Organisations*. Sage, 1999

Gabriel, Y. 'Glass Palaces and Glass Cages: Organisations in Times of Flexible Work, Fragmented Consumption and Fragile Selves'. *Ephemera*, vol. 3, no. 3, 2003, pp.166–84. http://users.wbs.warwick.ac.uk/ephemera/ephmeraweb/journal/3-3/3-3gabriel.pdf

Galinsky, E. *Ask the Children*. HarperCollins, 1999

Galinsky, E., Kim, S. and Bond, J. *Feeling Overworked: When Work becomes Too Much*. Families and Work Institute, New York, 2001

Gershuny, J. *Changing Times: Work and Leisure in Post-Industrial Society*. Oxford University Press, 2000

Gini, A. *My Job, My Self*. Routledge, 2000

Gorz, A. *Reclaiming Work*. Polity Press, 1999

Gray, J. *False Dawn: The Delusions of Global Capitalism*. Granta, 1998

Green, F. 'It's Been a Hard Day's Night: The Concentration and Intensification of Work in Late-Twentieth-Century Britain'. *British Journal of Industrial Relations*, 39 (1), March 2001, pp.53–80

Green, F. 'Rise and Decline of Job Insecurity'. Paper for ESRC seminar series, February 2003. http://www.lse.ac.uk/collections/worklife/

Gregg, P. and Wadsworth, J. (eds). *The State of Working Britain*. Manchester University Press, 1999

Grimshaw, J. *Employment and Health: Psychosocial Stress in the Workplace*. British Library, 1999

Grugulis, I. 'Emotions and Aesthetics for Work and Labour'. *Business & Management*, 2002/02

Hakim, C. *Work and Lifestyle Preferences in the Twenty-First Century*. Oxford, 2000

Hanauer, C. *The Bitch in the House*. HarperCollins, 2002

Handy, C. *The Empty Raincoat*. Random House, 1994

Handy, C. *The Hungry Spirit*. Arrow, Random House, 1997

Bibliography

Harkness, S. et al. 'Examining the Pin Money Hypothesis'. *Journal of Population Economics*, 10, pp.137–58

HSE. Surveys of Self-Reported Work-Related Ill-Health (SWI90 and SWI01/02). Available at http://www.hse.gov.uk/statistics/pdf/swi05.pdf

Heelas, P. *The New Age Movement*. Blackwell, 1996

Heelas, P. 'Work Ethics, Soft Capitalism and the "Turn to Life" ', in du Gay, P. and Pryke, M. (eds). *Cultural Economy*. Sage, 2002

HM Treasury and DTI. 'Balancing Work and Family Life'. HMSO, 2003

Hewitt, P. *About Time*. Rivers Oram Press, 1993

Heymann, J. *Families on the Edge*. Oxford University Press, forthcoming

Hochschild, A. *The Managed Heart*. University of California Press, 1983

Hochschild, A. *The Second Shift*. Viking Penguin, 1989

Hochschild, A. *Timebind: When Work Becomes Home and Home Becomes Work*. Henry Holt, 1997

Hochschild, A. *The Commercialisation of Intimate Life*. University of California, 2003

House of Commons, Public Administration Select Committee. 'On Target? Government by Measurement'. 2003

House of Commons, Work and Pensions Committee Report. 'Childcare for Working Parents'. July 2003

Houston, D. and Waumsley, J. 'Attitudes to Flexible Working and Family Life'. Joseph Rowntree Foundation/Policy Press, 2003

Hutton, W. *The World We're in*. Little, Brown, 2002

Hyman, J. et al. 'Balancing Work and Life: Not Just a Matter of Time Flexibility'. Paper presented at Work, Employment and Society Conference, Nottingham, 2001

Inglehart, R. *Culture Shift in Advanced Industrial Society*. Princeton, 1989

Jackson, M. *What's Happening to Home? Balancing Work, Life and Refuge in the Information Age*. Sorin Books, 2002

James, O. *Britain on the Couch*. Century, 1997

James, O. *They F*** You Up*. Bloomsbury, 2002

Jenkins, S. and Osberg, L. 'Nobody to Play With? The Implications of

Bibliography

Leisure Coordination'. IZA discussion paper, Bonn, 2003. Available at www.iza.org

Jones, A. 'About Time for Change'. Work Foundation, 2003

Keep, E. and Payne, J. 'What Can the UK Learn from the Norwegian and Finnish Experience of Attempts at Work Reorganisation?'. SKOPE research paper no. 41, spring 2002

Kellaway, L. *Sense and Nonsense in the Office*. Prentice Hall, 2000

Kendall, L. and Harker, L. 'An Equal Start'. IPPR, 2003

Kimmel, M. *The Gendered Society*. Oxford University Press, 2000

King, D. and Wickham-Jones, M. 'Bridging the Atlantic: The Democratic (Party) Origins of Welfare to Work', in Powell, M. (ed.). *New Labour, New Welfare State?*. Policy Press, 1999

Kivimäki, M., Leino-Arjas, P., Luukkonen, R., Riihimäki, H., Vahtera, J. and Kirjonen, J. 'Work Stress and Risk of Cardiovascular Mortality: Prospective Cohort Study of Industrial Employees'. *British Medical Journal*, vol. 325, October 2002

Klein, N. *No Logo*. HarperCollins, 2000

Knell, J. 'Most Wanted: The Quiet Birth of the Free Worker'. Industrial Society, 2000

Knell, J. and Reeves, R. 'Transforming Work'. Unpublished paper

Kodz, J., Harper, H. and Dench, S. 'Work–Life Balance: Beyond the Rhetoric'. Institute of Employment Studies, 2002

Kodz, J. et al. 'Breaking the Long Hours Culture'. Institute of Employment Studies, 1998

Korczynski, M. *Human Resource Management in Service Work*. Palgrave/ Macmillan, 2002

Kunde, J. *Corporate Religion*. Prentice Hall, 2000

Ladipo, D. and Mankelow, R. 'Can Managers Still Rely on the Loyalty of Their Workforce?'. Unpublished paper

Landsbergis, P. 'Don't Go Breaking My Heart'. *Hazards*, no. 83 (July–September 2003)

Lane, R. *The Loss of Happiness in Market Democracies*. Yale University Press, 2000

Bibliography

La Valle, I. et al. 'Happy Families? Atypical Working Hours and its Influence on Family Life'. Joseph Rowntree Foundation, 2002

Layard, R. 'Happiness: Has Social Science Got a Clue?' Lionel Robbins Memorial Lectures, London School of Economics, 3, 4 and 5 March 2003

Leach, P. *Children First*. Penguin, 1994

Leadbeater, C. *Up the Down Escalator*. Viking, 2002

Lewis, D. *Information Overload: Practical Strategies for Surviving in Today's Workplace*. Penguin, 1999

Lewis, S., Rapoport, R. and Gambles, R. 'Reflections on the Integration of Paid Work and the Rest of Life'. Unpublished paper, 2003

Lewis, S. 'Sense of Entitlement to Support the Reconciliation of Employment and Family Life'. Holt, H. and Thaulow, I., *The Role of Companies in Reconciling Working Life and Family Life*. Copenhagen, 1996

Little, A. 'Rethinking Civil Society'. *Contemporary Politics*, vol. 8, no. 2, 2002

Lundberg, U. 'Repetitive Work Stress, Muscle Tension and Musculo-skeletal Disorders', in *Conference Abstracts for Work, Stress, and Health '99: Organization of Work in a Global Economy*. American Psychological Association, 1999. Available at http://www.apa.org/pi/wpo/niosh/abstract13.html

Marx, K. *Selected Writings*, cited in Arrowsmith, J. 'The Struggle Over Working Time in Nineteenth- and Twentieth-Century Britain'. *Historical Studies in Industrial Relations*, no. 13, spring 2002, pp.83–117

Maslow, A. *Maslow on Management*. John Wiley & Sons, 1998

Menzies, I. 'The Functioning of Social Systems as a Defence Against Anxiety: A Report of a Study of the Nursing Service of a General Hospital'. *Human Relations*, 13, 1959

Micklethwait, J. and Wooldridge, A. *The Witch Doctors: What the Management Gurus are Saying, Why it Matters and How to Make Sense of it*. Heinemann, 1997

Mooney, A. 'Childminding in the 1990s'. Joseph Rowntree Foundation, 2001

Bibliography

Moynagh, M. and Worsley, R. 'Tomorrow's Workplace: Fulfilment or Stress?'. www.tomorrowproject.net, 2001

Murlis, H. and Schubert, P. 'Engage Employees and Boost Performance'. Hay Group working paper, 2002. www.haygroup.com

National Travel Survey. Transport 2000. Available from http://www.transport2000.org.uk/factsandfigures/Facts.asp

O'Brien, M. and Shemilt, I. 'Working Fathers: Earning and Caring'. Equal Opportunities Commission, 2003

Office of National Statistics. *Social Trends: British Social Attitudes Survey 30.* HMSO, 2000

O'Neill, O. *A Question of Trust: The BBC Reith Lectures 2003.* Cambridge University Press, 2003

Osborne, D. and Gaebler, T. *Reinventing Government: How the Entrepreneurial Spirit is Transforming the Public Sector.* Perseus, 1992

Pearson, A. *I Don't Know How She Does It.* Chatto & Windus, 2002

Peters, T. *In Search of Excellence.* HarperCollins, 1995

Peters, T. *Brand You 50: Reinventing Work.* Alfred A. Knopf, 1999

Phillips, J. Bernard, M. and Chittenden, M. 'Juggling Work and Care'. Joseph Rowntree Foundation/Policy Press, 2002

Powell, M. (ed.). *New Labour, New Welfare State? The 'Third Way' in British Social Policy.* Policy Press, 1999

Power, M. *The Audit Society: Rituals of Verification.* Oxford University Press, 1997

Public Administration Select Committee. 'Public Service Ethos'. HMSO, 2003

Putnam, R. *Bowling Alone.* Touchstone, 2000

Rake, K. 'Women's Income Over the Lifetime'. ONS Women's Unit, Cabinet Office, 2000

Rapoport, R. et al. *Beyond Work–Family Balance: Advancing Gender Equity and Workplace Performance.* John Wiley & Sons, 2002

Reeves, R. 'Mothers Versus Men'. Industrial Society, 2000

Reeves, R. *Happy Mondays.* Pearson Educational, 2001

Reeves, R. 'Dad's Army'. Industrial Society, 2002

Bibliography

Reich, R. *The Future of Success*. Alfred A. Knopf, 2001

Rick, J., Hillage, J., Honey, S. and Perryman, S. 'Stress: Big Issue, but What are the Problems?'. Institute of Employment Studies, Brighton, 1997

Rose, M. 'Employee Skill, Occupation and Work Involvement'. Future of Work Programme working paper no. 1, ESRC, 1999

Rose, M. 'Future Tense: Are Growing Occupations More Stressed-Out and Depressive?'. Future of Work Programme working paper no. 5, ESRC, 2000

Sammons, P. et al. 'Measuring the Impact of Pre-School on Children's Social/Behavioural Development Over the Pre-School Period'. The Effective Provision of Pre-School Education Project, Institute of Education, 2003

Scase, R. *Living in the Corporate Zoo*. Capstone, 2002

Schleifer, L., Ley, R. and Spalding, T. 'Job Stress, Psychophysiological Mechanisms and Musculoskeletal Disorders: Preliminary Results'. Abstract available on American Psychological Association site at: www.apa.org/pi/wpo/niosh/abstract13.html

Schor, J. *The Overworked American: The Unexpected Decline of Leisure*. Basic Books, 1991

Schor, J. *The Overspent American*. Basic Books, 1998

Scott, A. *Willing Slaves? British Workers Under Human Resource Management*. Cambridge University Press, 1994

Sennett, R. *The Corrosion of Character: Personal Consequences of Work in the New Capitalism*. Norton, 1998

Skinner, C. 'Running Around in Circles: Co-ordinating Childcare, Education and Work'. Joseph Rowntree Foundation/Policy Press, 2003

Smith, A.P., Brice, C., Collins, A., Matthews, V. and McNamara, R. 'The Scale of Occupational Stress: A Further Analysis of the Impact of Demographic Factors and Type of Job'. HSE, 2000

Smith, A.P., Wadsworth, E., Johal, S.S., Davey Smith, G. and Peters, T. 'The Scale of Occupational Stress'. The Bristol Stress and Health at Work Study, HSE, 2000

Bibliography

Smith, J.D. National Survey of Volunteering. Institute of Volunteering Research, 1997. Available at http://www.ivr.org.uk/nationalsurvey.htm

Stansfeld, S., Head, J. and Marmot, M. 'Work Related Factors and Ill-Health: The Whitehall II Study'. HSE, 2000

Statham, J. and Mooney, A. 'Around the Clock: Childcare Services at Atypical Times'. Joseph Rowntree Foundation/Policy Press, 2003

Strategy Unit Review of Childcare. 'Delivering for Families and Children'. www.number-10.gov.uk/su/childcare, 2002

Strategy Unit: 'Life Satisfaction: State of Knowledge and Implications for Government'. www.number-10.gov.uk/su/lifesatisfaction, 2002

Sutherland, V. and Cooper, C. *Understanding Stress*. Chapman & Hall, 1990

Taylor, L. and Taylor, M. *What are Children For?*. Short Books, 2003

Taylor, P., Hyman, J., Mulvey, G. and Bain, P. 'Work Organisation, Control and the Experience of Work in Call Centres'. *Work, Employment and Society*, 16(1), 2002, pp.133–50

Taylor, R. 'Britain's World of Work: Myths and Realities'. ESRC, 2002

Taylor, R. 'The Future of Work–Life Balance'. ESRC, 2002

Thompson, E.P. 'Time, Work-Discipline and Industrial Capitalism', in *Customs in Common*. Merlin, 1991

Thompson, P. and Warhurst, C. (eds). *Workplaces of the Future*. Palgrave/Macmillan, 1998

Timmins, N. and Cox, B. 'A Public Realm', *Prospect*, July 2001

Toynbee, P. *Hard Work: Life in Low Pay Britain*. Bloomsbury, 2003

Trades Union Congress. 'About Time: A New Agenda for Shaping Working Hours'. TUC, 2002

Trades Union Congress. 'Focus on Services for Injury Victims'. TUC, 2002

Turner, A. *Just Capital*. Macmillan, 2001

Wajcman, J. *Managing Like a Man*. Polity Press, 1998

Watson, T. *In Search of Management*. Thomson Learning, 1994

Wheatley, R. 'Taking the Strain: A Survey of Managers and Workplace Stress'. Institute of Management, 2000

Bibliography

White, M., Hill, S, McGovern, P., Mills, C. and Smeaton, D. 'High Performance Management Practices, Working Hours and Work–Life Balance'. *British Journal of Industrial Relations*, vol. 41, no. 2, pp.175–96

Wilkinson, H. 'Creche Barriers'. Demos, 2002

Wills, J. 'Union Futures'. Fabian Society, 2002

The Work Foundation. 'Working Capital'. 2002

Worrall, L. and Cooper, C. 'The Long Working Hours Culture'. EBF, issue 6, summer 2001

Worrall, L. and Cooper, C. 'The Quality of Working Life'. Institute of Management, 2001

Zeldin, T. *An Intimate History of Humanity*. Sinclair-Stevenson, 1994

Index

Index

Index

Index

Index

Index

internet 46: email correspondence 41, 42–4, 55; increase in volume of information made available 40

Isherwood, Kathy 100, 111

ISS 11, 13, 14, 274–5

Italy 18, 58

Jackson, Maggie: *What's Happening to Home* 245

James, Oliver 228

Japan 224

job insecurity 52–6, 189; fear of losing job 52–3, 54; and intensification of desire to control 55–6; white-collar and blue-collar workers compared 53

job satisfaction xxii, 10–11, 147, 185–6

Joseph Rowntree Foundation study 236

Joseph Rowntree Report on Job Insecurity and Intensification 30, 48

Jospin, Lionel 304

just-in-time working 32, 35–6

Kaletsky, Anatole 121

Keep, Ewart 57, 58

Kellaway, Lucy 82, 116–17

Kimmel, Michael: *The Gendered Society* 264, 266–7

Labour government 150; and public sector reforms 130–8, 142, 190; welfare-to-work proposals and new work ethic 160–4

Ladipo, David 48

Lane, Robert: *The Loss of Happiness in Market Democracies* 317–18

Lasch, Christopher 242

Layard, Richard 318

Leach, Penelope 226–7; *Children First* 210

Leadbeater, Charles 209; *Up the Down Escalator* 73–4

learndirect 57

leisure time 202

Lewis, David: *Information Overload* 40

Lindley, Elizabeth 142–3

Lippincott, Kristen 165

Little, Adrian 164

Little, Alan 80–1

Lloyds TSB: Work Options programme 294–5

local government 120, 129

lone parents 162–3

long hours 7–15, 189; correlation between job insecurity and 53; as determinant of success 55; and high salaries 148; impact on relationships 200– 1, 209, 210–11, 236–7; link with low pay 15, 148; and low productivity 56–7, 59; and overtime pay 149; public sector 120, 121; and stress 188, 189; and women 221

Louis, Nicole 107

low-paid, the 150, 157–8, 162

low-skill labour 11–14

lunch 'hour' 10

Luther, Martin 166

McKinsey's 297

Mahon, Simon 49, 50–1

Index

Index

Index

Index

Play is the Medicine Man

You're not designed for office life.

You're not designed to just sit there.

You're a hunter-gatherer, dammit.

That urge to get out there goes back a long way.

You need to feel the four winds.

To tell stories around a shared camp-fire.

To see the stars that will be famous for more than 15 minutes.

To leave the hubbub, humdrum and hoo-ha behind.

To listen to the stream trickle on its way.

To go to places 4x4's only get to in TV commercials.

To put some distance between you and your work.

To forget everything for a while.

To make some molehills out of mountains.

Play is best when not done to a deadline,

nor does it require a finish line.

Play is a multivitamin. Play is a de-tox. Play is head yoga.

Play is the natural enemy of stress.

Play is good. Play is great. Play is brilliant.

Play is splashing in puddles, climbing mountains,

and riding across them.

Play is juvenile, pointless and dumb.

And frankly, all the better for it.

Work is complicated. Play is simple.

Summer's coming. Go play.

Women's T-shirts

All our t-shirts are also available as blanks. They cost £17.50 and come in all our different colours and sizes. If your band, club, university or society etc. would like to print on our organic blanks, just give us a call for a price.

Index

Welch, Jack 110, 115, 198

welfare-to-work policies 160, 161, 163, 172

well-being, politics of 300, 301–25

West Dorset Hospitals NHS 193, 300

Whelham, Diana 122–3

Whitbread plc 49

White, Michael 147

Whitehall Study 188–9, 190

Whyte, William: *The Organisation Man* 167, 172

Wilkinson, Frank 48

Willans, Barry 192

Willis, Martin 121–2

Wilson, Sloan: *The Man in the Gray Flannel Suit* 167

'winner-takes-all' culture 151

Winsper, Kay 94, 95

wisdom ethic 324

women: and career progression 248; challenge of separation between public and private lives 217; delay in having children 248; demand for emotional skills of in labour market 84; and division of labour 216; and 'double shift' 246–7, 250–1, 257; and emotional labour 72–3; in employment 148, 220, 246, 267, 306; employment rate 217–18; and feminist agenda for workplace 251–2; gap in pay between men and 261; increase in 'timelessness' by flow of women into labour market 17; in information technology 297; non-recognition of female economy 216–17, 218; and part-time work 222, 247, 255, 311; and pay 151–2; personal experiences of overwork culture 252–7; and service sector 72–3; shift in employment patterns of 215–16; shift of labour from home to workplace 215–16; under-representation at top levels of professions 248–50; and 'work–life' balance 212–15; working hours 10

Women and Equality Unit 217

work ethic xxiii, 22, 112, 159–64, 172–3, 179, 207, 250, 313; alternative 320–1; and Labour Party 160; and Labour's welfare-to-work proposals 160–3; Protestant 160, 167, 168; and United States 168; and work as vocation 165–72

Work Foundation 25, 296

work intensification 28–30, 83; effect on children 231; company example 32–7; and 'functional flexibility' 31; and increased competition and de-industrialisation 36–7; and information technology 37–45; and need for competitiveness 47–8; reducing of 'porosity' 31; and stock market 48–9; and stress 187–8; surveys 29–30

work–life balance 212–15, 237, 240, 284–5, 295; and fathers 262–3; government campaign 298, 309; pioneering schemes by companies 294–5; and trade unions 285–6, 289

Index

P.S.

Ideas,
interviews
& features ...

Questioning the World

Louise Tucker talks to Madeleine Bunting

What did you want to be when you grew up? Have you always wanted to be a journalist and writer?

I first wanted to be a teacher, but after eight months teaching as a volunteer in Sri Lanka at 19 I switched tack and decided I wanted to write. I had too many questions about the world which I thought I'd only get a chance to answer, or even keep asking, if I was a writer. Once at university I decided the writing should be as a journalist first.

Did you always have a strong sense of social justice as expressed in the book? How did your background and family inform this?

I don't think I did grow up with a strong sense of social justice – I was very disturbed as a teenager by suffering and how that could be accommodated with the strongly Catholic upbringing I had. But my preoccupation became the issue of why people suffer, why might an all-powerful God allow them to suffer and whether there were any redeeming aspects of the experience of suffering – these are spiritual questions. Gradually at university and at the beginning of my working life I gained a political perspective, and it was at that point that I began to engage with the social justice issues on which I now write.

When writing your first book (*The Model Occupation*) did you find the transition from journalism to book-writing difficult?
I expected to find it much harder than I did. Of course there were tough patches – usually around questions of self-doubt, such as could I pull it off? – but the actual nuts and bolts of research, writing, revising come very easily to me and I loved being totally in charge of my work.

Which writers or journalists have most influenced your own work?
I'm always inspired by the work of Zygmunt Bauman. His mind is enormous, and his breadth of thought and intellectual scale always leave me awestruck. A sociologist, he knits together ideas from several academic disciplines with astonishing insight into the predicaments of our age. I think he is also a man of great humanity and his quest for understanding is always illuminated by a wonderful compassion. As if those many qualities were not enough, he is a man of great humility and personal charm; now, nearly 80, he is prolific, writing a book a year in his house in Leeds where he has lived since he left his home country Poland in the late sixties.

The inspiration for this book was, you say, the emails you used to receive as a *Guardian* columnist, but was there anything in your ▶

❛ At the heart of this book is my own personal experience of trying to combine motherhood and work. ❜

LIFE
at a Glance

BORN

19 March 1964, Westow,
North Yorkshire

EDUCATED

Convent of the
Assumption, Richmond,
North Yorkshire, 1974–80;
Brighton, Hove, Sussex VI
Form College, 1980–83;
History MA, Cambridge
University, 1983–6;
postgraduate fellowship,
Harvard University,
1986–7.

JOBS

Investor's Chronicle,
1986–7; Brook
Independent Television
Company, 1987–8;
Guardian, 1988–

LIVES

In Hackney, East London
with her husband and
three children.

◀ own life or those of your friends that inspired you?

As I write in my introduction, at the heart of this book is my own personal experience of trying to combine motherhood and work and the re-evaluation of my own professional aspirations that that prompted. I set out to write the book because there was a clear set of questions in my mind about the place of work in the lives of myself and many of the people around me. I wanted to try and answer them.

How long did it take to write the book, and did you have to compromise your own work–life balance to finish it?

The book took a year. I worked very hard four days a week from 9.30 to 6 p.m. I was very strict about keeping to those times – and the kids made sure I did: my son would appear in my study on the dot of 6 p.m. I think I suffered from the work intensification rather than long hours. It was very tiring as I tried to absorb and digest a huge range of material across many academic disciplines, many non-academic sources and the wide-ranging interviews. I started the book when my youngest child was seven months old, and looking back I remember being absolutely exhausted on frequent occasions.

Full-time workers in Britain have the longest hours in Europe. How did you manage a home, children, a job as well as writing the book?

Combining a job and writing a book would

have been impossible – I took leave from the first to do the second. What was crucial to the book was my husband's support. He scaled his work right down to look after the children. But the running of the house I think we split pretty evenly – he does all the cooking, I do most of the laundry and the bills! What added to the pressure was that we unexpectedly found the perfect house for our family bang in the middle of writing the book – so we added in a house move to the mix. That felt very demanding.

With three children of your own, have you ever thought of downsizing like Sarah? If so, would you move abroad like so many others?
I do sometimes think about downsizing because I yearn for the countryside; I passionately love big empty spaces. I grew up on the North Yorkshire moors and miss the wide, windswept moorland. We always go to very remote places in Scotland for our annual summer holiday, and no matter what the weather or the midges are like I find the sense of space in the mountains, beaches and horizons exhilarating. So any downsizing would have to be in the British Isles – I feel too much British blood runs in my veins, I have a Scottish, an Irish and an English grandparent – this is where I belong. But I also have a Jewish grandparent, which perhaps explains my love of good conversation, intellectual stimulation and new ideas which keeps me in the vibrancy of London life. ▶

Questioning the World *(continued)*

◄ **Do you think that downsizing is only available to wealthier sectors of the working population, or is it more an attitude?**
I think there is some truth to that. They always say it takes a lot of education to be poor. That was true of my parents. My father was by any conventional standards poor most of his life, but he never ever saw himself like that. He had downsized in the fifties to live a country life in a beautiful part of the world. He took great pleasure in very small things such as a good book, a glass of good beer or a bracing walk across the moors.

> ❛ They always say it takes a lot of education to be poor. ❜

Is work your life, or how do you stop it becoming so?
Work is a very important part of my life, but so is my family. I try to balance the two, and by and large I manage. The bit I feel I miss out is some space between the two – I wish I had more time for friends, and increasingly I'd like to pursue other interests such as painting.

One refrain in the book is that ambition is very costly. Have your ambitions changed over the course of your working life or while writing this book?
Yes, I think the ambition I had as a 25 year old has gone. There was a real drive for success and recognition which has thankfully faded considerably. But what is left is the continuing drive to better understand whatever issue confronts me, and the deep satisfaction of writing about it.

Time is something that you describe as being bought and sold for wages. What would you do with more?
I would take a course in print-making – particularly screen-printing – and another course in making mosaics, and then I would disregard my zero musical abilities and join a choir.

We have been encouraged to be fulfilled and satisfied by our work. What, apart from your writing, makes you happy?
My family. Windy walks on cliff tops. Pottering in the garden (it's so haphazard that I'm not sure it's right to call it gardening).

We now have a 'Work Your Proper Hours' Day. Do you think or hope that there will come a time when we no longer need such artificial incentives?
No, I think the love affair with work will intensify so I think challenges to that, as is often the case with an abusive relationship, will be required for the foreseeable future.

Is there any book that you wish you had written?
Dozens.

What is your next book?
I'm working up to it. These things shouldn't happen in a hurry – I think Slow Thinking is as much needed as Slow Food. But perhaps it will be something on Islam. ∎

> ❝ I think the love affair with work will intensify so I think challenges to that will be required for the foreseeable future. ❞

A Writing Life

Where do you write?
I have a lovely study overlooking the garden.

Why do you write?
It helps me work out what I think.

Pen or computer?
Computer

Silence or music?
Silence except for the birds in the back garden.

What started you writing?
The experience of living in Sri Lanka as a volunteer.

How do you start a book?
By reading and talking to people.

And finish?
By a painful process of rewriting the first, very fast, very rough draft.

Do you have any writing rituals or superstitions?
I periodically dedicate whatever I'm writing to the benefit of all living beings – it is a Buddhist dedication which I've picked up.

What or who inspires you?
My husband, my children and a wonderful collection of people – I meet people everywhere who fascinate and inspire me.

What's your guilty reading pleasure or favourite trashy read?
Trashy reads irritate the hell out of me, but I sometimes like a bit of trashy TV when I'm slumped on the sofa at the end of the day. ■

A New Generation
by Madeleine Bunting

AT ALL THE TALKS and lectures I've been asked to give around the country since the publication of *Willing Slaves*, one question has invariably been posed by the audience: 'Do you feel optimistic or pessimistic about the future?' Are things getting better or worse? Is our working culture changing to give more space to the care ethic? Is human sustainability finally reaching the mainstream political agenda? These are tough questions because I can't decide.

There have been several developments which make me very pessimistic. Throughout the last year there have been reports of how the working culture of Europe is being undermined. Several major manufacturers in Germany have announced that the working week for thousands of employees would increase; they threatened the unions with moving the jobs to Hungary and the Czech Republic if they refused to increase their hours. In France there have been huge protests as the government has initiated moves to dilute the thirty-five-hour working week. (However, even after these changes the French are still in a much better position than the UK – the limit is now put at thirty-nine hours a week.)

This is the background against which the UK has been renegotiating to continue its opt-out of the Working Time Directive which limits the working week throughout Europe to forty-eight hours. The Directive came into operation in 1998, and some countries used an opt-out to phase in the limit (such as Ireland) while the UK has been the only country to have stubbornly insisted that it still needed an opt-out. This is clearly in direct contradiction of everything else the UK government has said about trying to promote a work–life balance and family-friendly working. Unfortunately, the accession of Eastern European countries in 2004 has bolstered the UK's position – it now has the support of Slovenia, Poland and Malta – on keeping an opt-out. All the other countries of the twenty-five-strong European Union want the opt-out dropped outright or with strict conditions of use. The UK has taken a position of the 'sick man of Europe' – its economy is too fragile to support any restriction on working time.

But there are many other developments which make me very optimistic. It's been well trailed that Labour will, if elected at the next election, implement a series of commitments on reshaping our work culture. Paid maternity leave will be extended and the level of pay is likely to be improved; maternity leave may be transferable to the father for the first time. The right to request flexible working could be extended beyond just parents with children under 6: it could apply to those caring for the sick and elderly, and possibly to parents of older children as well. These would be major victories.

Equally heartening is the fact that the number of people working more than forty-eight hours a week has fallen by 100,000, ensuring that the average for full-time workers is now beginning to drop – by ▶

6 The UK has taken a position of the "sick man of Europe" – its economy is too fragile to support any restriction on working time. 9

A New Generation *(continued)*

◀ 1 hour 25 minutes since 2001. That's a step forward even if it's a small step – as the TUC points out, at the current rate of progress, it will be forty-five years before the hours of working fall to the EU average.

More broadly, across a wide spectrum there is increasing evidence of how the role of work in our lives and the quality of working life are being questioned and debated. These are social trends which I am confident will continue. The pervasive consumer culture puts huge emphasis on the quality of life, and that inevitably triggers much questioning in our society of what exactly constitutes 'quality of life'. Is it increasing affluence and consumer goods, or is it a quality of experience only possible when there is the luxury of time? We continue to interrogate ourselves on what exactly is the 'good life'; the 'happiness debate' pioneered by economists such as Richard Layard and Andrew Oswald flourishes.

Other questions of human sustainability are also increasingly coming to the fore, such as what constitutes a secure sense of personal identity and a strong sense of belonging. Given the insecurity, pressure and stress of our working culture, it is hard to see how work can provide either identity or belonging in the way it has done in the past.

The greatest potential danger of the current patterns of change is the emergence of a twin-track labour market. There will be a set of jobs which are compatible with caring responsibilities, and then there will be the highly paid, highly skilled elite. The childless and those who delegate their child-rearing

❝ We continue to interrogate ourselves on what exactly is the "good life"; the "happiness debate" flourishes. ❞

will be among the latter and break though the glass ceiling. But what will remain unchallenged is that outdated, old-fashioned male work ethic of single-minded total dedication to work. Caring will continue to effectively exact a tough penalty in terms of career progression, and being a good parent will be held against you by your employer. Inevitably, that will impact disproportionately on women, though there will be an increasing minority of men who take on the main carer role.

The interesting new ingredient is a generation of women who are far more challenging of the work culture, and a generation of men who want a new deal to give space to their relationships with their children. The women are not fighting the battles of their mothers in the eighties that they should be allowed to work and whether there is a place for them in the labour market. Such battles have been won; no one seriously disputes a woman's right – often need – to work. Meanwhile the men are beginning to lose their self-consciousness about their demands – house husbands are no longer a shockingly new concept.

The sense of entitlement of a new generation now in their twenties will give a positive edge to their confidence to renegotiate work. They will be able to take up that effort of debate, argument, campaigning and sheer stubbornness required. It's possible that it will succeed in edging the British working culture onto a more humane path. ∎

‘ Given the insecurity, pressure and stress of our working culture, it is hard to see how work can provide either identity or belonging in the way it has done in the past. ’

Have You Read?

The Model Occupation: The Channel Islands Under German Rule, 1940–45
Madeleine Bunting studied new documents and interviewed former slave workers from Russia, the Ukraine and Germany to tell the (sometimes controversial) human story of the only part of Britain to fall under Nazi rule in the Second World War.

'Much the best book so far to appear on the German occupation of the Channel Islands'
Times Literary Supplement

'If you want a classic example of the dilemmas of Resistance, here it is'
The Times

If You Loved This,
You Might Like ...

CORPORATE LIFE

Blood, Sweat and Tears: The Evolution of Work
Richard Donkin
Donkin studied the world of work for six years and presents its history and evolution from the moment when humans first used tools to the present-day landscape of dot-coms and management-speak.

The Corporation: The Pathological Pursuit of Profit and Power
Joel Bakan
Bakan, a Professor of Law at the University of British Columbia, offers a complete history of the corporation and its control of our lives. He argues that corporations have self-interest at their heart, to support themselves and their shareholders, and having rid themselves of most legal constraints they have no impetus to act morally or with concern for how their actions affect others.

The Affluent Society
John Kenneth Galbraith
A history and critique of economic and employment inequalities from one of the world's most respected economists. He questions why work is something revered when it frequently produces things we don't need, and why public works are such a low priority for government when it is acceptable to spend extravagantly in the private sector. ▶

If You Loved This ... *(continued)*

◀ RETHINKING YOUR RELATIONSHIP
TO WORK

It's Not How Good You Are, It's How Good You Want to Be
Paul Arden
Written by an advertising executive, this
short book encourages creativity, ideas and
getting out from under, whether a job you
hate or your own timidity.

YOU HAVE TO LAUGH OR ELSE ...

Dilbert
Scott Adams
Any of the Dilbert cartoon books offers a
hilarious, albeit sometimes too close for
comfort, take on the working world. Try
*Things You Don't Want to Hear During Your
Annual Performance Review*, *Don't Step in
the Leadership* and *Dilbert: Random Acts of
Management*.

Work is Hell
Matt Groening
Now much more famous for *The Simpsons*,
Groening also produced the *Life is Hell*
newspaper cartoon strip throughout the
1980s and 1990s, and this book focuses on all
the various hells of work, from the barmy
boss to the colleague who won't stop telling
you about all manner of tedium.

MOVING ON

If *Willing Slaves* has inspired you to downsize
or change jobs, there are heaps of books
available to help. The following is a small
selection.

Getting a Life! The Downshifting Guide to Happier, Simpler Living
Polly Ghazi and Judy Jones
In one of the classics of downsizing your life, Ghazi and Jones offer practical advice and plenty of anecdotes.

Your Money or Your Life
Joe Dominguez and Vicki Robin
Another downsizing and rethink-your-life classic, this is a practical nine-step approach to reorganizing how you spend your money and your life.

The Work We Were Born to Do
Nick Williams
Also distilled as *The 12 Principles of The Work We Were Born to Do*, Williams's book is a practical guidebook to help the reader find more fulfilling work.

How to Find the Work You Love
Laurence G. Boldt
Boldt is probably better known for *Zen and the Art of Making a Living*, but this short philosophical and anecdotal book is useful for anyone considering a job or life change. The second half of the book focuses on four elements – Integrity, Service, Enjoyment and Excellence – that Boldt considers essential for any genuine happiness at work. ■

Find Out More

www.employersforwork-lifebalance.org.uk
Information for employers and individuals
in the UK on how to achieve better work–life
balance. Run by the Work Foundation, the
Employers for Work-Life Balance initiative
aims to be a 'one-stop work-life resource' for
everyone who works. Also see:

- www.unison.org.uk/worklifebalance/
  index.asp for information on the public
  services union's work–life initiatives
- www.eoc.org.uk/cseng/policyand
  campaigns/worklife_balance_update.asp,
  for details on the Equal Opportunities
  Commission's campaign
- www.tuc.org.uk/work_life/index.cfm.
  Information about achieving a work–life
  balance aimed at employers and unions;
  lots of information about policy
  development, family-friendly initiatives
  and the TUC's campaigns.

www.worklifebalance.com
A US-based training company's site.

www.worklifebalancecentre.org
A UK-based training company's site.

www.dol.govt.nz/worklife/index.asp
The New Zealand Department of Labour's
work–life balance site.

www.w-lb.org.uk
The website of the Work-Life Balance Trust, a
charity established by Shirley Conran OBE to
raise awareness of this issue. At the time of

18

writing, the Trust was taking a sabbatical until early 2005 to preserve its own WLB, but it might be worth investigating online after this date.

www.flexecutiveclient.co.uk/client/ inf_01.asp
If you're interested in flexible working, visit this recruitment and consultancy specialist's website. Find out how to approach your boss about flexible hours, redo your CV in line with a jobshare and determine the best flexible solution for you.

WATCH ...

***The Office,* Series 1, 2 and Christmas Specials**
This television series focuses on the excruciating character of David Brent (played by Ricky Gervais) who considers himself a cool and with-it manager, much to the embarrassment and pain of his colleagues. A bit like Dilbert, *The Office* can sometimes be too close for comfort for anyone who works in corporate life. ■